Create Web
Charts with D3

Fabio Nelli

Apress®

Create Web Charts with D3

ISBN-13 (pbk): 978-1-4842-0866-3

ISBN-13 (electronic): 978-1-4842-0865-6

Managing Director: Welmoed Spahr
Lead Editor: Ben Renow-Clarke
Development Editors: James Markham and Chris Nelson
Technical Reviewers: Matthew Canning and Massimo Nardone
Editorial Board: Steve Anglin, Mark Beckner, Ewan Buckingham, Gary Cornell, Louise Corrigan, Jim DeWolf, Jonathan Gennick, Robert Hutchinson, Michelle Lowman, James Markham, Matthew Moodie, Jeff Olson, Jeffrey Pepper, Douglas Pundick, Ben Renow-Clarke, Dominic Shakeshaft, Gwenan Spearing, Matt Wade, Steve Weiss
Coordinating Editosr: Jill Balzano and Christine Ricketts
Copy Editors: Lisa Vecchione, Kezia Endsley, and Brendan Frost
Compositor: SPi Global
Indexer: SPi Global
Artist: SPi Global
Cover Designer: Anna Ishchenko

Distributed to the book trade worldwide by Springer Science+Business Media New York, 233 Spring Street, 6th Floor, New York, NY 10013. Phone 1-800-SPRINGER, fax (201) 348-4505, e-mail orders-ny@springer-sbm.com, or visit www.springeronline.com. Apress Media, LLC is a California LLC and the sole member (owner) is Springer Science + Business Media Finance Inc (SSBM Finance Inc). SSBM Finance Inc is a Delaware corporation.

For information on translations, please e-mail rights@apress.com, or visit www.apress.com.

Apress and friends of ED books may be purchased in bulk for academic, corporate, or promotional use. eBook versions and licenses are also available for most titles. For more information, reference our Special Bulk Sales–eBook Licensing web page at www.apress.com/bulk-sales.

Any source code or other supplementary material referenced by the author in this text is available to readers at www.apress.com/9781430248033. For detailed information about how to locate your book's source code, go to www.apress.com/source-code/.

This book is dedicated to my grandfather Polo and my grandmother Franca,
for all the support they have given me in life

Contents at a Glance

Contents

About the Author

Fabio Nelli is an information technology scientific application specialist at IRBM Science Park, a private research center in Pomezia, Italy. He was a computer consultant for many years at IBM, EDS, and Merck Sharp and Dohme, along with several banks and insurance companies. He worked as well as a specialist in information technology and automation systems at Beckman Coulter.

He holds a Master's degree in Organic Chemistry from La Sapienza University of Rome. He recently earned a Bachelor's degree in Automation and Computer Engineering from eCampus University of Novedrate.

Nelli is currently developing Java applications that interface Oracle databases, using scientific instrumentation to generate data, and web server applications that provide analysis to researchers in real time.

Web site: www.meccanismocomplesso.org.

About the Technical Reviewers

Matthew Canning is an author, speaker, and experienced technical leader who has served in engineering and management roles at some of the world's largest companies. Aside from technology, he writes and presents on subjects such as memory, mental calculation, and productivity. He currently lives outside Philadelphia with his wife and daughter.

 Twitter: @MatthewCanning.
 Web site: matthewcanning.com.

Massimo Nardone is an experienced Android, Java, PHP, Python, C++ programmer, technical reviewer and expert.

 He holds a Master of Science degree in Computing Science from the University of Salerno, Italy. He worked as a PCI QSA and Senior Lead IT Security/Cloud/ SCADA Architect for many years and currently works as Security, Cloud and SCADA Lead IT Architect for Hewlett Packard Finland. He has more than 20 years of work experience in IT including Security, SCADA, Cloud Computing, IT Infrastructure, Mobile, Security and WWW technology areas for both national and international projects. Massimo has worked as a Project Manager, Cloud/SCADA Lead IT Architect, Software Engineer, Research Engineer, Chief Security Architect, and Software Specialist. He worked as visiting lecturer and supervisor for exercises at the Networking Laboratory of the Helsinki University of Technology (Aalto University). He has been programming and teaching how to program with Perl, PHP, Java, VB, Python, C/C++ for almost 20 years.

 He holds four international patents (PKI, SIP, SAML and Proxy areas).

Acknowledgments

I would like to express my gratitude to all the people who played a part in developing this book. First, a special thanks to Ben Renow-Clarke for giving me the opportunity to write the book. Thanks to Jill Balzano and Mark Powers for their guidance and direction. Thanks also to everyone who took part in the review and editing of the book for their professionalism and enthusiasm: Chris Nelson, Matthew Canning, James Markham, Lisa Vecchione, Kezia Endsley, Brendan Frost, and Dhaneesh Kumar.

Introduction

Welcome to the world of charts. If you are holding this book in your hands, you are undoubtedly interested in data visualization, perhaps with the hope of developing web pages filled with interactive charts. Or, maybe your purpose is to improve your knowledge of the D3 library. Whatever your objective, I hope this book enables you to achieve it.

In addition to the various types of charts, this book covers a range of topics: the DOM elements and selections, HTML5 and the canvas, jQuery UI widgets and controls, graphic manipulation with scalable vector graphics (SVG) technology, and mathematical concepts (scales and domains, curve fitting and trend lines, clustering analysis, and much more).

I have enriched this wide range of topics with many examples, each tightly focused on a particular one and presented to you in an ordered sequence, with step-by-step instructions.

Chart development can be easy once you know the process and have the right tools at the ready. Therefore, in presenting this material, I have included helpful, reusable code snippets as well as explanations of underlying concepts. After reading this book, you will be equipped to create any type of data visualization, either traditional or newer, with confidence.

CHAPTER 1

■ ■ ■

Charting Technology Overview

When we need to represent data or qualitative structures graphically in order to show a relationship—to make a comparison or highlight a trend—we make use of charts. A chart is a graphic structure consisting of symbols, such as lines, in a line chart; bars, in a bar chart; or slices, in a pie chart. Charts serve as valid tools that can help us discern and understand the relationships underlying large quantities of data. It is easier for humans to read graphic representations, such as a chart, than raw numeric data. Nowadays, use of charts has become common practice in a wide variety of professional fields as well as in many other aspects of daily life. For this reason, charts have come to take on many forms, depending on the stucture of the data and the phenomenon that is being highlighted.

For example, if you have data separated into different groups and want to represent the percentage of each, with respect to the total, you usually display these groups of data in a pie chart or a bar chart. In contrast, if you want to show the trend of a variable over time, a line chart is typically the best choice.

In this book, you will learn how to create, draw, and adapt charts to your needs, using various technologies based on JavaScript. Before you start using JavaScript to develop charts, however, it is important that you understand the basic concepts that will be covered in the chapters of this book. In this chapter, I will provide a brief overview of these concepts.

First, I will show you how to recognize the most common elements that make up a chart. Knowledge of these elements will prove helpful, because you will find them in the form of components, variables, and objects defined within the specialized JavaScript libraries created for the realization of charts.

Next, I will present a list of the most common types of charts. The greater your knowledge of charts and their features, the easier it will be to choose the right representation for your data. Making the right choice is essential if you are to underline the relationships you want to represent, and just reading the data will not be sufficent. Only when you have become familiar with the most common types of charts will you be able to choose which is the most suitable for your purposes.

Once you have become familiar with these concepts, you will need to learn how it is possible to realize them via the Web and what the current technologies are that can help you achieve this aim. Thus, in the second part of the chapter, I will discuss these technical aspects, presenting one by one the technologies involved in the development of the examples provided in this book.

Finally, given that all our work will focus on the development of code in JavaScript, I thought it would be helpful to provide a brief description of certain types of data. Those who are not familiar with JavaScript can benefit from this quick reference source on the forms that the data will take within the code. However, I strongly recommend that the reader research in greater depth the concepts and technologies discussed in this chapter.

Elements in a Chart

As you will soon see, charts can assume a variety of forms. In a chart the data take on graphic structure through the use of symbols specific to the type of chart; there are, however, some features that are common to all charts.

Generally, every chart has a title, appearing at the top, that provides a short description of the data. Less frequently, subtitles or footnotes are used to supply additional descriptions (mostly data-related information, such as references, places, dates, and notes).

Charts often have axes—two perpendicular lines that allow the user to refer to the values of the coordinates (x, y) for each data point P(x, y), as shown in Figure 1-1. The horizontal line usually represents the x axis, and the vertical line, the y axis.

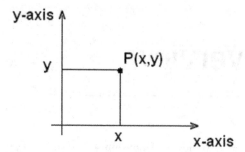

Figure 1-1. *A two-dimensional chart*

A scale is defined on each axis. The scale can be either numerical or categorical. Each axis is divided into segments corresponding to the particular range of values represented by the scale. The boundaries between one segment and the next are called ticks. Each tick reports the value of the scale associated with that axis. Generally, call these tick labels.

Figure 1-2 shows four axes with different scales. Axes a and b have numerical scales, with a being a linear scale, and b, a logarithmic scale. Axes c and d have categorical scales, with c being ordinal and therefore following an ascending order, whereas d is only a sequence of categories without any particular order.

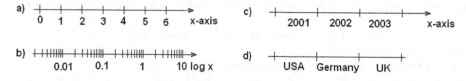

Figure 1-2. *Four axes with different scales*

Along with each axis, it is good practice to display a label briefly describing the dimension represented; these are called axis labels. If the scale is numerical, the label should show the units of measure in brackets. For instance, if you had an x axis reporting the timing for a set of data, you might write "time" as an axis label, with the second unit (in this case, seconds) in square brackets as [s] (see Figure 1-3).

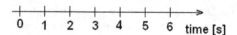

Figure 1-3. *An axis label*

In the drawing area displaying the chart, a line grid may be included to aid in the visual alignment of data. Figure 1-4 shows a grid for a chart with a linear time scale on the x axis and a logarithmic scale on the y axis.

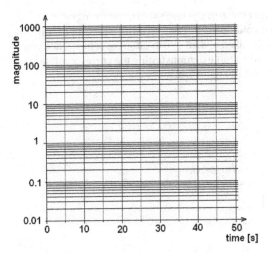

Figure 1-4. *A chart with two different scales*

You have seen how data can be represented symbolically. However, text labels can also be used to highlight specific data points. Point labels provide values in a chart right at the corresponding points in a chart, whereas tool tips are small frames that appear dynamically, when you pass the mouse over a given point. These two types of labels are shown in Figure 1-5.

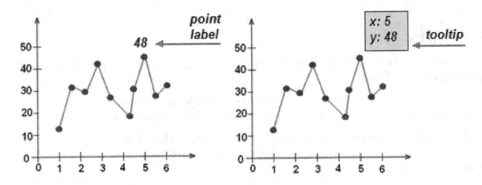

Figure 1-5. *The point label and the tooltip of a data point*

Data are often grouped in several series, and in order to represent these in the same chart, they must be distinguishable. The most common approach is to assign a different color to each series. In other cases, for example, with line charts, the line stroke (dashed, dotted, and so on) can also be used to distinguish different series. Once you have established a sequence of colors (or strokes), it is necessary to add a table demonstrating the correspondence between colors and groups. This table is called the legend and is shown in Figure 1-6.

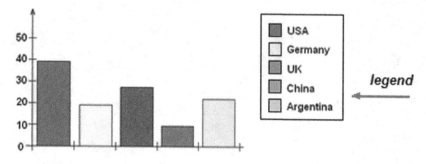

Figure 1-6. A legend

Although it may seem trivial to discuss the concepts covered in this section, it is important to define the terminology of the elements that I will be referring to throughout the book. They form the building blocks with which you will be building your charts. You will also see how JavaScript libraries specializing in the representation of charts use these terms, associating them with editing and setting components (see the section "Inserting Options" in Chapter 8).

Most Common Charts

This section contains a brief overview of the most common types of charts. These charts will each be described more thoroughly in the following chapters of the book.

> **Histogram:** Adjacent rectangles erected on the x axis, split into discrete intervals (bins) and with an area proportional to the frequency of the observation for that bin (see Figure 1-7).

> **Bar chart:** Similar in shape to a histogram, but different in essence, this is a chart with rectangular bars of a length proportional to the values they represent. Each bar identifies a group of data (see Figure 1-7).

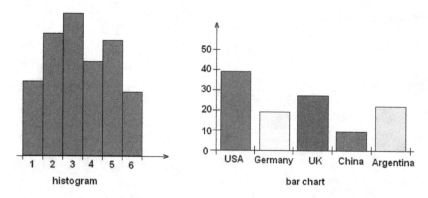

Figure 1-7. A histogram and a bar chart

4

Line chart: A sequence of ordered data points connected by a line. Data points P(x, y) are reported in the chart, representing the scales of two axes, x and y (see Figure 1-8).

Pie chart: A circle (pie) divided into segments (slices). Each slice represents a group of data, and its size is proportional to the percentage value (see Figure 1-8).

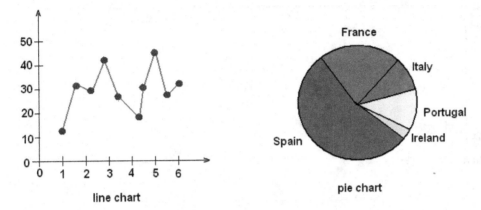

Figure 1-8. A line chart and a pie chart

Bubble chart: A two-dimensional scatterplot in which a third variable is represented by the size of the data points (see Figure 1-9).

Radar chart: A chart in which a series of data is represented on many axes, starting radially from a point of origin at the center of the chart. This chart often takes on the appearance of a spiderweb (see Figure 1-9).

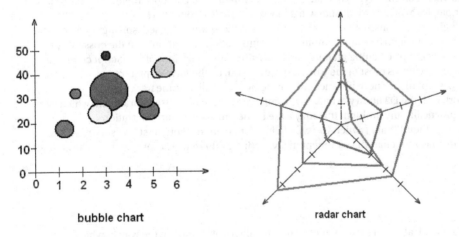

Figure 1-9. A bubble chart and a radar chart

Candlestick chart: A type of chart specifically used to describe price trends over time. Each data point consists of four values, generally known as open-high-low-close (OHLC) values, and assumes a shape resembling a candlestick (see Figure 1-10).

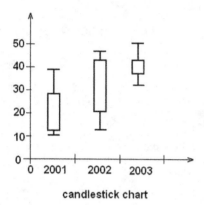

candlestick chart

Figure 1-10. *A candlestick chart*

■ **Note**   Open-high-low-close (OHLC) are four numeric values typically used to illustrate movement in the price of a financial instrument over time.

How to Realize Charts on the Web

Now that I have described the most common types of charts and the elements that compose them, the next step is to take a quick look at the technologies available today that will allow you to realize your chart.

Nowadays, web technologies are in constant flux: each day, new solutions are proposed, solving problems that only a short time ago would have proven to be quite complex. These innovations will afford you the possibility to realize highly interactive charts, with eye-catching graphics, all by writing only a few lines of JavaScript code. The whole thing can be done fast and easily, as most of the work is done for you, by the JavaScript libraries, which are highly specialized in chart representation. These libraries are now to be found all over the network.

In this book, you will work with the D3 library, which is currently the most widely used library and which can provide general solutions to practically any problem that may arise in the process of chart realization.

But, before stepping through theis library (which you will do in later chapters), you must first survey all the technologies that constitute the basis for chart development in JavaScript, as these will accompany you throughout the rest of the book.

HTML5

Recently, there has been a lot of talk about HTML5, which is practically revolutionizing the way in which web applications are developed. Before its advent, if you wanted to introduce interactive graphical content, the use of applications such as Adobe Flash was pretty much the obligatory path. But, dealing with Flash or similar applications for developing charts or other graphic representations on the Web involves an obvious limitation: dependency on a plug-in, to be installed on the end user's machine. In addition, these kinds of applications are not supported on smartphones. Thanks to HTML5, developers can now create advanced graphics and animation without relying on Flash.

As you read through this book, you will see how HTML5 has also led to the birth of many other technologies, some new, others old but renewed, such as JavaScript. In fact, as a language, JavaScript is experiencing a rebirth, as a result of the new libraries developed precicely to take advantage of the innovations introduced by HTML5. HTML5 has many new syntactical features, including the <canvas> elements and the integration of scalar vector graphics (SVG) content. Owing to these elements, it will be very easy to integrate multimedia and graphical content on the Web without using Flash.

In Flash's place, you will be using the D3 library. Currently, this is the most widespread and complete library available for the realization tasks such as the graphic visualization of data. The world of web technologies is constantly evolving, however; on the Internet, you can always find new libraries, with characteristics similar to the D3 library.

Charting with SVG and CANVAS

Among all the possible graphic applications that can be implemented with the new technologies introduced by HTML5, I will focus on the representation and visualization of data through charts. Using JavaScript as a programming language, we can now take advantage of the powerful rendering engines embedded in new browsers. As the basis of the new capabilities of this language, I will refer to the HTML5 canvas and SVG. Instead of drawing static images on the server and then downloading them into the browser, SVG and canvas allow you to develop fully interactive charts and thus to enrich your graphic representations with built-in animation, transitions, and tool tips. This is because SVG and canvas content is drawn in the browser, and so the graphic elements that make up the chart can be transformed without refreshing the page. This feature is essential for visualizing real-time data, which require that the chart be continually updated, as the data change. Operating in this way will ensure a true client-side charting. In fact, by making use of these technologies, charts are actually drawn on the client and only require that the data be passed from the server. This aspect affords a considerable number of advantages, the foremost being elimination of the need for large graphics files to be downloaded from the server.

Canvas vs SVG

Both HTML5 canvas and SVG are web technologies that allow you to create rich graphics in the browser, but they are fundamentally different. Throughout this text, you will see mainly how **D3 makes use of the SVG technology**. Other libraries similar to D3 (i.e. jqPlot and Highcharts), instead, make use of the HTML5 <canvas> element to draw its charts. In contrast, D3 does not make use of canvas; it relies on SVG technology for graphic representations.

SVG is an XML-based vector graphic format. SVG content can be static, dynamic, interactive, or animated, which makes it very flexible. You can also style the SVG elements with Cascading Style Sheets (CSS) and add dynamic behavior to them, using the application programming interface (API) methods provided by the SVG document object model (DOM). In choosing this format, you can, therefore, obtain much more than simple vector graphics and animation: you can develop highly interactive web applications, with scripting, advanced animation, events, filters, and almost anything else your imagination might suggest.

The HTML5 canvas specification is a versatile JavaScript API, allowing you to code programmatic drawing operations. Canvas, by itself, lets you define a canvas context object, shown as a <canvas> element on your HTML page. This element can then be drawn inside, using either a two-dimensional or three-dimensional drawing context, with Web Graphics Library (WebGL).

The advantages of canvas, compared with SVG, are high drawing performance and faster graphics and image editing. Whenever it is necessary to work at the pixel level, canvas is preferable. However, with canvas, not having DOM nodes on which to work can be a disadvantage, especially if you do not use a JavaScript framework. Another disadvantage is poor text-rendering capabilities.

The advantages of SVG, compared with canvas, are resolution independence, good support for animation, and the ability to animate elements, using a declarative syntax. Most important, though, is having full control over each element, using the SVG DOM API in JavaScript. Yet, when complexity increases, slow rendering can be a problem, but browser providers are working hard to make browsers faster (see Tables 1-1 and 1-2).

Table 1-1. *Web Browsers and Engines*

Browser	Current	Engine	Developer	License
Google Chrome	29	Blink	Google, Opera, Samsung, Intel, others	GNU Lesser General Public License (LGPL), Berkeley Software Distribution (BSD) style
Mozilla Firefox	23	Gecko	Netscape/Mozilla Foundation	Mozilla Public License (MPL)
Internet Explorer	10	Trident	Microsoft	Proprietary
Apple Safari	6	WebKit	Apple, KDE, Nokia, Blackberry, Palm, others	GNU LGPL, BSD style

Table 1-2. *Web Technology Support: Comparison of Web Browsers*

Technology	Browser			
	Internet Explorer 10	Chrome 29	Firefox 23	Safari 6
SVG (v.1.1)				
Filters	Yes (from 10)	Yes	Yes	Yes (from 6)
Synchronized Multimedia Integration Language (SMIL) animation	No	Yes	Yes	Partial
Fonts	No	Yes	No	Yes
Fragment identifiers	Yes	No	Yes	No
HTML effects	Partial	Partial	Yes	Partial
CSS backgrounds	Yes	Yes	Partial	Yes
CSS	Yes	Yes	Yes	Yes
HTML5				
Canvas	Yes(from 9)	Yes	Yes	Yes
New elements	Yes	Yes	Yes	Yes
Video elements	Yes(from 9)	Yes	Yes	Yes
JavaScript API				
JavaScript Object Notation (JSON) parsing	Yes	Yes	Yes	Yes
WebGL	No	Yes	Partial	Partial

The DOM

Working with libraries that act at the level of the structural elements of an HTML page, we cannot avoid talking about the DOM. I will be referring to this concept often, as it is the basic structure underlying every web page. The World Wide Web Consortium (W3C) felt the need, and rightly so, to create an official standard for the representation of structured documents, so as to develop guidelines for all programming languages and platforms.The tree structure of

HTML documents, as well as those of XML, follows the guidelines developed by this standard perfectly. Following is an example of an HTML document:

```
<HTML>
    <HEAD>
      <TITLE>A title</TITLE>
    </HEAD>
    <BODY>
      Hello
      <BR>
    </BODY>
</HTML>
```

The DOM tree of this document can be represented as shown in Figure 1-11.

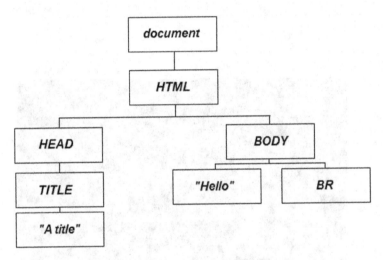

Figure 1-11. *An example of tree structure of the DOM*

But, the DOM standard is not limited to developing guidelines on how the DOM should be structured in a document; the standard also defines a number of features designed to act on the elements that compose a document. Thus, any action pertaining to a document (creating, inserting, deleting) should follow the DOM standard. As a result, regardless of the programming language that you are using or the platform on which you are working, you will always find the same functionality expressed by this standard. Often, the term *DOM* also applies to the API, which manages all the elements of a web page.

All this is important, because anyone choosing to read this book is interested in developing charts that not only use the DOM, but that are also part of it and whose every aspect can be inspected and manipulated in JavaScript. Throughout the book, you will learn how to make the best use of the D3 library. Thanks to this JavaScript library, you can access every chart element, such as changing the color and position of objects.

Developing in JavaScript

Although it is likely that most people who have chosen to read this book already have a good knowledge of JavaScript, this may not in fact be the case. For this reason, I have structured the book in a practical way, giving step-by-step examples and providing all the code that must be written in the examples. As such, this book offers newcomers an opportunity to study the language and those who have not used it for some time a chance to refresh their memories.

To start working with the JavaScript libraries that you will be using to develop your charts, it is necessary to prepare a development environment. It is true that to develop JavaScript code, you could simply use a text editor, such as Notepad (or, even better, Notepad++), but developers generally prefer to use specialized applications, usually called integrated development enviroments (IDEs), to develop code. As well as providing a text editor with differentiated colors corresponding to the keywords used in the code, such applications also contain a set of tools designed to facilitate the work. These applications can check if there are any errors in the code, supply debugging tools, make it easy to manage files, and assist in deployment on the server, among many other operations.

Nowadays, there are many JavaScript IDEs on the network, but some of the most prominent are **Aptana Studio** (see Figure 1-12); **Eclipse Web Developer**, with the JavaScript test driver (JSTD) plug-in installed; and **NetBeans**. These editors also allow you to develop Hypertext Preprocessor (PHP), CSS, and HTML (for information on how to use the Aptana Studio IDE to set up a workspace in which to implement the code for this book, see Appendix A, or use the source code accompanying the book directly; you can find the code samples in the Source Code/Download area of the Apress web site [www.apress.com]).

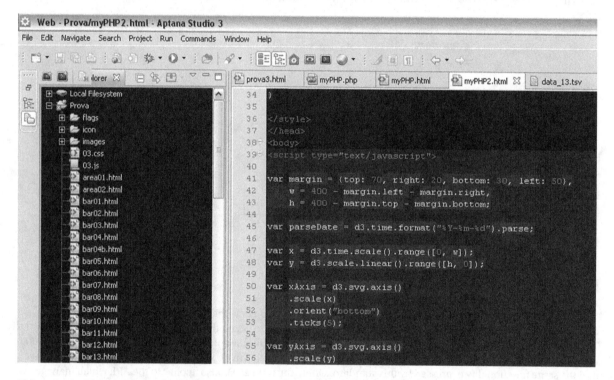

Figure 1-12. *The Aptana Studio 3 IDE*

For those who prefer not to install too many applications on their computer, there are online JavaScript IDEs. These allow users to edit JavaScript code in a web page working as an IDE and to check their result directly from the same web page. Unfortunately, many of these IDEs charge a fee. However, **jsFiddle** (http://jsfiddle.net) is an online IDE that requires no payment and that, in addition to editing, provides code sharing and the option of adding libraries, such as jQuery and D3.(see Figure 1-13).

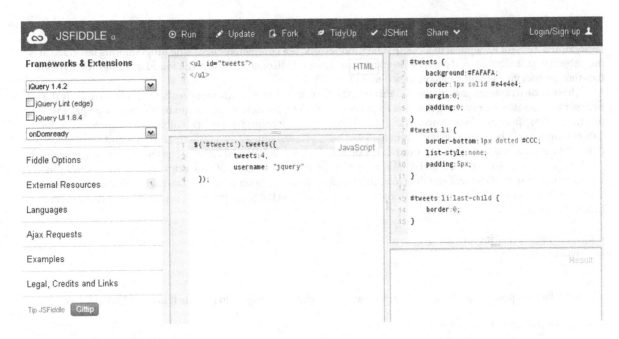

Figure 1-13. *The online IDE jsFiddle*

jsFiddle can prove very useful. As well as letting the user include many JavaScript libraries (see Figure 1-14), it offers the respective different versions released, thus allowing him or her to test any incompatibilities in real time.

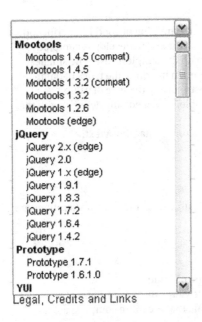

Figure 1-14. *jsFiddle offers a set of the most popular JavaScript libraries*

Running and Debugging JavaScript

JavaScript, if we want to define it in a client–server framework, is a completely client-side programming language. It is not subject to compilation, and parts of the code, apart from HTML documents, can be found in many other types of files that are specific to other languages, such as .JSP or .PHP.

These code fragments pass unaffected through the application servers without ever being processed. Only the browser is responsible for running the JavaScript code. Therefore, JavaScript code is run only when a web page is downloaded or afterward, in response to an event. If the JavaScript code is of a considerable size or might be useful subsequently, it can be defined externally in a .JS file; here, you will find all the JavaScript libraries and frameworks that will be mentioned throughout this text. Regardless of its form, however, JavaScript runs directly from the browser.

So, even if you do not use a real IDE for the development and debugging of JavaScript code, you can simply insert the code in an empty HTML file and then load this file directly in a browser (Chrome, Internet Explorer, and Firefox are the most common). To distinguish it from the rest of the text on the page, you must separate the code by putting it inside the <script></scripts> tags:

```
<script type="text/javascript">
// JavaScript code
</script>
```

If the JavaScript code resides in an external file, then it will be necessary to include it in the HTML page, writing

```
<script type="text/javascript" src="library.js"></script>
```

Therefore, as long as the execution of JavaScript is not required for the purpose of installing something, you have everything you need. Who does not have a web browser on his or her operating system?

Data Types in JavaScript

As mentioned earlier, this book will neither explain the rules and syntax for the programming of good JavaScript code nor will it linger too long on programming details. Nevertheless, the code that we are going to develop is centered on charts, or rather the processing of data and how to display them. Let us start with the simplest case. The smallest building block of all data structures is the variable (when it contains a single value). In handling the types of data, JavaScript is very different from other programming languages. , You do not have to specify the type of value (int, string, float, boolean, and so on) when you want to store JavaScript in a variable; you need only define it with the var keyword.

In Java or C a variable containing an integer value is declared differently from one containing a text:

```
int value = 3;
String text = "This is a string value";
```

In JavaScript the type of stored value does not matter. Everything is declared with var, so the same declarations are

```
var value = 3;
var text = "This is a string value";
```

Thus, in JavaScript we can think of variables as containers for storing any type of value.

For the sake of simplicity, here the variables are seen as containers of a single value, thus representing the simplest data structure. Actually, however, variables may also contain types of data that are more complex: arrays and objects.

■ **Note**   The use of variables in JavaScript is actually a bit more complicated. You can also use a variable without ever declaring it with the var keyword. The var keyword will declare the variable within the current scope. If var is missing, JavaScript will search for a variable with the same name declared at an upper level of scope. If JavaScript does not find this variable, a new one is declared; otherwise, JavaScript will use the values in the variable found. As a result, an incorrect use of variables can sometimes lead to errors that are difficult to detect.

Arrays

An array is a sequence of values separated by a comma and enclosed in square brackets [ ]:

```
var array = [ 1, 6, 3, 8, 2, 4 ];
```

Arrays are the simplest and most widely used data structure in JavaScript, so you should become very familiar with them. It is possible to access any value in an array by specifying its index (position in the array) in the brackets, immediately following the name of the array. In JavaScript the indexes start from 0:

```
array[3]   //returns 8
```

Arrays can contain any type of data, not just integers:

```
var fruits = [ "banana", "apple", "peach" ];
```

There are a many functions that can help us handle this kind of object. Because of its usefulness, I will be using this object frequently throughout the book, and it therefore seems proper to give it a quick look.

It is possible to know the number of the values in an array by writing

```
fruits.length   //returns 3
```

Or, if you know the values, you can get the corresponding index with

```
fruits.indexOf("apple") //returns 1
```

Moreover, there is a set of functions that allow us to add and remove items in an array. **push()** and **pop()** functions add and remove the last element in an array, whereas **shift()** and **unshift()** functions add and remove the first element in an array:

```
fruits.push("strawberry");
// Now the array is ["banana", "apple", "peach", "strawberry"];
fruits.pop();   //returns "strawberry"
// Now the array is ["banana", "apple", "peach"];
fruits.unshift("orange", "pear");
// Now the array is ["orange", "pear", "banana", "apple", "peach"];
fruits.shift(); //returns "orange"
// Now the array is ["pear", "banana", "apple", "peach"];
```

Sometimes, it is necessary to make a loop through every value in an array in order to perform some action with it. An approach that is widely used in other programming languages is the use of the function for(). For example, to calculate the sum of the values in an array, you would write

```
var sum = 0;
for (var i = 0; i < array.length; i++) {
    sum += array[i];
}
```

But, in JavaScript it is more common to use the forEach() function, where d assumes the values in the array, one by one, following the sequence:

```
var sum = 0;
array.forEach(function(d) {
    sum += d;
});
```

Objects

Arrays are useful for simple lists of values, but if you want structured data, you need to define an object. An object is a custom data structure whose properties and values you define. You can define an object by enclosing its properties between two curly brackets { }; every property is defined by a name followed by a colon (:) and the assigned value, and commas separate each property/value pair:

```
var animal = {
    species: "lion",
    class: "mammalia",
    order: "carnivora",
    extinct: false,
    number: 123456
};
```

In JavaScript code, dot notation refers to each value, specifying the name of the property:

```
animal.species        //Returns "lion"
```

Now that you have learned about both objects and arrays, you can see how it is possible to combine them in order to get more complex data structures in JavaScript. You can create arrays of objects or objects of arrays, or even objects of objects. Square brackets are used to indicate an array, curly brackets, an object. For example, let us define an array of objects in this way:

```
var animals = [
    {
        species: "lion",
        class: "mammalia",
        order: "carnivora",
        extinct: false,
        number: 123456
    },
    {
        species: "gorilla",
        class: "mammalia",
        order: "primates",
        extinct: false,
        number: 555234
    },
```

```
    {
        species: "octopus",
        class: "cephalopoda",
        order: "octopoda",
        extinct: false,
        number: 333421
    }
];
```

To get the values of these data structures, you need to use both the square brackets with the index and the name of the property:

```
animals[0].extinct //return false
animals[2].species //return "octopus"
```

Firebug and DevTools

To debug, if you are using an IDE, you can easily make use of the various debugging tools that are included with it. If you do not have access to an IDE, however, you can still avail yourself of external tools. Think of the browser as a development environment, where debugging tools can be integrated through plug-ins that are downloadable from Internet. There are many tools currently available on the Internet, but the one I want to propose is Firebug, a web development tool for those who prefer to use the browser Mozilla Firefox. Firebug is an add-in that integrates seamlessly into the Firefox browser, as demonstrated in Figure 1-15.

Figure 1-15. *Firebug is an extention of Mozilla Firefox and is fully integrated into the browser*

Firebug will prove a very useful tool throughout, especially when using use the jQuery and D3 libraries, which require that the structure of the DOM always be kept under control. This tool will allow you to monitor the structure of the DOM directly.

For those who prefer to use Google Chrome, however, there is DevTools, which is already integrated into the browser (see Figure 1-16). To access this tool, simply click the button at the top-right corner of the browser.

Figure 1-16. *With DevTools it is possible to monitor a lot of information about your web page*

Next, select Tools ➤ Developer Tools, or simply right-click any page element, and then select Inspect element in the context menu.

With these two tools, you can easily inspect not only each element of the DOM—its attributes and their values—but also the CSS styles applied to them. You can also input changes to these values to observe the effects in real time without having to modify the code on file and save it every time. Firebug and DevTools also include various tools for monitoring the performance of the page, for both rendering and networking.

With DevTools, particular attention should be paid to the use of the console as well. Through it, you can access diagnostic information, using methods such as `console.log()`. This method is frequently used to display the values of many variables through the console, passing the name of the variable as an argument, with the addition of text as an indication:

```
var x = 3;
console.log("The value of x is " + x); // The value of x is 3
```

It is also possible to enter commands and perform interactions with the document, using methods such as $() or profile(). For further information on these methods, see the documentation regarding the Console API (https://developers.google.com/chrome-developer-tools/docs/console-api) and the Command Line API (https://developers.google.com/chrome-developer-tools/docs/commandline-api).

JSON

JSON is a specific syntax for organizing data as JavaScript objects. This format is generally used in browser-based code, especially in JavaScript. JSON represents a valid alternative to XML for organizing data. Both are independent from the programming language, but JSON is faster and easier to parse with JavaScript than XML, which is a full-markup language. Moreover, D3 works well with JSON. Its structure follows perfectly the rules that we have seen for objects and arrays defined in JavaScript:

```
var company = {
    "name": "Elusive Dinamics",
    "location": "France",
    "sites": 2,
    "employees": 234,
    "updated": true
};
```

Summary

This first chapter has introduced you to many of the fundamental concepts that will accompany you throughout the book. First, you examined the most common types of charts and the elements that compose them. You also took a quick look at many of the technical aspects you need to know when setting about developing a chart on the Web. Finally, you briefly explored the types of data used in the JavaScript examples in this book.

I mentioned that the majority of your work will be done by a specialized JavaScript library. The next chapter will cover the highlights of the D3 library. Through a series of examples, you will see how to manipulate DOM elements by changing their attributes, and by creating new ones when needed. In the second part of the chapter, you will learn what the main object of manipulations with the D3 library is: **SVG elements**.

■ ■ ■

CHAPTER 2

Working with D3

In the various sections of this chapter, and as you delve deeper into the aspects of the library in the next chapters, you'll be able to appreciate that D3 has a unique and innovative structure. First of all, it does not use jQuery, but it reproduces all the features necessary for data visualization. Whereas in the jqPlot and Highcharts libraries, chart components are already created, requiring the users only to adjust their properties via the options object, D3 has virtually the opposite approach.

The D3 library allows you to build any representation, starting with the most basic graphical elements such as circles, lines, squares, and so on. Certainly, such an approach greatly complicates the implementation of a chart, but at the same time, it allows you to develop completely new graphical representations, free from having to follow the preset patterns that the other graphic libraries provide.

Thus, in the course of this chapter, you'll become acquainted with the basic concepts that underlie this library. You'll also find out how to manipulate the various Document Object Model (DOM) elements, especially the creation of Scalable Vector Graphics (SVG) elements, which are the essential building blocks of the graphical representations.

The chapter closes with a brief introduction to the transformations and transitions of SVG elements.

You'll start with an introduction to this wonderful library.

FIREBUG: DEBUGGING D3 CODE

Before beginning with some practical examples, I would like to remind you to use FireBug for debugging. At the least, be sure to get a good debugging tool in JavaScript that allows you to view the DOM tree of the web page upon which you'll be working (see the "FireBug and DevTool" section in Chapter 1).

Using a debugging tool with the D3 library is essential, given that unlike the other libraries you have seen, it is not structured with premodeled objects. With D3, it is necessary to start from scratch, implementing all the chart elements one by one. Therefore, those who are familiar with development will realize that choosing a good debugging tool is essential to solving any problems that arise.

With FireBug it is possible to edit, debug, and monitor CSS, SVG, and HTML. You can change their values in real time and see the effects. It also provides a console where you can read out the log, which is suitably placed within the JavaScript code to monitor the content of the variables used. This can be achieved by calling the `log()` function of the console object and passing the variable interested as argument:

```
console.log (variable);
It is possible to add some text for reference, as well:
console.log ("this is the value:");
```

You will see that, when working with D3, FireBug is crucial for inspecting the dynamic structures of SVG elements that JavaScript generates in the DOM.

Introducing D3

D3 is a JavaScript library that allows direct inspection and manipulation of the DOM, but is intended solely for data visualization. It really does its job excellently. In fact, the name D3 is derived from *data-driven documents*. D3 was developed by Mike Bostock, the creator of the Protovis library, which D3 is designed to replace.

This library is proving to be very versatile and powerful, thanks to the technologies upon which it is based: JavaScript, SVG, and CSS. D3 combines powerful visualization components with a data-driven approach to DOM manipulation. In so doing, D3 takes full advantage of the capabilities of the modern browser.

D3 allows you to bind arbitrary data to the DOM. Its strength is its capability to affect several transformations of the document. For example, a set of data could be converted into an interactive SVG graphical structure such as a chart.

If you are familiar with other JavaScript frameworks specialized in web chart representation (i.e. jqPlot), you know that their strength is that they provide structured solutions, which you manipulate through the settings of options. Instead, the strength of D3 is precisely the opposite. It provides the building blocks and tools to assemble structures based on SVG. The result of this approach is the continuous development of new structures, which are graphically rich and open to all sorts of interactions and animations. D3 is the perfect tool for those who want to develop new graphics solutions for aspects not covered by existing frameworks.

Differently from the other JavaScript graphic libraries, D3 does not use the jQuery library to handle the DOM elements, but it has many similar concepts in it, including the method-chaining paradigm and the selections. It provides a jQuery-like interface to the DOM, which means you don't need to know all the features of SVG in much detail. In order to handle the D3 code, you need to be able to use objects and functions and to understand the basics of SVG and CSS, which are used extensively. The sacrifices that go into mastering all of this knowledge are rewarded with the amazing visualizations you can create.

SVG provides the building blocks for the artwork; it allows you to draw all the basic shape primitives such as lines, rectangles, and circles, as well as text. It allows you to build complex shapes with paths.

Starting with a Blank HTML Page

It's time to practice the concepts just outlined. First, start with a blank page, shown in Listing 2-1. This will be the starting point for all of the D3 examples.

Listing 2-1. Ch2_01a.html

```
<!DOCTYPE html>
<html>
<head>
<meta charset="utf-8">
<script src="http://d3js.org/d3.v3.js"></script>
<style>

    // CSS Style here

</style>
</head>
<body>

    <!-- HTML elements here -->
```

```
<script type="text/javascript">

    // D3 code here

</script>
</body>
</html>
```

Although, at first glance, you see only a simple HTML blank page, there are some small measures you must take when you work with D3. The most simple and clear measure is to include the library D3:

```
<script src="../src/d3.v3.js"></script>
```

Or if you prefer to use a content delivery network (CDN) service:

```
<script src="http://d3js.org/d3.v3.js"></script>
```

When entering the URL of the remote D3 library, make sure that the website always includes the latest version. Another measure, which is less obvious, is to add the <head> of the page:

```
<meta charset="utf-8">
```

If you do not specify this row, you will soon find out that the D3 code you added does not run. Last, but not least, where you add the various parts of the code is very important. It is advisable to include all the JavaScript code of D3 at the end of the <body> section, after all the HTML elements.

Using Selections and Operators

To start working with D3, it is necessary to become familiar with the concept of *selections*. Having to deal with selections involves the use of three basic objects:

- **Selections**
- **Selectors**
- **Operators**

A **selection** is an array of node elements extracted from the current document. In order to extract a specific set of elements (selection), you need to use **selectors**. These are patterns that match elements in the tree structure of the document. Once you get a selection, you might wish to perform some operations on it and so you use **operators**. As a result of their operation, you get a new selection, and so it is possible to apply another operator, and so on.

Selectors and operators are defined by the W3C (World Wide Web Consortium) APIs and are supported by all modern browsers. Generally, you'll operate on HTML documents, and so you'll work on the selection of HTML elements.

Selections and Selectors

To extract a selection from a document, D3 provides two methods:

- select
- selectAll

d3.select("selector") selects the first element that matches the selector, returning a selection with only one element.

d3.selectAll("selector") instead selects all elements that match the selector, returning a selection with all these elements.

There is no better way to understand these concepts than to do so gradually, with some simple examples. Starting from the HTML page just described, add two paragraphs containing some text and then make a selection with D3 (see Listing 2-2).

Listing 2-2. Ch2_01a.html

```
<body>
<p>First paragraph</p>
<p>Second paragraph</p>
<script type="text/javascript">
    var selection = d3.select("p");
    console.log(selection);
</script>
</body>
```

d3.select is the top-level operator; "p" is the selector; and the selection is the returned value of the operator you assign to a variable. With this D3 command, you want to select the first element <p> in the web page. Using the log function, you can see the selection with FireBug in Figure 2-1.

Figure 2-1. *The FireBug console enables you to see the content of the selection*

Since you used the select() method, you have a selection with only one element, although in the web page there are two. If you want to select both, you use selectAll(), as in Listing 2-3.

Listing 2-3. Ch2_01b.html

```
<script type="text/javascript">
    var selection = d3.selectAll("p");
    console.log(selection);
</script>
```

Figure 2-2 shows both elements.

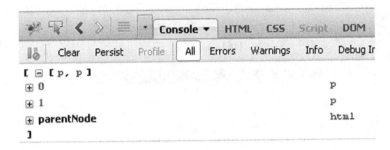

Figure 2-2. *FireBug shows the selection of all the <p> elements in the web page*

Now you have a selection with two elements. The great innovation that jQuery and D3 introduce with the concept of selection is that for loops are no long necessary. Instead of coding recursive functions to modify elements, you can operate on entire selections at once.

Operators

Once you have learned to make selections, it is time to apply operators to them.

An operator is a method that's applied to a selection, or generally to a set of elements, and it specifically "operates" a manipulation. For example, it can get or set a property of the elements in the selection, or can act in some way on their content. For example, you may want to replace existing text with new text. For this purpose, you use the text() operator, shown in Listing 2-4.

Listing 2-4. Ch2_02.html

```
<body>
<p>First paragraph</p>
<p>Second paragraph</p>
<script type="text/javascript">
    var selection = d3.selectAll("p");
    selection.text("we add this new text");
</script>
</body>
```

The page now reports twice for the same text, where before there were two paragraphs (see Figure 2-3).

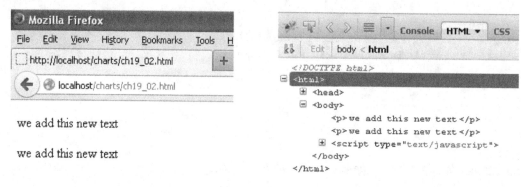

Figure 2-3. *The text contained in the two <p> elements has been replaced in the browser on the left and is shown in FireBug on the right*

You defined the variable selection and then applied the operator to this variable. But there is another way to write all this; you can use the methods of chain functionality, especially when you apply multiple operators to the same selection.

```
d3.selectAll("p").text("we add this new text");
```

You have seen that by passing a parameter to the text() operator, you are going to replace the existing text. So it is as if the function were setText("new text"). But you do not always want that. If you do not pass any arguments, the function will have a different behavior. It will return the value of the text already present. This can be very useful for further processing, or for assigning this string value to a variable or an array. Therefore, without parameters, it is as if it were getText().

```
var text = d3.select("p").text();
console.log(text);
```

The text variable contains the "First paragraph" string (see Figure 2-4).

Figure 2-4. *The FireBug console shows the text contained in the selection*

There are operators for every kind of object upon which you'd want operate. These operators can set the content of:

- **Attributes**
- **Styles**
- **Properties**
- **HTML**
- **Text**

You just saw the text() operator in action. Next, you'll see some of the other operators.

■ **Note** If you want to learn more about operators, I suggest you visit the API reference for the D3 library at this link: https://github.com/mbostock/d3/wiki/API-Reference.

For example, it is helpful to be able to change a CSS style and you can do so with the style() operator. Listing 2-5 replaces the existing text using text() and then modifies its style to be written in red, adding the style() operator to the methods chain.

Listing 2-5. Ch2_03.html

```
<body>
<p>Existing black text</p>
<script type="text/javascript">
    d3.selectAll("p").style('color','red').text("New red text");
</script>
</body>
```

Figure 2-5 shows the original text on the left and the newly styled text on the right.

Existing black text

New red text

Figure 2-5. *The original text is replaced by the new red text, applying the chain method upon the selection*

Another operator, attr(), acts at the level of attributes of elements. This operator will be used when you create new SVG elements; in fact, it allows you to define the attributes while you are creating the tags, before inserting them in the web page. Here you can see how it can modify an existing attribute. In Listing 2-6, you're changing the alignment of a title to be displayed in the middle of the page (see Figure 2-6).

Listing 2-6. ch2_04.html

```
<body>
<h1>Title</h1>
<script type="text/javascript">
    d3.select('h1').attr('align','center');
</script>
</body>
```

Title

Figure 2-6. *With the D3 library it is possible to dynamically add a title to a web page*

Creating New Elements

Now that you have seen how to act at the level of elements and how to modify both attributes and content, it is time to see how to create new items. To do this, D3 provides a number of operators (https://github.com/mbostock/d3/wiki/API-Reference), among which the most commonly used are:

- html()
- append()
- insert()

The html( ) Method

This section shows how the html() method operates. You always start from a selection and then apply this operator to add an element inside. For example, you select a particular tag as a container, and then write a string that is passed as an argument. The string then becomes the content of the tag (see Listing 2-7).

Listing 2-7. Ch2_05.html

```
<body>
<p>A paragraph</p>
<script type="text/javascript">
    d3.select('p').html("<h1>New Paragraph</h1>");
</script>
</body>
```

Here, you first select the <p> tag with select() and then with html() you replace its contents with a new element, <h1>. Figure 2-7 shows the original text on the left and the newly formatted version on the right.

Figure 2-7. *The text in a paragraph element <p> is replaced with a heading element <h>*

You can see this change better, using FireBug (see Figure 2-8)

Figure 2-8. *FireBug clearly shows the insertion of the head element (on the right) to replace the content of the paragraph element (on the left)*

Practically, the html() function replaces the contents of the selection with the HTML code passed as an argument. Exactly as its name suggests, this function allows you to dynamically write HTML code within the elements of the selection.

The append( ) Method

Another popular method for adding elements is append().

Recall that when you're using the html() operator, the content of the selected tag, if any, is replaced with the new one passed as an argument. The append() operator instead adds a new element, passed as its argument, to the end of all the existing elements contained in the selected tag. The content of the newly created element must be added to the chain of methods, using text() if it is only a string, or append(), html() or insert() if it is a further element.

In order to understand this last point, add an unordered list <ul> with some items containing fruit names to the page (see Figure 2-9).

* Apples
* Pears
* Bananas

Figure 2-9. *An unordered list of three fruits*

Say that you now want to add Oranges to this list. In order to do this, you must select the unordered list tag <ul> and then use append() to add a list item tag <li>. But append() creates only the tag, so in order to insert the string "Oranges" inside it, you need to add the text() operator to the chain of methods (see Listing 2-8).

Listing 2-8. Ch2_06.html

```
<body>
<ul>
    <li>Apples</li>
    <li>Pears</li>
    <li>Bananas</li>
</ul>
<script type="text/javascript">
    d3.select('ul').append('li').text("Oranges");
</script>
</body>
```

Figure 2-10 shows the list with the added element.

- Apples
- Pears
- Bananas
- Oranges

Figure 2-10. *Using the append() operator, you have added the Oranges item to the end of the list*

Figure 2-11 shows it in FireBug.

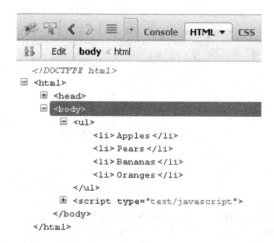

Figure 2-11. *FireBug shows the HTML structure with the added <li> element*

In this case, you have used simple text as the content for the new element added to the list, but the append() operator can do more. In fact, as previously noted, the content of an element may be yet another element. This allows you to create an entire tree of HTML elements, all by exploiting a chain method. In fact, the content of the new element created by the append() operator can in turn be created by another operator, such as another append() operator. Look at Listing 2-9. It is a simple example that will help you better understand this concept.

Listing 2-9. Ch2_06b.html

```
<body>
<ul>
    <li>Apples</li>
    <li>Pears</li>
    <li>Bananas</li>
</ul>
<script type="text/javascript">
    d3.select('ul').append('li').text("Citrus fruits");
    d3.select('ul').append('ul').append('li').text("Oranges");
    d3.select('ul').select('ul').append('li').text("Lemons");
    d3.select('ul').select('ul').append('li').text("Grapefruits");
</script>
</body>
```

This time, you want to create a sub-category of fruits, Citrus fruits, in which we shall assign the Oranges, Lemons, and Grapefruits items. In order to do this, you need to add a new list item <li> with the string "Citrus fruits" as its content. This works the same way as in the previous example, concatenating the text() operator just after the append() operator. Then you need to create a new list item. This time, its content is an unordered list. Thus, you need to concatenate two append() operators in order to create a list item <li> element nested in an unordered list <ul> element. You can then add two other new elements to the nested unordered list, again with the append() operator.

Figure 2-12 shows the new nested list of citrus fruits on the browser and the HTML structure that generates it on FireBug.

Figure 2-12. *FireBug shows the HTML structure with a nested unordered list in the browser on the left and in FireBug on the right*

The insert( ) Method

The last operator, insert(), has a particular behavior. If you use it with only one argument, it behaves as if you were using append(). Normally, it is used with two arguments. The first indicates the tag to add, and the second is the matching tag where you want to insert it. In fact, replace append() with insert() in the preceding fruit list example, and you will obtain a different result, shown in Figure 2-13 (the original list is on the left and new one with Oranges added is on the right).

```
d3.select('ul').insert('li','li').text("Oranges");
```

Figure 2-13. *Using the* insert() *operator, you can insert the Oranges item at the top of the list*

Now the new element is at the top of the unordered list. But if you wanted to insert a new item in a different location than the first? You can use the CSS selector nth-child(i) to do this, where i is the index of the element. Therefore, if you use the selector li:nth-child(i), you are going to select the i-th <li> element. Thus, if you want to insert an element between the second and the third element, you need to call the third <li> element in the insert() operator (remember that this operator puts the new element before the one called):

```
d3.select('ul').insert('li','li:nth-child(2)').text("Oranges");
```

This will insert the new Orange item between the second and the third items in the list, as shown in Figure 2-14 (in the browser on the left and in FireBug on the right).

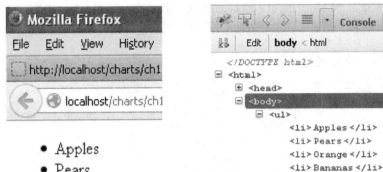

Figure 2-14. *Using the CSS selector nth-child, you can add the Oranges item in any position in the list*

HTML(), APPEND(), AND INSERT() OPERATORS: A BETTER UNDERSTANDING

Sometimes, understanding the functionality of these three operators isn't easy. Consider this schematic HTML structure, containing a generic parent tag and some children tags inside:

```
<parent>
    <child></child>
    <child></child>
    <child></child>
</parent>
```

The following simple diagrams show what each operator does exactly, in order to better understand the different behaviors. It is crucial that you fully understand the functionality of these three operators if you want to exploit the full potential of the D3 library.

When you need to create a new tag element at the end of a list of other tags at the same level of the HTML structure, use the append() operator. Figure 2-15 shows the behavior of this operator.

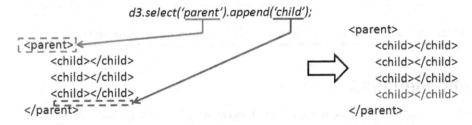

Figure 2-15. *The append() operator adds a child tag to the end of the list*

When you need to create a new tag element at the beginning of a list of other tags at the same level of the HTML structure, use the insert() operator. Figure 2-16 shows the behavior of this operator.

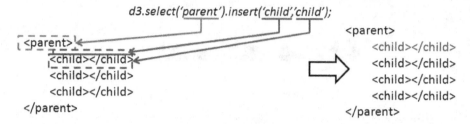

Figure 2-16. *The insert() operator adds a child tag before the child tag is passed as a second argument*

When you need to create a new tag element at a specific position in a list of other tags, always at the same level of the HTML structure, use the insert() operator. Figure 2-17 shows the behavior of this operator.

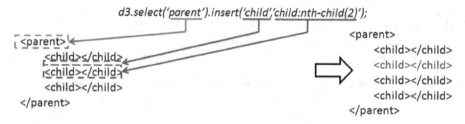

Figure 2-17. *You can pass a child of the list as the argument using the CSS selector nth-child()*

When you need to create a new tag element in place of another tag or in place of a list of other tags at the same level of the HTML structure, use the html() operator. Figure 2-18 illustrates the behavior of this operator.

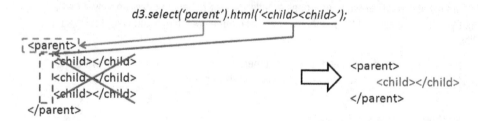

Figure 2-18. *The html() operator replaces the contents of the parent tag with the tag passed as the argument*

Inserting Data into Elements

You have just seen how to create new elements in your document. But how can you put the data inside? This is where the data() operator comes in, by passing an array of data as an argument.

For each element in the selection, a value will be assigned in the array following the same order of the sequence. This correspondence is indicated by a generic function in which d and i are passed as arguments.

```
function(d,i) {
    // code with d and i
    // return some elaboration of d;
}
```

This function will be executed as many times as there are elements in the list: i is the index of the sequence and d is the value in the data array corresponding to that index. Many times you are not interested in the value of i and use only d.

For those familiar with the for loop, it is as if you had written:

```
for(i=0; i < selection.length; i++){
    d = input_array[i];
    //  code with d and i
    //return output_array[i];
}
```

To understand the whole thing, there is no better way than to provide an example. Define an array containing the names of three fruits. You'll create an unordered list with three empty items and create a selection of these items with selectAll(). You must have a corresponding number of items in the selection and values in the array; otherwise, the values in surplus will not be evaluated. You associate the array to the selection and then, applying function(d), write the values of each item within the list (see Listing 2-10).

Listing 2-10. Ch2_07.html

```
<body>
<ul>
    <li></li>
    <li></li>
    <li></li>
</ul>
<script type="text/javascript">
    var fruits = ['Apples', 'Pears', 'Bananas'];

    d3.selectAll('li').data(fruits).text( function(d){
        return d;
    });
</script>
</body>
```

Figure 2-19 shows the result in the browser on the left and in FireBug on the right. In FireBug, you can see the HTML structure used for each list item <li> content, which was not present when you wrote Listing 2-10. These added text items are the values of the fruits array.

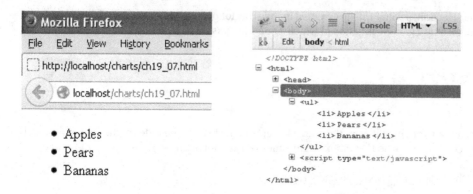

Figure 2-19. *It is possible to fill the content of HTML elements with array values*

The data() operator does not just bind data to elements, it computes a connection between the element of the selection and the data provided. All goes well as long as the length of the array is equal to the number of elements in the selection. But what if it is not so? If you have a selection with three elements and provide an array with five values, the two extra values will be stored in a special selection called "enter." This selection is accessible via the enter() operator on the return value of a call to data. You can see this in the example in Listing 2-11.

Listing 2-11. Ch2_08.html

```
<body>
<ul>
    <li></li>
    <li></li>
    <li></li>
</ul>
<script type="text/javascript">
    var fruits = ['Apples', 'Pears', 'Bananas', 'Oranges', 'Strawberries'];
    var list = d3.select('ul');
    var fruits = list.selectAll('li').data(fruits);
    fruits.enter().append('li').text( function(d){
        return d;
    });
    fruits.text( function(d){
        return d;
    });
</script>
</body>
```

First, you define the array with five different fruits. Then, you make a selection that contains the list and assign it to the variable list. From this selection, you make a further selection containing the three empty list items and assign the fruits array to it. From this association, the last two values of the array will advance (Oranges and Strawberries), and thus they will be stored in the enter selection. Now you must pay particular attention to this point: usually it is best to deal with the enter selection first. Therefore, you have to access the enter selection and use append() in order to create two new list items with the two fruits advanced. Then you write the values in the fruit selection within the three existing list items.

You get a list with all five fruits, in the order in which they were entered. Figure 2-20 shows the change in the browser on the top and in FireBug on the bottom.

Figure 2-20. *It is possible to fill the content of HTML elements with array values and to integrate them with other elements if they are not enough*

Applying Dynamic Properties

You have seen how to define and modify styles, attributes, and other properties with the use of functions provided by the D3 framework. But so far, they have been treated as constants. It is time to take a leap forward. One of the advantages of the JavaScript language and especially of the D3 (and jQuery) library lies in its ability to make the content of a page dynamic. In fact, you have just seen how to delete, create, and manipulate the element tags in a web page. A similar approach is also applicable to other types of values such as CSS styles or the attributes of elements you created or manipulated through the selections mechanism. You could even create different options relating to events or controls.

D3 provides you with a set of specific functions for this purpose. Despite their apparent simplicity, these functions can be a powerful tool for those who know how to make full use of their mechanisms.

In the example in Listing 2-12, you use a generic function to assign a random color to the paragraphs. Every time the page is loaded, it shows a different set of colors.

Listing 2-12. Ch2_09.html

```
<body>
<p>the first paragraph</p>
<p>the second paragraph</p>
<p>the third paragraph</p>
<p>the last paragraph</p>
<script>
d3.selectAll("p").style("color", function() {

    r = Math.round((Math.random() * 255));
    g = Math.round((Math.random() * 255));
    b = Math.round((Math.random() * 255));
    return "rgb("+r+", "+g+", "+b+")";

});
</script>
</body>
```

Figure 2-21 on the left shows the results of one loaded page and another, on the right, with different colors applied to it. Every time you load the page, you get a different color combination.

Figure 2-21. *The colors change each time the page loads*

Certainly, this is a very trivial example, but it shows the basic idea. Any value that you assign to an attribute, a text, or a style can be dynamically generated from a function.

Adding SVG Elements

You have finally arrived at the point where you can apply what you learned to create beautiful displays. In this section, you'll begin to learn about the peculiarities of the D3 library, with the creation and manipulation of graphic elements such as lines, squares, circles, and more. All of this will be done primarily by using nested structures of two tags: <svg> for graphic elements and <g> for application groups.

First, you'll learn how to create an SVG element and how to nest it in a group using the <g> tag. Later, you'll discover what SVG transformations are and how to apply them to groups of elements. Finally, with a further example, you'll see how to animate these elements with SVG transitions, in order to get nice animations.

Creating an SVG Element

You can start from a `<div>` tag, which will be used as a container for the visualization, similarly to what jQuery does with `<canvas>`. From this `<div>` tag, you create the root tag `<svg>` using the `append()` operator. Then you can set the size of the visualization by acting on the `height` and `width` attributes using the `attr()` operator (see Listing 2-13).

Listing 2-13. Ch2_10.html

```
<body>
<div id="circle"></div>
<script type="text/javascript">
    var svg = d3.select('#circle')
        .append('svg')
        .attr('width', 200)
        .attr('height', 200);
</script>
</body>
```

From FireBug, you can see the `<body>` structure with the new `<svg>` element and its attributes (see Figure 2-22).

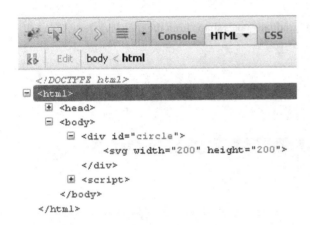

Figure 2-22. *FireBug shows the `<svg>` tag you just created*

You can also add a basic shape to the root tag `<svg>`. Let's add a yellow circle (see Listing 2-14). Once you understand this principle, it is very simple to repeat it whenever you wish.

Listing 2-14. ch19_10.html

```
<script type="text/javascript">
    var svg = d3.select('#circle')
        .append('svg')
        .attr('width', 200)
        .attr('height', 200);
```

```
svg.append('circle')
    .style('stroke', 'black')
    .style('fill', 'yellow')
    .attr('r', 40)
    .attr('cx', 50)
    .attr('cy', 50);
</script>
```

Figure 2-23 shows the perfect yellow circle.

Figure 2-23. *A perfect yellow circle*

In FireBug, you can see how the tree structure of the tags gradually takes shape from the root `<svg>`, specifying all the attributes (see Figure 2-24).

```
Console   HTML ▼   CSS   Script   DOM   Net   Cookies

Edit   body < html

<!DOCTYPE html>
<html>
  ⊞ <head>
  ⊟ <body>
      ⊟ <div id="circle">
          ⊟ <svg width="200" height="200">
                <circle style="stroke: black; fill: yellow;" r="40" cx="50" cy="50">
              </svg>
          </div>
      ⊞ <script>
  </body>
</html>
```

Figure 2-24. *In FireBug, it is possible to follow the development of the tag structure*

Now that you have seen how to create graphics using SVG tags, the next step is to apply transformations to them.

Transformations

A key aspect of D3 is its transformation capability. This extends the concept of SVG transformations in JavaScript. Once an object is created in SVG, from a simple square to more complex structures, it can be subjected to various transformations. The most common transformations include:

- **Scale**

- **Translate**

- **Rotate**

■ **Note**   If you are interested in learning more about transformations, I suggest that you visit this page: `https://developer.mozilla.org/en-US/docs/Web/SVG/Attribute/transform`. It lists all the available transformations, with simple explanations.

Typically, you use sequences of these basic transformations to obtain more complex transformations. As always, you'll see a series of small examples to illustrate the concept of transformations. First, you'll draw a small red square in the same way you drew the yellow circle (see Listing 2-15). For this purpose, you use the `<rect>` tag. The only difference from `<circle>` is that for rectangles, you need to specify the position of the rectangle's top-left corner with x and y instead of the center of the circle. Then you have to specify the size of the rectangle, and since it is a square, the sides will be equal.

Listing 2-15. Ch2_11a.html

```
<div id="square"></div>
<script type="text/javascript">
    var svg = d3.select('#square')
        .append('svg')
        .attr('width', 200)
        .attr('height', 200);
    svg.append('rect')
        .style('stroke', 'black')
        .style('fill', 'red')
        .attr('x', 50)
        .attr('y', 50)
        .attr('width', 50)
        .attr('height', 50);
</script>
```

It's a good time to introduce another concept that will be useful when in dealing with SVG elements: *groups* of elements. You'll often need to apply a series of operations, including only the transformations at times, to a group of shapes or to a complex shape (consisting of multiple basic shapes). This is possible by grouping several items together in a group, which is reflected in SVG by putting all the elements in a tag `<g>`. So if you want to apply a transformation to the red square for example, you need to insert it within a group (see Listing 2-16).

Listing 2-16. Ch2_11a.html

```
var svg = d3.select('#square')
    .append('svg')
    .attr('width', 200)
    .attr('height', 200);

var g = svg.append("svg:g");

g.append('rect')
    .style('stroke', 'black')
    .style('fill', 'red')
    .attr('x', 50)
    .attr('y', 50)
    .attr('width', 50)
    .attr('height', 50);
```

Figure 2-25 shows how the SVG structure appears in FireBug.

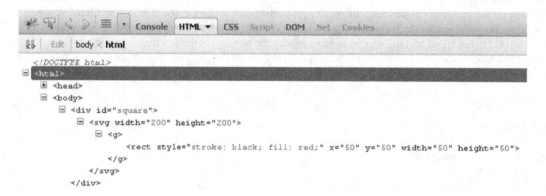

Figure 2-25. *FireBug shows the SVG structure corresponding to the red square*

In the browser, you'll a small red square like the one shown in Figure 2-26.

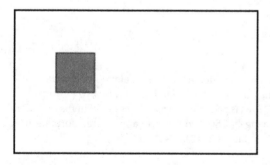

Figure 2-26. *A red square is a good object upon which to apply transformations*

Now you'll apply all the transformations, one by one. Start with the *translation*, which in SVG is expressed by the `translate(x, y)` function, where x and y are the amount of pixels by which the square will be moved (see Listing 2-17).

Listing 2-17. Ch2_11b.html

```
var g = svg.append("svg:g")
    .attr("transform", "translate(" + 100 + ",0)");
```

Here I put the value 100 outside of the string passed as an attribute, to understand that at that point you can insert a previously defined variable. This will make the transformation more dynamic. With this line, you moved the square to the right 100 pixels (see Figure 2-27).

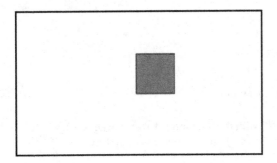

Figure 2-27. *Now the red square appears right-shifted by 100 pixels*

Another transformation that you can apply to the square is called *scaling*. In this SVG, it is expressed through the function `scale(s)` or `scale(sx, sy)`. If you pass a single parameter in the function, the scaling will be uniform, but if you pass two parameters, you can apply the expansion of the square in a different way horizontally and vertically. Listing 2-18 increases the size of the red square by two times. Thus, you need to apply the `scale()` transformation and to pass the value 2 as a parameter. The number passed is the factor by which the size of the square will be multiplied. Since you've passed a single parameter, scaling is uniform.

Listing 2-18. Ch2_11c.html

```
var g = svg.append("svg:g")
    .attr("transform","scale(2)");
```

Figure 2-28 shows the square scaled by two times. The square has doubled in height and width.

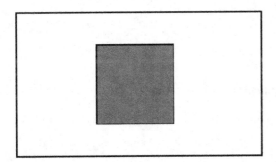

Figure 2-28. *The red square has doubled its size*

If you want non-uniform scaling, you can use something like Listing 2-19 to obtain a result similar to Figure 2-29. Non-uniform scaling can distort a figure to give another picture. In this case, you get a rectangle from a square.

Listing 2-19. Ch2_11d.html

```
var g = svg.append("svg:g")
       .attr("transform","scale(2, 1)");
```

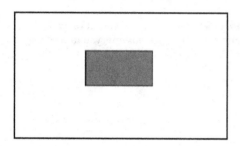

Figure 2-29. *A rectangle obtained by applying non-uniform scaling to a square*

The last kind of transformation is *rotation*. It is expressed in SVG with the function rotate(degree,x,y), where the first argument is the angle of rotation (clockwise) in degrees, and x and y are the coordinates of the center of rotation.

Say you want the center of rotation to correspond with the center of the square, which is located at x = 75 and y = 75. If you wish to draw a rhombus, you need to perform a rotation of 45 degrees on the square (see Listing 2-20).

Listing 2-20. Ch2_11e.html

```
var g = svg.append("svg:g")
       .attr("transform","rotate(45, 75, 75)");
```

You get the rhombus (see Figure 2-30).

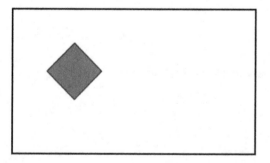

Figure 2-30. *A rhombus is the result you obtain when you rotate a square*

But the most interesting effect involves applying the transformations in a sequence, thereby creating a chain (see Listing 2-21).

Listing 2-21. Ch2_11f.html

```
var g = svg.append("svg:g")
    .attr("transform", "translate(-30, 0),scale(2, 1),rotate(45, 75, 75)");
```

From this listing, you obtain the shape in Figure 2-31.

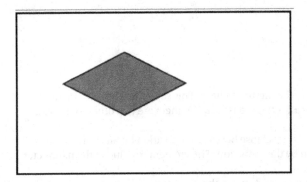

Figure 2-31. *A rhombus obtained by applying a chain of transformations to a square*

Transitions

You have seen that values of attributes, styles, and so forth, can be dynamic, according to the definition set with the help of certain functions. But D3 offers more—you can even animate your shapes. D3 provides three functions to this purpose:

- `transition()`
- `delay()`
- `duration()`

Naturally, you'll apply these functions to the SVG elements, thanks to D3, which can recognize any kind of values and interpolate them.

You define a transition when an SVG shape passes from one state to another. Both the starting state and the final state are characterized by several parameters that define the color, the shape, the size, and the position of an object. You take as the initial state the one defined in the yellow circle example (refer to Listing 2-14). In Listing 2-22, you subject the circle to a transition consisting of three different mutations: the circle changes its color to black (setting `fill` to `black`), it reduces its area (changing `r` from 40 to 10), and it moves slightly to the right (changing `cx` from 50 to 150).

Listing 2-22. Ch2_12.html

```
<div id="circle"></div>
<script>
var svg = d3.select('#circle')
    .append('svg')
    .attr('width', 200)
    .attr('height', 200);
```

```
svg.append('circle')
    .style('stroke', 'black')
    .style('fill', 'yellow')
    .attr('r', 40)
    .attr('cx', 50)
    .attr('cy', 50)
    .transition()
    .delay(100)
    .duration(4000)
    .attr("r", 10)
    .attr("cx", 150)
    .style("fill", "black");
</script>
```

So, in this example, you add the `transition()` method to the methods chain. This separates the initial state from the final one and warns D3 of a transition. Immediately after the `transition()`, there are two other functions: `delay()` and `duration()`.

The `delay()` function takes one argument: the time that must elapse before the transition begins. The `duration()` function, in contrast, is defined as the time taken by the transition. The greater the value of the parameter passed, the slower the transition will be.

Following these three functions, you add all the attributes characterizing the final state of the figure to the method chain. D3 interpolates the intermediate values depending on the time you have established, and will generate all the intermediate figures with those values. What appears before your eyes is an animation in which the yellow circle turns black, moving to the left and decreasing in size. All of this takes four seconds.

Figure 2-32 shows the transition sequence whereby you can see the changes to the circle.

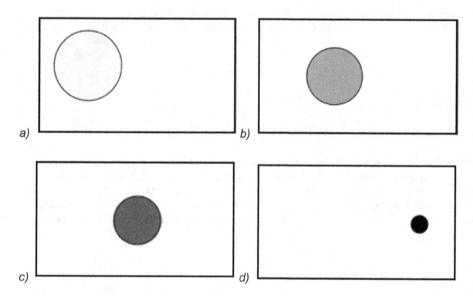

Figure 2-32. *Different instances of the animation of a circle subjected to transitions*

The simple examples you have seen so far were applied to one graphic element at a time. The next step is to apply what you have learned to groups of elements, so as to create more complex graphics. Subsequent chapters provide good examples in which this basic concept of the D3 library will be put into practice.

Summary

This chapter covered the highlights of the D3 library. The D3 library can manage **selections**, **selectors** and **operators** without making use of jQuery JavaScript library. Through a series of examples, you have seen how to manipulate DOM elements by changing their attributes, and by creating new ones when needed. In the second part of the chapter, you learned what the main object of manipulations with the D3 library is: **SVG elements**. These are the graphic building blocks with which you build your charts. Finally, you took a quick look at how to apply **SVG transformations** to these graphic elements and then at how to exploit **SVG transitions** to generate nice animations.

The next chapter puts what you have learned so far about the D3 library into practice, by implementing line charts. Taking one SVG element after another, you'll see how to achieve attractive graphical representations.

CHAPTER 3

■ ■ ■

Line Charts with D3

In this chapter, you are going to create a line chart with ticks and labels. You will find out how to add Scalable Vector Graphics (SVG) elements to a document, and by manipulating these elements, how you can create any kind of visualization. Such flexibility enables you to build any type of chart, building it up brick by brick.

You'll begin by looking at how to build the basic elements of a line chart using the D3 commands introduced in the previous chapter. In particular, you'll be analyzing the concepts of scales, domains, and ranges, which you'll be encountering frequently. These constitute a typical aspect of the D3 library, in terms of how it manages sets of values.

Once you understand how to manage values in their domains, scales, and intervals, you'll be ready to move on to the realization of the chart components, such as axes, axis labels, the title, and the grid. These components form the basis upon which you'll be drawing the line chart. Unlike in jqPlot, these components are not readily available but must be developed gradually. This will result in additional work, but it will also enable you to create special features. Your D3 charts will be able to respond to particular needs, or at least, they will have a totally original look. By way of example, you'll see how to add arrows to the axes.

Another peculiarity of the D3 library is the use of functions that read data contained in a file. You'll see how these functions work and how to exploit them for your needs.

Once you have the basic knowledge necessary to implement a line chart, you'll see how to implement a multiseries line chart. You'll also read about how to implement a legend and how to associate it with the chart.

Finally, to conclude, you'll analyze a particular case of line chart: the difference line chart. This will help you understand clip area paths—what they are and what their uses are.

Developing a Line Chart with D3

You'll begin to finally implement your chart using the D3 library. In this and in the following sections, you'll discover a different approach toward chart implementation compared to the one adopted with libraries such as jqPlot and Highcharts. Here the implementation is at a lower level and the code is much longer and more complex; however, nothing beyond your reach.

Now, step by step, or better, brick by brick, you'll discover how to produce a line chart and the elements that compose it.

Starting with the First Bricks

The first "brick" to start is to include the D3 library in your web page (for further information, see Appendix A):

```
<script src="../src/d3.v3.min.js"></script>
```

Or if you prefer to use a content delivery network (CDN) service:

```
<script src="http://d3js.org/d3.v3.min.js"></script>
```

The next "brick" consists of the input data array in Listing 3-1. This array contains the y values of the data series.

Listing 3-1. Ch3_01.html

```
var data = [100, 110, 140, 130, 80, 75, 120, 130, 100];
```

Listing 3-2 you define a set of variables related to the size of the visualization where you're drawing the chart. The w and h variables are the width and height of the chart; the margins are used to create room at the edges of the chart.

Listing 3-2. Ch3_01.html

```
w = 400;
h = 300;
margin_x = 32;
margin_y = 20;
```

Because you're working on a graph based on an x-axis and y-axis, in D3 it is necessary to define a scale, a domain, and a range of values for each of these two axes. Let's first clarify these concepts and learn how they are managed in D3.

Scales, Domains, and Ranges

You have already had to deal with scales, even though you might not realize it. The linear scale is more natural to understand, although in some examples, you have used a logarithmic scale (see the Sidebar "LOG SCALE" below)

LOG SCALE

The log scale uses intervals corresponding to orders of magnitude (generally ten) rather than a standard linear scale. This allows you to represent a large range of values (v) on an axis.

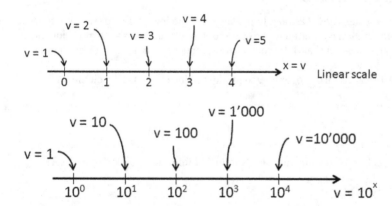

The logarithm is another way of writing exponentials, and you can use it to separate the exponent (x) and place it on an axis.

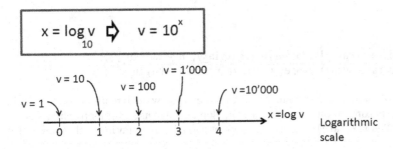

For example, an increase of one point on a log scale corresponds to an increase of 10 times that value. Similarly, an increase of two points corresponds to an increase of 100 times that value. And so on.

A **scale** is simply a function that converts a value in a certain interval, called a **domain**, into another value belonging to another interval, called a **range**. But what does all this mean exactly? How does this help you?

Actually, this can serve you every time you want to affect the conversion of a value between two variables belonging to different intervals, but keeping its "meaning" with respect to the current interval. This relates to the concept of normalization.

Suppose that you want to convert a value from an instrument, such as the voltage reported by a multimeter. You know that the voltage value would read between 0 and 5 volts, which is the range of values, also known as the domain.

You want to convert the voltage measured on a scale of red. Using Red-Green-Blue (RGB) codes, this value will be between 0 and 255. You have now defined another color range, which is the range.

Now suppose the voltage on the multimeter reads 2.7 volts, and the color scale shown in red corresponds to 138 (actually 137.7). You have just applied a linear scale for the conversion of values. Figure 3-1 shows the conversion of the voltage value into the corresponding R value on the RGB scale. This conversion operates within a linear scale, since the values are converted linearly.

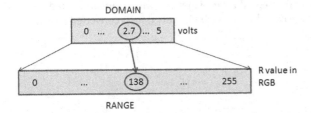

Figure 3-1. *The conversion from the voltage to the R value is managed by the D3 library*

But of what use is all of this? First, conversions between different intervals are not so uncommon when you aim to visualize data in a chart, and second, such conversions are managed completely by the D3 library. You do not need to do any calculations; you just need to define the domains, the range, and the scale to apply.

Translating this example into D3 code, you can write:

```
var scale = d3.scale.linear(),
        .domain([0,5]),
        .range([0,255]);
console.log(Math.round(scale(2.7)));    //it returns 138 on FireBug console
```

Inside the Code

You can define the scale, the domain, and the range; therefore, you can continue to implement the line chart by adding Listing 3-3 to your code.

Listing 3-3. Ch3_01.html

```
y = d3.scale.linear().domain([0, d3.max(data)]).range([0 + margin_y, h - margin_y]);
x = d3.scale.linear().domain([0, data.length]).range([0 + margin_x, w - margin_x]);
```

Because the input data array is one-dimensional and contains the values that you want to represent on the y-axis, you can extend the domain from 0 to the maximum value of the array. You don't need to use a for loop to find this value. D3 provides a specific function called max(date), where the argument passed is the array in which you want to find the maximum.

Now is the time to begin adding SVG elements. The first element to add is the <svg> element that represents the root of all the other elements you're going to add. The function of the <svg> tag is somewhat similar to that of the canvas in jQuery and jqPlot. As such, you need to specify the canvas size with w and h. Inside the <svg> element, you append a <g> element so that all the elements added to it internally will be grouped together.

Subsequently, apply a transformation to this group <g> of elements. In this case, the transformation consists of a translation of the coordinate grid, moving it down by h pixels, as shown in Listing 3-4.

Listing 3-4. Ch3_01.html

```
var svg = d3.select("body")
    .append("svg:svg")
    .attr("width", w)
    .attr("height", h);

var g = svg.append("svg:g")
    .attr("transform", "translate(0," + h + ")");
```

Another fundamental thing you need in order to create a line chart is the **path element**. This path is filled with the data using the d attribute.

The manual entry of all these values is too arduous and in this regard D3 provides you with a function that does it for you: d3.svg.line. So, in Listing 3-5, you declare a variable called line in which every data is converted into a point (x,y).

Listing 3-5. Ch3_01.html

```
var line = d3.svg.line()
    .x(function(d,i) { return x(i); })
    .y(function(d) { return -1 * y(d); });
```

As you'll see in all the cases where you need to make a scan of an array (a for loop), in D3 such a scan is handled differently through the use of the parameters d and i. The index of the current item of the array is indicated with i, whereas the current item is indicated with d. Recall that you translated the y-axis down with a transformation. You need to keep that mind; if you want to draw a line correctly, you must use the negative values of y. This is why you multiply the d values by -1.

The next step is to assign a line to a path element (see Listing 3-6).

Listing 3-6. Ch3_01.html

```
g.append("svg:path").attr("d", line(data));
```

If you stopped here and launch the web browser on the page, you would get the image shown in Figure 3-2.

Figure 3-2. *The default behavior of an SVG path element is to draw filled areas*

This seems to be wrong somehow, but you must consider that in the creation of images with SVG, the role managed by CSS styles is preponderant. In fact, you can simply add the CSS classes in Listing 3-7 to have the line of data.

Listing 3-7. Ch3_01.html

```
<style>
path {
    stroke: steelblue;
    stroke-width: 3;
    fill: none;
}

line {
    stroke: black;
}
</style>
```

Thus, with the CSS style classes suitably defined, you'll get a line as shown in Figure 3-3.

Figure 3-3. *The SVG path element draws a line if the CSS style classes are suitably defined*

But you are still far from having a line chart. You must add the two axes. To draw these two objects, you use simple SVG lines, as shown in Listing 3-8.

Listing 3-8. Ch3_01.html

```
// draw the x axis
g.append("svg:line")
    .attr("x1", x(0))
    .attr("y1", -y(0))
    .attr("x2", x(w))
    .attr("y2", -y(0))
```

```
// draw the y axis
g.append("svg:line")
    .attr("x1", x(0))
    .attr("y1", -y(0))
    .attr("x2", x(0))
    .attr("y2", -y(d3.max(data))-10)
```

Now is the time to add labels. For this purpose there is a D3 function that greatly simplifies the job: ticks(). This function is applied to a D3 scale such as x or y, and returns rounded numbers to use as ticks. You need to use the function text(String) to obtain the string value of the current d (see Listing 3-9).

Listing 3-9. ch3_01.html

```
//draw the xLabels
g.selectAll(".xLabel")
    .data(x.ticks(5))
    .enter().append("svg:text")
    .attr("class", "xLabel")
    .text(String)
    .attr("x", function(d) { return x(d) })
    .attr("y", 0)
    .attr("text-anchor", "middle");

// draw the yLabels
g.selectAll(".yLabel")
    .data(y.ticks(5))
    .enter().append("svg:text")
    .attr("class", "yLabel")
    .text(String)
    .attr("x", 25)
    .attr("y", function(d) { return -y(d) })
    .attr("text-anchor", "end");
```

To align the labels, you need to specify the attribute text-anchor. Its possible values are middle, start, and end, depending on whether you want the labels aligned in the center, to the left, or to the right, respectively.

Here, you use the D3 function attr() to specify the attribute, but it is possible to specify it in the CSS style as well, as shown in Listing 3-10.

Listing 3-10. ch3_01.html

```
.xLabel {
    text-anchor: middle;
}

.yLabel {
    text-anchor: end;
}
```

In fact, writing these lines is pretty much the same thing. Usually, however, you'll prefer to set these values in the CSS style when you plan to change them—they are understood as parameters. Instead, in this case, or if you want them to be a fixed property of an object, it is preferable to insert them using the attr() function.

Now you can add the ticks to the axes. This is obtained by drawing a short line for each tick. What you did for tick labels you now do for ticks, as shown in Listing 3-11.

Listing 3-11. ch3_01.html

```
//draw the x ticks
g.selectAll(".xTicks")
    .data(x.ticks(5))
    .enter().append("svg:line")
    .attr("class", "xTicks")
    .attr("x1", function(d) { return x(d); })
    .attr("y1", -y(0))
    .attr("x2", function(d) { return x(d); })
    .attr("y2", -y(0)-5)

// draw the y ticks
g.selectAll(".yTicks")
    .data(y.ticks(5))
    .enter().append("svg:line")
    .attr("class", "yTicks")
    .attr("y1", function(d) { return -y(d); })
    .attr("x1", x(0)+5)
    .attr("y2", function(d) { return -y(d); })
    .attr("x2", x(0))
```

Figure 3-4 shows the line chart at this stage.

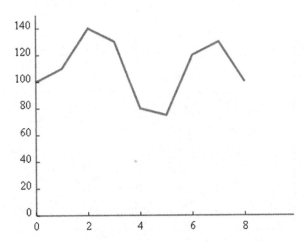

Figure 3-4. *Adding the two axes and the labels on them, you finally get a simple line chart*

As you can see, you already have a line chart. Perhaps by adding a grid, as shown in Listing 3-12, you can make things look better.

Listing 3-12. Ch3_01.html

```
//draw the x grid
g.selectAll(".xGrids")
    .data(x.ticks(5))
    .enter().append("svg:line")
    .attr("class", "xGrids")
    .attr("x1", function(d) { return x(d); })
    .attr("y1", -y(0))
    .attr("x2", function(d) { return x(d); })
    .attr("y2", -y(d3.max(data))-10);
// draw the y grid
g.selectAll(".yGrids")
    .data(y.ticks(5))
    .enter().append("svg:line")
    .attr("class", "yGrids")
    .attr("y1", function(d) { return -y(d); })
    .attr("x1", x(w))
    .attr("y2", function(d) { return -y(d); })
    .attr("x2", x(0));
```

You can make a few small additions to the CSS style (see Listing 3-13) in order to get a light gray grid as the background of the line chart. Moreover, you can define the text style as it seems more appropriate, for example by selecting Verdana for the font, with size 9.

Listing 3-13. Ch3_01.html

```
<style>
path {
    stroke: steelblue;
    stroke-width: 3;
    fill: none;
}
line {
    stroke: black;
}
.xGrids {
    stroke: lightgray;
}
.yGrids {
    stroke: lightgray;
}
text {
    font-family: Verdana;
    font-size: 9pt;
}
</style>
```

The line chart is now drawn with a light gray grid, as shown in Figure 3-5.

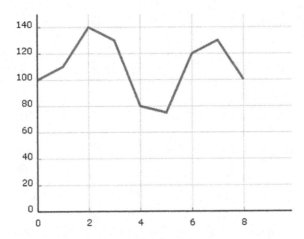

Figure 3-5. *A line chart with a grid covering the blue lines*

Look carefully at the Figure 3-5. The gray lines of the grid are drawn above the blue line representing the data. In other words, to be more explicit, you must be careful about the order in which you draw the SVG elements. In fact it is convenient to first draw the axes and the grid and then eventually to move on to the representation of the input data. Thus, you need to put all items that you want to draw in the right order, as shown in Listing 3-14.

Listing 3-14. ch3_01.html

```
<script>
var data = [100,110,140,130,80,75,120,130,100];
w = 400;
h = 300;
margin_x = 32;
margin_y = 20;
y = d3.scale.linear().domain([0, d3.max(data)]).range([0 + margin_y, h - margin_y]);
x = d3.scale.linear().domain([0, data.length]).range([0 + margin_x, w - margin_x]);
var svg = d3.select("body")
    .append("svg:svg")
    .attr("width", w)
    .attr("height", h);

var g = svg.append("svg:g")
    .attr("transform", "translate(0," + h + ")");

var line = d3.svg.line()
    .x(function(d,i) { return x(i); })
    .y(function(d) { return -y(d); });

// draw the y axis
g.append("svg:line")
    .attr("x1", x(0))
    .attr("y1", -y(0))
    .attr("x2", x(w))
    .attr("y2", -y(0));
```

```
// draw the x axis
g.append("svg:line")
    .attr("x1", x(0))
    .attr("y1", -y(0))
    .attr("x2", x(0))
    .attr("y2", -y(d3.max(data))-10);

//draw the xLabels
g.selectAll(".xLabel")
    .data(x.ticks(5))
    .enter().append("svg:text")
    .attr("class", "xLabel")
    .text(String)
    .attr("x", function(d) { return x(d) })
    .attr("y", 0)
    .attr("text-anchor", "middle");

// draw the yLabels
g.selectAll(".yLabel")
    .data(y.ticks(5))
    .enter().append("svg:text")
    .attr("class", "yLabel")
    .text(String)
    .attr("x", 25)
    .attr("y", function(d) { return -y(d) })
    .attr("text-anchor", "end");

//draw the x ticks
g.selectAll(".xTicks")
    .data(x.ticks(5))
    .enter().append("svg:line")
    .attr("class", "xTicks")
    .attr("x1", function(d) { return x(d); })
    .attr("y1", -y(0))
    .attr("x2", function(d) { return x(d); })
    .attr("y2", -y(0)-5);

// draw the y ticks
g.selectAll(".yTicks")
    .data(y.ticks(5))
    .enter().append("svg:line")
    .attr("class", "yTicks")
    .attr("y1", function(d) { return -1 * y(d); })
    .attr("x1", x(0)+5)
    .attr("y2", function(d) { return -1 * y(d); })
    .attr("x2", x(0));

//draw the x grid
g.selectAll(".xGrids")
    .data(x.ticks(5))
    .enter().append("svg:line")
    .attr("class", "xGrids")
    .attr("x1", function(d) { return x(d); })
```

```
        .attr("y1", -y(0))
        .attr("x2", function(d) { return x(d); })
        .attr("y2", -y(d3.max(data))-10);

// draw the y grid
g.selectAll(".yGrids")
    .data(y.ticks(5))
    .enter().append("svg:line")
    .attr("class", "yGrids")
    .attr("y1", function(d) { return -1 * y(d); })
    .attr("x1", x(w))
    .attr("y2", function(d) { return -y(d); })
    .attr("x2", x(0));

// draw the x axis
g.append("svg:line")
    .attr("x1", x(0))
    .attr("y1", -y(0))
    .attr("x2", x(w))
    .attr("y2", -y(0));

// draw the y axis
g.append("svg:line")
    .attr("x1", x(0))
    .attr("y1", -y(0))
    .attr("x2", x(0))
    .attr("y2", -y(d3.max(data))+10);

// draw the line of data points
g.append("svg:path").attr("d", line(data));
</script>
```

Figure 3-6 shows the line chart with the elements drawn in the correct sequence. In fact, the blue line representing the input data is now on the foreground covering the grid and not vice versa.

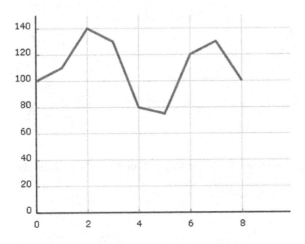

Figure 3-6. *A line chart with a grid drawn correctly*

Using Data with (x,y) Values

So far, you have used an input data array containing only the values of y. In general, you'll want to represent points that have x and y values assigned to them. Therefore, you'll extend the previous case by using the input data array in Listing 3-15.

Listing 3-15. Ch3_02.html

```
var data = [{x: 0, y: 100}, {x: 10, y: 110}, {x: 20, y: 140},
            {x: 30, y: 130}, {x: 40, y: 80}, {x: 50, y: 75},
            {x: 60, y: 120}, {x: 70, y: 130}, {x: 80, y: 100}];
```

You can now see how the data is represented by dots containing both the values of x and y. When you use a sequence of data, you'll often need to immediately identify the maximum values of both x and y (and sometimes the minimum values too). In the previous case, you used the d3.max and d3.min functions, but these operate only on arrays, not on objects. The input data array you inserted is an array of objects. How do you solve this? There are several approaches. Perhaps the most direct way is to affect a scan of the data and find the maximum values for both x and y. In Listing 3-16, you define two variables that will contain the two maximums. Then scanning the values of x and y of each object at a time, you compare the current value of x and y with the values of xMax and yMax, in order to see which value is larger. The greater of the two will become the new maximum.

Listing 3-16. Ch3_02.html

```
var xMax = 0, yMax = 0;
data.forEach(function(d) {
    if(d.x > xMax)
        xMax =  d.x;
    if(d.y > yMax)
        yMax =  d.y;
});
```

Several useful D3 functions work on arrays, so why not create two arrays directly from the input array of objects—one containing the values of x and the other containing the values of y? You can use these two arrays whenever necessary, instead of using the array of objects, which is far more complex (see Listing 3-17).

Listing 3-17. Ch3_02.html

```
var ax = [];
var ay = [];
data.forEach(function(d,i){
    ax[i] = d.x;
    ay[i] = d.y;
})
var xMax = d3.max(ax);
var yMax = d3.max(ay);
```

This time you assign both x and y to the line of data points, as shown in Listing 3-18. This operation is very simple even when you're working with an array of objects.

Listing 3-18. Ch3_02.html

```
var line = d3.svg.line()
    .x(function(d) { return x(d.x); })
    .y(function(d) { return -y(d.y); })
```

As for the rest of the code, there is not much to be changed—only a few corrections to the values of x and y bounds, as shown in Listing 3-19.

Listing 3-19. Ch3_02.html

```
y = d3.scale.linear().domain([0, yMax]).range([0 + margin_y, h - margin_y]);
x = d3.scale.linear().domain([0, xMax]).range([0 + margin_x, w - margin_x]);
...
// draw the y axis
g.append("svg:line")
    .attr("x1", x(0))
    .attr("y1", -y(0))
    .attr("x2", x(0))
    .attr("y2", -y(yMax)-20)
...
//draw the x grid
g.selectAll(".xGrids")
    .data(x.ticks(5))
    .enter().append("svg:line")
    .attr("class", "xGrids")
    .attr("x1", function(d) { return x(d); })
    .attr("y1", -y(0))
    .attr("x2", function(d) { return x(d); })
    .attr("y2", -y(yMax)-10)

// draw the y grid
g.selectAll(".yGrids")
    .data(y.ticks(5))
    .enter().append("svg:line")
    .attr("class", "yGrids")
    .attr("y1", function(d) { return -1 * y(d); })
    .attr("x1", x(xMax)+20)
    .attr("y2", function(d) { return -1 * y(d); })
    .attr("x2", x(0))
```

Figure 3-7 shows the outcome resulting from the changes made to handle the y values introduced by the input data array.

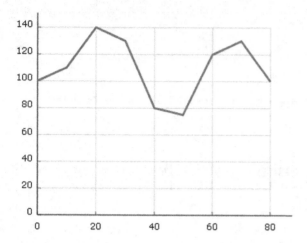

Figure 3-7. *A line chart with a grid and axis labels that take into account the y values entered with the input array*

Controlling the Axes' Range

In the line chart you just drew in the code, the data line will always be at the top of the chart. If your data oscillates at very high levels, with the scale of y starting at 0, you risk having a flattened trend line. It is also not optimal when the upper limit of the y-axis is the maximum value of y. Here, you'll add a check on the range of the axes. For this purpose in Listing 3-20, you define four variables that specify the lower and upper limits of the x- and y-axes.

Listing 3-20. Ch3_03.html

```
var xLowLim = 0;
var xUpLim = d3.max(ax);
var yUpLim = 1.2 * d3.max(ay);
var yLowLim = 0.8 * d3.min(ay);
```

You consequently replace all the limit references with these variables. Note that the code becomes somewhat more readable. Specifying these four limits in a direct manner enables you to modify them easily as the need arises. In this case, only the range covered by the experimental data on y, plus a margin of 20%, is represented, as shown in Listing 3-21.

Listing 3-21. ch3_03.html

```
y = d3.scale.linear().domain([yLowLim, yUpLim]).range([0 + margin_y, h - margin_y]);
x = d3.scale.linear().domain([xLowLim, xUpLim]).range([0 + margin_x, w - margin_x]);

...

//draw the x ticks
g.selectAll(".xTicks")
    .data(x.ticks(5))
    .enter().append("svg:line")
    .attr("class", "xTicks")
    .attr("x1", function(d) { return x(d); })
```

```
        .attr("y1", -y(yLowLim))
        .attr("x2", function(d) { return x(d); })
        .attr("y2", -y(yLowLim)-5)

// draw the y ticks
g.selectAll(".yTicks")
    .data(y.ticks(5))
    .enter().append("svg:line")
    .attr("class", "yTicks")
    .attr("y1", function(d) { return -y(d); })
    .attr("x1", x(xLowLim))
    .attr("y2", function(d) { return -y(d); })
    .attr("x2", x(xLowLim)+5)

//draw the x grid
g.selectAll(".xGrids")
    .data(x.ticks(5))
    .enter().append("svg:line")
    .attr("class", "xGrids")
    .attr("x1", function(d) { return x(d); })
    .attr("y1", -y(yLowLim))
    .attr("x2", function(d) { return x(d); })
    .attr("y2", -y(yUpLim))

// draw the y grid
g.selectAll(".yGrids")
    .data(y.ticks(5))
    .enter().append("svg:line")
    .attr("class", "yGrids")
    .attr("y1", function(d) { return -y(d); })
    .attr("x1", x(xUpLim)+20)
    .attr("y2", function(d) { return -y(d); })
    .attr("x2", x(xLowLim))

// draw the x axis
g.append("svg:line")
    .attr("x1", x(xLowLim))
    .attr("y1", -y(yLowLim))
    .attr("x2", 1.2*x(xUpLim))
    .attr("y2", -y(yLowLim))

// draw the y axis
g.append("svg:line")
    .attr("x1", x(xLowLim))
    .attr("y1", -y(yLowLim))
    .attr("x2", x(xLowLim))
    .attr("y2", -1.2*y(yUpLim))
```

Figure 3-8 shows the new line chart with the y-axis range between 60 and 160, which displays the line better.

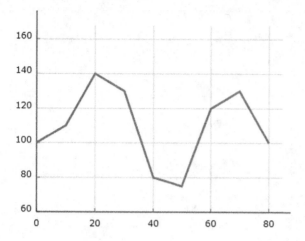

Figure 3-8. *A line chart with y-axis range focused around the y values*

Adding the Axis Arrows

In order to better understand the graphical versatility of D3, especially in the implementation of new features, you'll learn to add arrows to the x- and y-axes. To do this, you must add the two paths in Listing 3-22, as they will draw the arrows at the ends of both axes.

Listing 3-22. Ch3_04.html

```
g.append("svg:path")
      .attr("class", "axisArrow")
      .attr("d", function() {
         var x1 = x(xUpLim)+23, x2 = x(xUpLim)+30;
         var y2 = -y(yLowLim),y1 = y2-3, y3 = y2+3
         return 'M'+x1+','+y1+','+x2+','+y2+','+x1+','+y3;
});

g.append("svg:path")
      .attr("class", "axisArrow")
      .attr("d", function() {
         var y1 = -y(yUpLim)-13, y2 = -y(yUpLim)-20;
         var x2 = x(xLowLim),x1 = x2-3, x3 = x2+3
         return 'M'+x1+','+y1+','+x2+','+y2+','+x3+','+y1;
});
```

In the CCS style, you add the axisArrow class, as shown in Listing 3-23. You can also choose to enable the fill attribute to obtain a filled arrow.

Listing 3-23. Ch3_04.html

```
.axisArrow {
    stroke: black;
    stroke-width: 1;
    /*fill: black; */
}
```

Figure 3-9 shows the results, with and without filling.

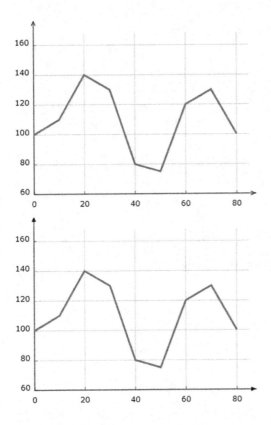

Figure 3-9. *Two different ways to represent the arrows on the axes*

Adding a Title and Axis Labels

In this section, you'll add a title to the chart. It is quite a simple thing to do, and you will use the SVG element called text with appropriate changes to the style, as shown in Listing 3-24. This code will place the title in the center, on top.

Listing 3-24. Ch3_05.html

```
g.append("svg:text")
        .attr("x", (w / 2))
        .attr("y", -h + margin_y )
        .attr("text-anchor", "middle")
        .style("font-size", "22px")
        .text("My first D3 line chart");
```

Figure 3-10 shows the title added to the top of the line chart.

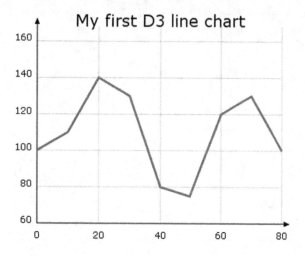

Figure 3-10. *A line chart with a title*

Following a similar procedure, you can add labels to the axes as well (see Listing 3-25).

Listing 3-25. Ch3_05.html

```
g.append("svg:text")
        .attr("x", 25)
        .attr("y", -h + margin_y)
        .attr("text-anchor", "end")
        .style("font-size", "11px")
        .text("[#]");

g.append("svg:text")
        .attr("x", w - 40)
        .attr("y", -8 )
        .attr("text-anchor", "end")
        .style("font-size", "11px")
        .text("time [s]");
```

Figure 3-11 shows the two new axis labels put beside their corresponding axes.

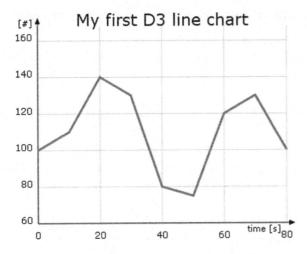

Figure 3-11. *A more complete line chart with title and axes labels*

Now that you have learned how to make a line chart, you're ready to try some more complex charts. Generally, the data you want to display in a chart are not present in the web page, but rather in external files. You'll integrate the following session on how to read data from external files with what you have learned so far.

Drawing a Line Chart from Data in a CSV File

When designing a chart, you typically refer to data of varied formats. This data often come from several different sources. In the most common case, you have applications on the server (which your web page is addressed to) that extract data from a database or by instrumentation, or you might even have data files collected in these servers. The example here uses a comma-separated value (CSV) file residing on the server as a source of data. This CSV file contains the data and could be loaded directly on the server or, as is more often the case, could be generated by other applications.

It is no coincidence that D3 has been prepared to deal with this type of file. For this purpose, D3 provides the function d3.csv(). You'll learn more about this topic with an example.

Reading and Parsing Data

First of all, you need to define the size of the "canvas," or better, the size and margins of the area where you want to draw the chart. This time, you define four margins. This will give you more control over the drawing area (see Listing 3-26).

Listing 3-26. Ch3_06a.html

```
<!DOCTYPE html>
<meta charset="utf-8">
<style>
</style>
<body>
<script src="http://d3js.org/d3.v3.js"></script>
<script>
var margin = {top: 70, right: 20, bottom: 30, left: 50},
    w = 400 - margin.left - margin.right,
    h = 400 - margin.top - margin.bottom;
```

Now you deal with the data; write the data in Listing 3-27 with a text editor into a file and save it as data_01.csv.

Listing 3-27. data_01.csv

```
date,attendee
12-Feb-12,80
27-Feb-12,56
02-Mar-12,42
14-Mar-12,63
30-Mar-12,64
07-Apr-12,72
18-Apr-12,65
02-May-12,80
19-May-12,76
28-May-12,66
03-Jun-12,64
18-Jun-12,53
29-Jun-12,59
```

This data contain two sets of values separated by a comma (recall that CSV stands for comma-separated values). The first is in date format and lists the days on which there was a particular event, such as a conference or a meeting. The second column lists the number of attendees. Note that the dates are not enclosed in any quote marks.

In a manner similar to jqPlot, D3 has a number of tools that the control time formats. In fact, to handle dates contained in the CSV file, you must specify a parser, as shown in Listing 3-28.

Listing 3-28. Ch3_06a.html

```
var parseDate = d3.time.format("%d-%b-%y").parse;
```

Here you need to specify the format contained in the CSV file: %d indicates the number format of the days, %b indicates the month reported with the first three characters, and %y indicates the year reported with the last two digits. You can specify the x and y values, assigning them with a scale and a range, as shown in Listing 3-29.

Listing 3-29. ch3_06a.html

```
var x = d3.time.scale().range([0, w]);
var y = d3.scale.linear().range([h, 0]);
```

Now that you have dealt with the correct processing of input data, you can begin to create the graphical components.

Implementing Axes and the Grid

You'll begin by learning how to graphically realize the two Cartesian axes. In this example, shown in Listing 3-30, you follow the most appropriate way to specify the x-axis and y-axis through the function d3.svg.axis().

Listing 3-30. ch3_06a.html

```
var xAxis = d3.svg.axis()
    .scale(x)
    .orient("bottom")
    .ticks(5);
```

```
var yAxis = d3.svg.axis()
    .scale(y)
    .orient("left")
    .ticks(5);
```

This allows you to focus on the data, while all the axes-related concerns (ticks, labels, and so on) are automatically handled by the axis components. Thus, after you create xAxis and yAxis, you assign the scale of x and y to them and set the orientation. Is it simple? Yes; this time you don't have to specify all that tedious stuff about axes—their limits, where to put ticks and labels, and so on. Unlike the previous example, all this is automatically done with very few rows. I chose to introduce this concept now, because in the previous example, I wanted to emphasize the fact that every item you design is a brick that you can manage with D3, regardless of whether this process is then automated within the D3 library.

Now you can add the SVG elements to the page, as shown in Listing 3-31.

Listing 3-31. ch3_06a.html

```
var svg = d3.select("body").append("svg")
    .attr("width", w + margin.left + margin.right)
    .attr("height", h + margin.top + margin.bottom)
    .append("g")
    .attr("transform", "translate(" + margin.left + "," + margin.top + ")");

  svg.append("g")
      .attr("class", "x axis")
      .attr("transform", "translate(0," + h + ")")
      .call(xAxis);

  svg.append("g")
      .attr("class", "y axis")
      .call(yAxis);
```

Notice how the x-axis is subjected to translation. In fact, in the absence of specifications, the x-axis would be drawn at the top of the drawing area. Moreover, you also need to add to the CSS style. See Listing 3-32.

Listing 3-32. Ch3_06a.html

```
<style>
body {
  font: 10px verdana;
}
.axis path,
.axis line {
  fill: none;
  stroke: #333;
}
</style>
```

Figure 3-12 shows the result.

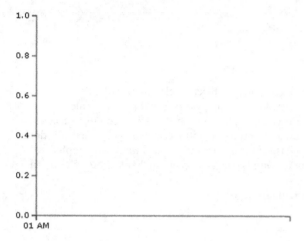

Figure 3-12. *An empty chart ready to be filled with data*

Using FireBug, you can see the structure of the SVG elements as you have just defined them (see Figure 3-13).

```
<!DOCTYPE html>
⊟ <html>
   ⊞ <head>
   ⊟ <body>
      ⊞ <script src="http://d3js.org/d3.v3.js">
      ⊞ <script>
      ⊟ <svg width="400" height="400">
         ⊟ <g transform="translate(50,70)">
            ⊞ <g class="x axis" transform="translate(0,300)">
            ⊞ <g class="y axis">
            </g>
         </svg>
      </body>
   </html>
```

Figure 3-13. *FireBug shows the structure of the SVG elements created dynamically to display the axes*

You can see that all the elements are automatically grouped within the group <g> tag. This gives you more control to apply possible transformations to the separate elements.

You can also add a grid if you want. You build the grid the same way you built the axes. In fact, in the same manner, you define two grid variables—xGrid and yGrid—using the axis() function in Listing 3-33.

Listing 3-33. Ch3_06a.html

```
var yAxis = d3.svg.axis()
  ...
var xGrid = d3.svg.axis()
    .scale(x)
    .orient("bottom")
    .ticks(5)
    .tickSize(-h, 0, 0)
    .tickFormat("");
```

```
var yGrid = d3.svg.axis()
    .scale(y)
    .orient("left")
    .ticks(5)
    .tickSize(-w, 0, 0)
    .tickFormat("");
```

And in the bottom of the JavaScript code, you add the two new SVG elements to the others, as shown in Listing 3-34.

Listing 3-34. ch3_06a.html

```
svg.append("g")
    .attr("class", "y axis")
    .call(yAxis)

svg.append("g")
    .attr("class", "grid")
    .attr("transform", "translate(0," + h + ")")
    .call(xGrid);

svg.append("g")
    .attr("class", "grid")
    .call(yGrid);
```

Both elements are named with the same class name: grid. Thus, you can style them as a single element (see Listing 3-35).

Listing 3-35. Ch3_06a.html

```
<style>
...
.grid .tick {
    stroke: lightgrey;
    opacity: 0.7;
}
.grid path {
    stroke-width: 0;
}
</style>
```

Figure 3-14 shows the horizontal grid lines you have just defined as SVG elements.

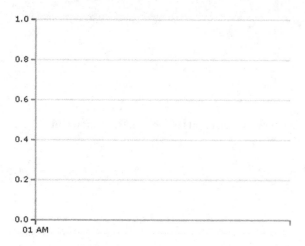

Figure 3-14. *Beginning to draw the horizontal grid lines*

Your chart is now ready to display the data from the CSV file.

Drawing Data with the csv() Function

It's now time to display the data in the chart, and you can do so with the D3 function d3.csv(), as shown in Listing 3-36.

Listing 3-36. ch3_06a.html

```
d3.csv("data_01.csv", function(error, data) {
// Here we will put all the SVG elements affected by the data
// on the file!!!
});
```

The first argument is the name of the CSV file; the second argument is a function where all the data within the file is handled. All the D3 functions that are in some way influenced by these values must be placed in this function. For example, you use svg.append() to create new SVG elements, but many of these functions need to know the x and y values of data. So you'll need to put them inside the csv() function as a second argument.

All the data in the CSV file is collected in an object called data. The different fields of the CSV file are recognized through their headers. The first thing you'll add is an iterative function where the data object is read item by item. Here, date values are parsed. You must ensure that all attendee values are read as numeric (this can be done by assigning each value to itself with a plus sign before it). See Listing 3-37.

Listing 3-37. Ch3_06a.html

```
d3.csv("data_01.csv", function(error, data) {
    data.forEach(function(d) {
        d.date = parseDate(d.date);
        d.attendee = +d.attendee;
    });
});
```

Only now is it possible to define the domain on x and y in Listing 3-38, because only now do you know the values of this data.

Listing 3-38. Ch3_06a.html

```
d3.csv("data_01.csv", function(error, data) {
    data.forEach(function(d) {
    ...
    });

    x.domain(d3.extent(data, function(d) { return d.date; }));
    y.domain(d3.extent(data, function(d) { return d.attendee; }));
});
```

Once data from the file is read and collected, it constitutes a set of points (x, y) that must be connected by a line. You'll use the SVG element path to build this line, as shown in Listing 3-39. As you saw previously, the function d3.svg.line() makes the work easier.

Listing 3-39. Ch3_06a.html

```
d3.csv("data_01.csv", function(error, data) {
    data.forEach(function(d) {
    ...
    });
...
var line = d3.svg.line()
    .x(function(d) { return x(d.date); })
    .y(function(d) { return y(d.attendee); });
});
```

You can also add the two axes labels and a title to the chart. This is a good example of how to build <g> groups manually. Previously the group and all the elements inside were created by functions; now you need to do this explicitly. If you wanted to add the two axis labels to one group and the title to another, you'd need to specify two different variables: labels and title (see Listing 3-40).

In each case you create an SVG element <g> with the append() method, and define the group with a class name. Subsequently, you assign the SVG elements to the two groups, using append() on these variables.

Listing 3-40. ch3_06a.html

```
d3.csv("data_01.csv", function(error, data) {
    data.forEach(function(d) {
    ...
    });
...
    var labels = svg.append("g")
        .attr("class", "labels")

    labels.append("text")
        .attr("transform", "translate(0," + h + ")")
        .attr("x", (w-margin.right))
        .attr("dx", "-1.0em")
        .attr("dy", "2.0em")
        .text("[Months]");
```

```
    labels.append("text")
        .attr("transform", "rotate(-90)")
        .attr("y", -40)
        .attr("dy", ".71em")
        .style("text-anchor", "end")
        .text("Attendees");

    var title = svg.append("g")
        .attr("class", "title");

    title.append("text")
        .attr("x", (w / 2))
        .attr("y", -30 )
        .attr("text-anchor", "middle")
        .style("font-size", "22px")
        .text("A D3 line chart from CSV file");
});
```

Finally, you can add the path element, which draws the line representing the data values (see Listing 3-41).

Listing 3-41. Ch3_06a.html

```
d3.csv("data_01.csv", function(error, data) {
    data.forEach(function(d) {
    ...
    });
...

    svg.append("path")
        .datum(data)
        .attr("class", "line")
        .attr("d", line);
});
```

Even for this new SVG element, you must not forget to add its CSS style settings, as shown in Listing 3-42.

Listing 3-42. Ch3_06a.html

```
<style>
...
.line {
    fill: none;
    stroke: steelblue;
    stroke-width: 1.5px;
}
</style>
```

Figure 3-15 shows the nice line chart reporting all the data in the CSV file.

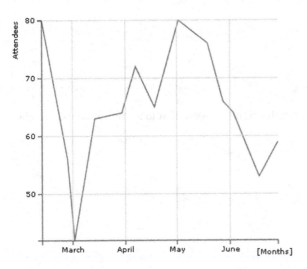

Figure 3-15. *A complete line chart with all of its main components*

Adding Marks to the Line

As you have seen for the line chart of jqPlot, even here it is possible to make further additions. For example, you could put data marker on the line.

Inside the d3.csv() function at the end of all the added SVG elements, you can add markers (see Listing 3-43). Remember that these elements depend on the data, so they must be inserted inside the csv() function.

Listing 3-43. Ch3_06b.html

```
d3.csv("data_01.csv", function(error, data) {
    data.forEach(function(d) {
    ...
    });
...

    svg.selectAll(".dot")
        .data(data)
        .enter().append("circle")
        .attr("class", "dot")
        .attr("r", 3.5)
        .attr("cx", function(d) { return x(d.date); })
        .attr("cy", function(d) { return y(d.attendee); });
});
```

In the style part of the file, you add the CSS style definition of the `.dot` class in Listing 3-44.

Listing 3-44. Ch3_06b.html

```
.dot {
    stroke: steelblue;
    fill: lightblue;
}
```

Figure 3-16 shows a line chart with small circles as markers; this result is very similar to the one obtained with the jqPlot library.

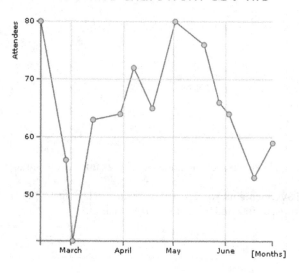

A D3 line chart from CSV file

Figure 3-16. *A complete line chart with markers*

These markers have a circle shape, but it is possible to give them many other shapes and colors. For example, you can use markers with a square shape (see Listing 3-45).

Listing 3-45. Ch3_06c.html

```
<style>
.dot {
    stroke: darkred;
    fill: red;
}
</style>
...
svg.selectAll(".dot")
    .data(data)
    .enter().append("rect")
    .attr("class", "dot")
```

```
    .attr("width", 7)
    .attr("height", 7)
    .attr("x", function(d) { return x(d.date)-3.5; })
    .attr("y", function(d) { return y(d.attendee)-3.5; });
```

Figure 3-17 shows the same line chart, but this time it uses small red squares for markers.

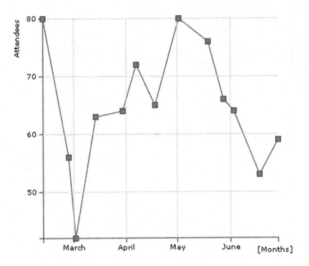

Figure 3-17. *One of the many marker options*

You could also use markers in the form of a yellow rhombus, often referred to as diamonds (see Listing 3-46).

Listing 3-46. Ch3_06d.html

```
<style>
.dot {
    stroke: orange;
    fill: yellow;
}
</style>
...
svg.selectAll(".dot")
    .data(data)
    .enter().append("rect")
    .attr("class", "dot")
    .attr("transform", function(d) {
        var str = "rotate(45," + x(d.date) + "," + y(d.attendee) + ")";
        return str;
    })
    .attr("width", 7)
    .attr("height", 7)
    .attr("x", function(d) { return x(d.date)-3.5; })
    .attr("y", function(d) { return y(d.attendee)-3.5; });
```

Figure 3-18 shows markers in the form of a yellow rhombus.

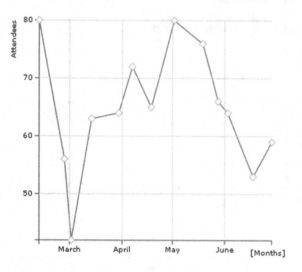

Figure 3-18. *Another marker option*

Line Charts with Filled Areas

In this section, you put point markers aside and return to the basic line chart. Another interesting feature you can add to your chart is to fill in the area below the line. Do you remember the d3.svg.line() function? Well, here you are using the d3.svg.area() function. Just as you have a line object in D3, you have an area object as well. Therefore, to define an area object, you can add the rows in bold in Listing 3-47 to the code, in the section just below the definition of the line object.

Listing 3-47. Ch3_07.html

```
var line = d3.svg.line()
    .x(function(d) { return x(d.date); })
    .y(function(d) { return y(d.attendee); });

var area = d3.svg.area()
    .x(function(d) { return x(d.date); })
    .y0(h)
    .y1(function(d) { return y(d.attendee); });

var labels = svg.append("g")
...
```

As you can see, to define an area you need to specify the three functions that delimit the edges: x, y0, and y1. In this case, y0 is constant, corresponding to the bottom of the drawing area (the x-axis). You now need to create the corresponding element in SVG, which is represented by a path element, as shown in Listing 3-48.

Listing 3-48. Ch3_07.html

```
d3.csv("data_01.csv", function(error, data) {

  data.forEach(function(d) {
    d.date = parseDate(d.date);
    d.attendee = +d.attendee;
  });

...
svg.append("path")
    .datum(data)
    .attr("class", "line")
    .attr("d", line);

svg.append("path")
    .datum(data)
    .attr("class", "area")
    .attr("d", area);
});
```

As shown in Listing 3-49, you need to specify the color setting in the corresponding CSS style class.

Listing 3-49. Ch3_07.html

```
.area {
    fill: lightblue;
}
```

Figure 3-19 shows an area chart derived from the line chart.

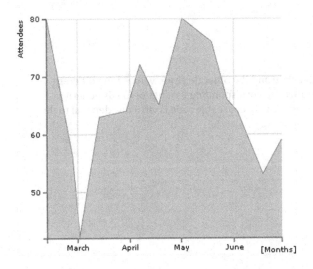

A D3 line chart from CSV file

Figure 3-19. *An area chart*

Multiseries Line Charts

Now that you're familiar with the creation of the basic components of a line chart using SVG elements, the next step is to start dealing with multiple data series: multiseries line charts. The most important element covered in this section is the legend. You'll learn to create one by exploiting the basic graphical elements that SVG provides.

Working with Multiple Series of Data

So far, you've been working with a single series of data. It is now time to move on to multiseries. In the previous example, you used a CSV file as a source of data. Now, you'll look at another D3 function: d3.tsv(). It performs the same task as csv(), but operates on tab-separated value (TSV) files.

Copy Listing 3-50 into your text editor and save it as data_02.tsv (see the following note).

■ **Note** The values in a TSV file are tab-separated, so when you write or copy Listing 3-50, remember to check that there is only one tab character between each value.

Listing 3-50. data_02.tsv

Date	europa	asia	america
12-Feb-12	52	40	65
27-Feb-12	56	35	70
02-Mar-12	51	45	62
14-Mar-12	63	44	82
30-Mar-12	64	54	85
07-Apr-12	70	34	72
18-Apr-12	65	36	69
02-May-12	56	40	71
19-May-12	71	55	75
28-May-12	45	32	68
03-Jun-12	64	44	75
18-Jun-12	53	36	78
29-Jun-12	59	42	79

Listing 3-50 has four columns, where the first column is a date and the other three are values from different continents. The first column contains the x values; the others are the corresponding y values of the three series.

Start writing the code in Listing 3-51; there isn't any explanation, because this code is virtually identical to the previous example.

Listing 3-51. Ch3_08a.html

```
<!DOCTYPE html>
<html>
<head>
<meta charset="utf-8">
<script src="http://d3js.org/d3.v3.js"></script>
<style>
```

```css
body {
    font: 10px verdana;
}
.axis path,
.axis line {
    fill: none;
    stroke: #333;
}

.grid .tick {
    stroke: lightgrey;
    opacity: 0.7;
}
.grid path {
    stroke-width: 0;
}

.line {
    fill: none;
    stroke: steelblue;
    stroke-width: 1.5px;
}
</style>
</head>
<body>
<script type="text/javascript">
var margin = {top: 70, right: 20, bottom: 30, left: 50},
    w = 400 - margin.left - margin.right,
    h = 400 - margin.top - margin.bottom;
var parseDate = d3.time.format("%d-%b-%y").parse;
var x = d3.time.scale().range([0, w]);
var y = d3.scale.linear().range([h, 0]);

var xAxis = d3.svg.axis()
    .scale(x)
    .orient("bottom")
    .ticks(5);

var yAxis = d3.svg.axis()
    .scale(y)
    .orient("left")
    .ticks(5);

var xGrid = d3.svg.axis()
    .scale(x)
    .orient("bottom")
    .ticks(5)
    .tickSize(-h, 0, 0)
    .tickFormat("");
```

```
var yGrid = d3.svg.axis()
    .scale(y)
    .orient("left")
    .ticks(5)
    .tickSize(-w, 0, 0)
    .tickFormat("");

var svg = d3.select("body").append("svg")
    .attr("width", w + margin.left + margin.right)
    .attr("height", h + margin.top + margin.bottom)
    .append("g")
    .attr("transform", "translate(" + margin.left + "," + margin.top + ")");

var line = d3.svg.line()
    .x(function(d) { return x(d.date); })
    .y(function(d) { return y(d.attendee); });

// Here we add the d3.tsv function
// start of the part of code to include in the d3.tsv() function
d3.tsv("data_02.tsv", function(error, data) {

    svg.append("g")
        .attr("class", "x axis")
        .attr("transform", "translate(0," + h + ")")
        .call(xAxis);

    svg.append("g")
        .attr("class", "y axis")
        .call(yAxis);

    svg.append("g")
        .attr("class", "grid")
        .attr("transform", "translate(0," + h + ")")
        .call(xGrid);

    svg.append("g")
        .attr("class", "grid")
        .call(yGrid);
});
//end of the part of code to include in the d3.tsv() function

var labels = svg.append("g")
    .attr("class","labels");

labels.append("text")
    .attr("transform", "translate(0," + h + ")")
    .attr("x", (w-margin.right))
    .attr("dx", "-1.0em")
    .attr("dy", "2.0em")
    .text("[Months]");
labels.append("text")
```

```
        .attr("transform", "rotate(-90)")
        .attr("y", -40)
        .attr("dy", ".71em")
        .style("text-anchor", "end")
        .text("Attendees");

var title = svg.append("g")
        .attr("class", "title");

title.append("text")
        .attr("x", (w / 2))
        .attr("y", -30 )
        .attr("text-anchor", "middle")
        .style("font-size", "22px")
        .text("A multiseries line chart");
</script>
</body>
</html>
```

When you deal with multiseries data in a single chart, you need to be able to identify the data quickly and as a result you need to use different colors. D3 provides some functions generating an already defined sequence of colors. For example, there is the category10() function, which provides a sequence of 10 different colors. You can create a color set for the multiseries line chart just by writing the line in Listing 3-52.

Listing 3-52. Ch3_08a.html

```
...
var x = d3.time.scale().range([0, w]);
var y = d3.scale.linear().range([h, 0]);
var color = d3.scale.category10();
var xAxis = d3.svg.axis()
...
```

You now need to read the data in the TSV file. As in the previous example, just after the call of the d3.tsv() function, you add a parser, as shown in Listing 3-53. Since you have to do with date values on the x-axis, you have to parse this type of value. You'll use the parseDate() function.

Listing 3-53. Ch3_08a.html

```
d3.tsv("data_02.tsv", function(error, data) {
    data.forEach(function(d) {
        d.date = parseDate(d.date);
    });
...
});
```

You've defined a color set, using the category10() function in a chain with a scale() function. This means that D3 handles color sequence as a scale. You need to create a domain, as shown in Listing 3-54 (in this case it will be composed of discrete values, not continuous values such as those for x or y). This domain consists of the headers in the TSV file. In this example, you have three continents. Consequently, you'll have a domain of three values and a color sequence of three colors.

Listing 3-54. Ch3_08a.html

```
d3.tsv("data_02.tsv", function(error, data) {
    data.forEach(function(d) {
        d.date = parseDate(d.date);
    });
    color.domain(d3.keys(data[0]).filter(function(key) {
        return key !== "date";
    }));
    ...
});
```

In Listing 3-53, you can see that data[0] is passed as an argument to the d3.keys() function. data[0] is the object corresponding to the first row of the TSV file:

```
Object {date=Date {Sun Feb 12 2012 00:00:00 GMT+0100},
europa="52", asia="40", america="65"}.
```

The d3.keys() function extracts the name of the values from inside an object, the same name which we find as a header in the TSV file. So using d3.keys(data[0]), you get the array of strings:

```
["date","europa","asia","america"]
```

You are interested only in the last three values, so you need to filter this array in order to exclude the key "date". You can do so with the filter() function. Finally, you'll assign the three continents to the domain of colors.

```
["europa","asia","america"]
```

The command in Listing 3-55 reorganizes all the data in an array of structured objects. This is done by the function map() with an inner function, which maps the values following a defined structure.

Listing 3-55. Ch3_08a.html

```
d3.tsv("data_02.tsv", function(error, data) {
...
    color.domain(d3.keys(data[0]).filter(function(key) {
        return key !== "date";
    }));

    var continents = color.domain().map(function(name) {
        return {
            name: name,
            values: data.map(function(d) {
                return {date: d.date, attendee: +d[name]};
            })
        };
    });
...
});
```

So this is the array of three objects called continents.

```
[ Object { name="europa", values=[13]},
  Object { name="asia", values=[13]},
  Object { name="america", values=[13]} ]
```

Every object has a continent name and a values array of 13 objects:

```
[ Object { date=Date, attendee=52 },
  Object { date=Date, attendee=56 },
  Object { date=Date, attendee=51 },
  ...]
```

You have the data structured in a way that allows for subsequent handling. In fact, when you need to specify the y domain of the chart, you can find the maximum and minimum of all values (not of each single one) in the series with a double iteration (see Listing 3-56). With function(c), you make an iteration of all the continents and with function(v), you make an iteration of all values inside them. In the end, d3.min and d3.max will extract only one value.

Listing 3-56. Ch3_08a.html

```
d3.tsv("data_02.tsv", function(error, data) {
...
    var continents = color.domain().map(function(name) {
    ...
    });

    x.domain(d3.extent(data, function(d) { return d.date; }));
    y.domain([
        d3.min(continents, function(c) {
            return d3.min(c.values, function(v) { return v.attendee; });
        }),
        d3.max(continents, function(c) {
            return d3.max(c.values, function(v) { return v.attendee; });
        })
    ]);
...
});
```

Thanks to the new data structure, you can add an SVG element <g> for each continent containing a line path, as shown in Listing 3-57.

Listing 3-57. Ch3_08a.html

```
d3.tsv("data_02.tsv", function(error, data) {
...

    svg.append("g")
        .attr("class", "grid")
        .call(yGrid);
```

```
var continent = svg.selectAll(".continent")
    .data(continents)
    .enter().append("g")
    .attr("class", "continent");

continent.append("path")
    .attr("class", "line")
    .attr("d", function(d) { return line(d.values); })
    .style("stroke", function(d) { return color(d.name); });
});
```

The resulting multiseries line chart is shown in Figure 3-20.

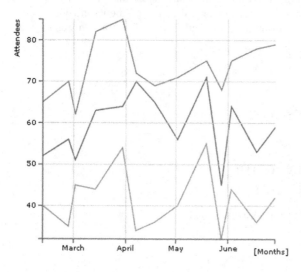

Figure 3-20. *A multiseries line chart*

Legend

When you are dealing with multiseries charts, the next logical step is to add a legend in order to categorize the series with colors and labels. Since a legend is a graphical object like any other, you need to add the SVG elements that allow you to draw it on the chart (see Listing 3-58).

Listing 3-58. Ch3_08a.html

```
d3.tsv("data_02.tsv", function(error, data) {
...
    continent.append("path")
        .attr("class", "line")
        .attr("d", function(d) { return line(d.values); })
        .style("stroke", function(d) { return color(d.name); });
```

```
var legend = svg.selectAll(".legend")
    .data(color.domain().slice().reverse())
    .enter().append("g")
    .attr("class", "legend")
    .attr("transform", function(d, i) { return "translate(0," + i * 20 + ")"; });

legend.append("rect")
    .attr("x", w - 18)
    .attr("y", 4)
    .attr("width", 10)
    .attr("height", 10)
    .style("fill", color);

legend.append("text")
    .attr("x", w - 24)
    .attr("y", 9)
    .attr("dy", ".35em")
    .style("text-anchor", "end")
    .text(function(d) { return d; });
});
```

The resulting multiseries line chart is shown in Figure 3-21, with a legend.

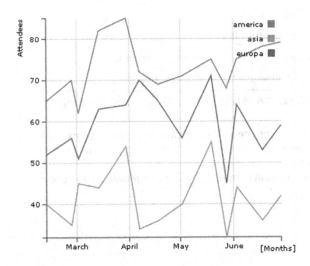

Figure 3-21. *A multiseries line chart with a legend*

Interpolating Lines

In a line chart, you usually have the data points connected by sequence, one by one, in a straight line. Sometimes, you can see some line chart representation with all the points joined into a curved line. In fact, the effect was obtained via an interpolation. The D3 library covers interpolations of data points in a more correct way from a mathematical point of view. You, therefore, need to delve a little deeper into this concept.

When you have a set of values and want to represent them using a line chart, you essentially want to know the trend that these values suggest. From this trend, you can evaluate which values may be obtained at intermediate points between a data point and the next. Well, with such an estimate you are actually affecting an **interpolation**. Depending on the trend and the degree of accuracy you want to achieve, you can use various mathematical methods that regulate the shape of the curve that will connect the data points.

The most commonly used method is the spline. (If you want to deepen your knowledge of the topic, visit `http://paulbourke.net/miscellaneous/interpolation/`.) Table 3-1 lists the various types of interpolation that the D3 library makes available.

Table 3-1. *The options for interpolating lines available within the D3 library*

Options	Description
basis	A B-spline, with control point duplication on the ends.
basis-open	An open B-spline; may not intersect the start or end.
basis-closed	A closed B-spline, as in a loop.
bundle	Equivalent to basis, except the tension parameter is used to straighten the spline.
cardinal	A Cardinal spline, with control point duplication on the ends.
cardinal-open	An open Cardinal spline; may not intersect the start or end, but will intersect other control points.
cardinal-closed	A closed Cardinal spline, as in a loop.
Linear	Piecewise linear segments, as in a polyline.
linear-closed	Close the linear segments to form a polygon.
monotone	Cubic interpolation that preserves a monotone effect in y.
step-before	Alternate between vertical and horizontal segments, as in a step function.
step-after	Alternate between horizontal and vertical segments, as in a step function.

You find these options by visiting https://github.com/mbostock/d3/wiki/SVG-Shapes#wiki-line_interpolate.

Now that you understand better what an interpolation is, you can see a practical case. In the previous example, you had three series represented by differently colored lines and made up of segments connecting the data points (x,y). But it is possible to draw corresponding interpolating lines instead.

As shown in Listing 3-59, you just add the `interpolate()` method to the `d3.svg.line` to get the desired effect.

Listing 3-59. Ch3_08b.html

```
var line = d3.svg.line()
    .interpolate("basis")
    .x(function(d) { return x(d.date); })
    .y(function(d) { return y(d.attendee); });
```

Figure 3-22 shows the interpolating lines applied to the three series in the chart. The straight lines connecting the data points have been replaced by curves.

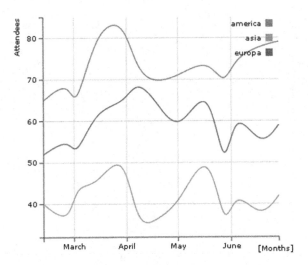

Figure 3-22. *A smooth multiseries line chart*

Difference Line Chart

This kind of chart portrays the area between two series. In the range where the first series is greater than the second series, the area has one color, where it is less the area has a different color. A good example of this kind of chart compares the trend of income and expense across time. When the income is greater than the expenses, the area will be green (usually the green color stands for OK), whereas when it is less, the area is red (meaning BAD). Write the values in Listing 3-60 in a TSV (or CSV) file and name it data_03.tsv (see the note).

■ **Note** The values in a TSV file are tab-separated, so when you write or copy Listing 3-60, remember to check that there is only one tab character between each value.

Listing 3-60. data_03.tsv

Date	income	expense
12-Feb-12	52	40
27-Feb-12	56	35
02-Mar-12	31	45
14-Mar-12	33	44
30-Mar-12	44	54
07-Apr-12	50	34
18-Apr-12	65	36
02-May-12	56	40
19-May-12	41	56
28-May-12	45	32
03-Jun-12	54	44
18-Jun-12	43	46
29-Jun-12	39	52

Start writing the code in Listing 3-61; explanations aren't included this time, as the example is virtually identical to the previous one.

Listing 3-61. Ch3_09.html

```
<!DOCTYPE html>
<html>
<head>
<meta charset="utf-8">
<script src="http://d3js.org/d3.v3.js"></script>
<style>
body {
  font: 10px verdana;
}
.axis path,
.axis line {
  fill: none;
  stroke: #333;
}
.grid .tick {
    stroke: lightgrey;
    opacity: 0.7;
}
.grid path {
    stroke-width: 0;
}
</style>
</head>
<body>
<script type="text/javascript">

var margin = {top: 70, right: 20, bottom: 30, left: 50},
    w = 400 - margin.left - margin.right,
    h = 400 - margin.top - margin.bottom;

var parseDate = d3.time.format("%d-%b-%y").parse;
var x = d3.time.scale().range([0, w]);
var y = d3.scale.linear().range([h, 0]);

var xAxis = d3.svg.axis()
    .scale(x)
    .orient("bottom")
    .ticks(5);

var yAxis = d3.svg.axis()
    .scale(y)
    .orient("left")
    .ticks(5);

var xGrid = d3.svg.axis()
    .scale(x)
    .orient("bottom")
```

```
        .ticks(5)
        .tickSize(-h, 0, 0)
        .tickFormat("");

var yGrid = d3.svg.axis()
        .scale(y)
        .orient("left")
        .ticks(5)
        .tickSize(-w, 0, 0)
        .tickFormat("");

var svg = d3.select("body").append("svg")
        .attr("width", w + margin.left + margin.right)
        .attr("height", h + margin.top + margin.bottom)
        .append("g")
        .attr("transform", "translate(" + margin.left + "," + margin.top + ")");

// Here we add the d3.tsv function
// start of the part of code to include in the d3.tsv() function
d3.tsv("data_03.tsv", function(error, data) {

    svg.append("g")
        .attr("class", "x axis")
        .attr("transform", "translate(0," + h + ")")
        .call(xAxis);

    svg.append("g")
        .attr("class", "y axis")
        .call(yAxis);

    svg.append("g")
        .attr("class", "grid")
        .attr("transform", "translate(0," + h + ")")
        .call(xGrid);

    svg.append("g")
        .attr("class", "grid")
        .call(yGrid);

});
//end of the part of code to include in the d3.tsv() function

var labels = svg.append("g")
        .attr("class", "labels");

labels.append("text")
        .attr("transform", "translate(0," + h + ")")
        .attr("x", (w-margin.right))
        .attr("dx", "-1.0em")
        .attr("dy", "2.0em")
        .text("[Months]");
```

```
labels.append("text")
    .attr("transform", "rotate(-90)")
    .attr("y", -40)
    .attr("dy", ".71em")
    .style("text-anchor", "end")
    .text("Millions ($)");

var title = svg.append("g")
    .attr("class", "title");

title.append("text")
    .attr("x", (w / 2))
    .attr("y", -30 )
    .attr("text-anchor", "middle")
    .style("font-size", "22px")
    .text("A difference chart");
</script>
</body>
</html>
```

First you read the TSV file to check whether the income and expense values are positive. Then you parse all the date values (see Listing 3-62).

Listing 3-62. Ch3_09.html

```
d3.tsv("data_03.tsv", function(error, data) {

    data.forEach(function(d) {
        d.date = parseDate(d.date);
        d.income = +d.income;
        d.expense = +d.expense;
    });
    ...
});
```

Here, unlike the example shown earlier (the multiseries line chart), there is no need to restructure the data, so you can create a domain on x and y, as shown in Listing 3-63. The maximum and minimum are obtained by comparing income and expense values with Math.max and Math.min at every step, and then finding the values affecting the iteration at each step with d3.min and d3.max.

Listing 3-63. Ch3_09.html

```
d3.tsv("data_03.tsv", function(error, data) {
    data.forEach(function(d) {
        ...
    });
```

```
        x.domain(d3.extent(data, function(d) { return d.date; }));
        y.domain([
            d3.min(data, function(d) {return Math.min(d.income, d.expense); }),
            d3.max(data, function(d) {return Math.max(d.income, d.expense); })
        ]);
        ...
});
```

Before adding SVG elements, you need to define some CSS classes. You'll use the color red when expenses are greater than income, and green otherwise. You need to define these colors, as shown in Listing 3-64.

Listing 3-64. Ch3_09.html

```
<style>
...
.area.above {
    fill: darkred;
}

.area.below {
    fill: lightgreen;
}

.line {
    fill: none;
    stroke: #000;
    stroke-width: 1.5px;
}
</style>
```

Since you need to represent lines and areas, you define them by using the interpolation between data points (see Listing 3-65).

Listing 3-65. Ch3_09.html

```
d3.tsv("data_03.tsv", function(error, data) {
    ...

    svg.append("g")
        .attr("class", "grid")
        .call(yGrid);

    var line = d3.svg.area()
        .interpolate("basis")
        .x(function(d) { return x(d.date); })
        .y(function(d) { return y(d["income"]); });

    var area = d3.svg.area()
        .interpolate("basis")
        .x(function(d) { return x(d.date); })
        .y1(function(d) { return y(d["income"]); });

});
```

As you can see, you are actually defining only the line of income points; there is no reference to expense values. But you are interested in the area between the two lines of income and expenditure, so when you define the path element, in order to draw this area, you can put the expense values as a border, with a generic function iterating the d values (see Listing 3-66).

Listing 3-66. Ch3_09.html

```
d3.tsv("data_03.tsv", function(error, data) {
    ...

    var area = d3.svg.area()
        .interpolate("basis")
        .x(function(d) { return x(d.date); })
        .y1(function(d) { return y(d["income"]); });

    svg.datum(data);

    svg.append("path")
        .attr("class", "area below")
        .attr("d", area.y0(function(d) { return y(d.expense); }));

    svg.append("path")
        .attr("class", "line")
        .attr("d", line);

});
```

If you load the web page now, you should get the desired area (see Figure 3-23).

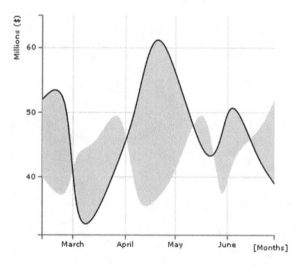

Figure 3-23. *An initial representation of the area between both trends*

But all the areas are green. Instead, you want some of these areas to be red. You need to select the areas enclosed by the income and expense lines, where the income line is above the expense line, and exclude the areas that do not correspond to this scheme. When you deal with areas, portions of which must be added or subtracted, it is necessary to introduce the **clip path** SVG element.

Clip paths are SVG elements that can be attached to previously drawn figures with a path element. The clip path describes a "window" area, which shows only in the area defined by the path. The other areas of the figure remain hidden.

Take a look at Figure 3-24. You can see that the line of income is black and thick. All green areas (light gray in the printed book version) above this line should be hidden by a clip path. But what clip path do you need? You need the clip path described by the path that delimits the lower area above the income line.

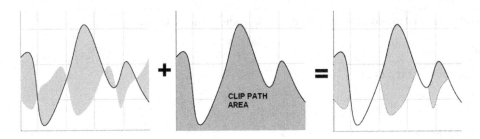

Figure 3-24. *Selection of the positive area with a clip path area*

You need to make some changes to the code, as shown in Listing 3-67.

Listing 3-67. ch3_09.html

```
d3.tsv("data_03.tsv", function(error, data) {
    ...

    svg.datum(data);

    svg.append("clipPath")
        .attr("id", "clip-below")
        .append("path")
        .attr("d", area.y0(h));

    svg.append("path")
        .attr("class", "area below")
        .attr("clip-path", "url(#clip-below)")
        .attr("d", area.y0(function(d) { return y(d.expense); }));

    svg.append("path")
        .attr("class", "line")
        .attr("d", line);

});
```

Now you need to do to same thing for the red areas (dark gray in the printed book version). Always starting from the area enclosed between the income and expense lines, you must eliminate the areas below the income line. So, as shown in Figure 3-25, you can use the clip path that describes the area above the income line as the window area.

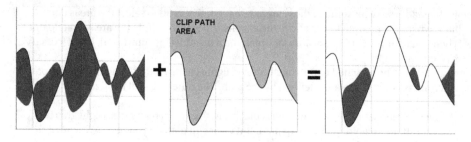

Figure 3-25. *Selection of the negative area with a clip path area*

Translating this into code, you need to add another clipPath to the code, as shown in Listing 3-68.

Listing 3-68. Ch3_09.html

```
d3.tsv("data_03.tsv", function(error, data) {
    ...

    svg.append("path")
        .attr("class", "area below")
        .attr("clip-path", "url(#clip-below)")
        .attr("d", area.y0(function(d) { return y(d.expense); }));

    svg.append("clipPath")
        .attr("id", "clip-above")
        .append("path")
        .attr("d", area.y0(0));

    svg.append("path")
        .attr("class", "area above")
        .attr("clip-path", "url(#clip-above)")
        .attr("d", area.y0(function(d) { return y(d.expense); }));

    svg.append("path")
        .attr("class", "line")
        .attr("d", line);

});
```

In the end, both areas are drawn simultaneously, and you get the desired chart (see Figure 3-26).

A difference chart

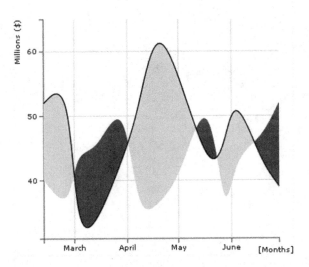

Figure 3-26. *The final representation of the difference area chart*

Summary

This chapter shows how to build the basic elements of a **line chart**, including axes, axis labels, titles, and grids. In particular you have read about the concepts of scales, domains, and ranges.

You then learned how to **read data from external files**, particularly CSV and TSV files. Furthermore, in starting to work with multiple series of data, you learned how to realize multiseries line charts, including learning about all the elements needed to complete them, such as legends.

Finally, you learned how to create a particular type of line chart: the **difference line chart**. This has helped you to understand **clip area paths**.

In the next chapter, you'll deal with **bar charts**. Exploiting all you've learned so far about D3, you'll see how it is possible to realize all the graphic components needed to build a bar chart, using only SVG elements. More specifically, you'll see how, using the same techniques, to implement all the possible types of **multiseries bar charts**, from stacked to grouped bars, both horizontally and vertically orientated.

CHAPTER 4

Bar Charts with D3

In this chapter, you will see how, using the D3 library, you can build the most commonly used type of chart: the bar chart. As a first example, you will start from a simple bar chart to practice the implementation of all the components using scalar vector graphic (SVG) elements.

Drawing a Bar Chart

In this regard, as an example to work with we choose to represent the income of some countries by vertical bars, so that we may compare them. As category labels, you will use the names of the countries themselves. Here, as you did for line charts, you decide to use an external file, such as a comma-separated values (CSV) file, which contains all the data. Your web page will then read the data contained within the file using the d3.csv() function. Therefore, write the data from Listing 4-1 in a file and save it as data_04.csv.

Listing 4-1. data_04.csv

```
country,income
France,14
Russia,22
Japan,13
South Korea,34
Argentina,28
```

Listing 4-2 shows a blank web page as a starting point for the development of your bar chart. You must remember to include the D3 library in the web page (see Appendix A for further information). If you prefer to use a content delivery network (CDN) service, you can replace the reference with this:

```
<script src="http://d3js.org/d3.v3.min.js"></script>
```

Listing 4-2. Ch4_01.html

```
<!DOCTYPE html>
<html>
<head>
<meta charset="utf-8">
<script src="../src/d3.v3.js"></script>
</head>
```

```
<body>
<script type="text/javascript">
// add the D3 code here
</script>
</body>
</html>
```

First, it is good practice to define the size of the drawing area on which you wish to represent your bar chart. The dimensions are specified by the w and h (width and height) variables, but you must also take the space for margins into account. These margin values must be subtracted from w and h, suitably restricting the area to be allocated to your chart (see Listing 4-3).

Listing 4-3. Ch4_01.html

```
<script type="text/javascript">
var margin = {top: 70, right: 20, bottom: 30, left: 40},
    w = 500 - margin.left - margin.right,
    h = 350 - margin.top - margin.bottom;
var color = d3.scale.category10();
</script>
```

Moreover, if you look at the data in the CSV file (see Listing 4-1), you will find a series of five countries with their relative values. If you want to have a color for identifying each country, it is necessary to define a color scale, and this, as you have already seen, could be done with the category10() function.

The next step is to define a scale on the x axis and y axis. You do not have numeric values on the x axis but string values identifying the country of origin. Thus, for this type of value, you have to define an ordinal scale as shown in Listing 4-4. In fact, the function rangeRoundBands divides the range passed as argument into discrete bands, which is just what you need in a bar chart. For the y axis, since it represents a variable in numerical values, you simply choose a linear scale.

Listing 4-4. Ch4_01.html

```
<script type="text/javascript">
...
var color = d3.scale.category10();
var x = d3.scale.ordinal()
    .rangeRoundBands([0, w], .1);
var y = d3.scale.linear()
    .range([h, 0]);
<script type="text/javascript">
```

Now you need to assign the two scales to the corresponding axes, using the d3.svg.axis() function. When you are dealing with bar charts, it is not uncommon that the values reported on the y axis are not the nominal values, but their percentage of the total value. So, you can define a percentage format through d3.format(), and then you assign it to tick labels on the y axis through the tickFormat() function (see Listing 4-5).

Listing 4-5. Ch4_01.html

```
<script type="text/javascript">
...
var y = d3.scale.linear()
    .range([h, 0]);

var formatPercent = d3.format(".0%");
var xAxis = d3.svg.axis()
    .scale(x)
    .orient("bottom");
var yAxis = d3.svg.axis()
    .scale(y)
    .orient("left")
    .tickFormat(formatPercent);
<script type="text/javascript">
```

Finally, it is time to start creating SVG elements in your web page. Start with the root as shown in Listing 4-6.

Listing 4-6. Ch4_01.html

```
<script type="text/javascript">
...
var yAxis = d3.svg.axis()
    .scale(y)
    .orient("left")
    .tickFormat(formatPercent);

var svg = d3.select("body").append("svg")
    .attr("width", w + margin.left + margin.right)
    .attr("height", h + margin.top + margin.bottom)
    .append("g")
    .attr("transform", "translate(" + margin.left + ", " + margin.top + ")");
<script type="text/javascript">
```

And now, to access the values contained in the CSV file, you have to use the d3.csv() function, as you have done already, passing the file name as first argument and the iterative function on the data contained within as the second argument (see Listing 4-7).

Listing 4-7. Ch4_01.html

```
<script type="text/javascript">
...
var svg = d3.select("body").append("svg")
    .attr("width", w + margin.left + margin.right)
    .attr("height", h + margin.top + margin.bottom)
    .append("g")
    .attr("transform", "translate(" + margin.left + ", " + margin.top + ")");
```

```
d3.csv("data_04.csv", function(error, data) {
    var sum = 0;
    data.forEach(function(d) {
        d.income = +d.income;
        sum += d.income;
    });
//insert here all the svg elements depending on data in the file
});
<script type="text/javascript">
```

During the scan of the values stored in the file through the forEach() loop, you ensure that all values of income will be read as numeric values and not as a string: this is possible by assigning every value to itself with a plus sign before it.

```
values = +values
```

And in the meantime, you also carry out the sum of all income values. This sum is necessary for you to compute the percentages. In fact, as shown in Listing 4-8, while you are defining the domains for both the axes, the "single income"/sum ratio is assigned to the y axis, thus obtaining a domain of percentages.

Listing 4-8. Ch4_01.html

```
...
d3.csv("data_04.csv", function(error, data) {
    data.forEach(function(d) {
        ...
    });

    x.domain(data.map(function(d) { return d.country; }));
    y.domain([0, d3.max(data, function(d) { return d.income/sum; })]);

});
```

After setting the values on both axes, you can draw them adding the corresponding SVG elements in Listing 4-9.

Listing 4-9. Ch4_01.html

```
d3.csv("data_04.csv", function(error, data) {
...
    y.domain([0, d3.max(data, function(d) { return d.income/sum; })]);

    svg.append("g")
        .attr("class", "x axis")
        .attr("transform", "translate(0, " + h + ")")
        .call(xAxis);

    svg.append("g")
        .attr("class", "y axis")
        .call(yAxis);
});
```

Usually, for bar charts, the grid is required only on one axis: the one on which the numeric values are shown. Since you are working with a vertical bar chart, you draw grid lines only on the y axis (see Listing 4-10). On the other hand, grid lines are not necessary on the x axis, because you already have a kind of classification in areas of discrete values, often referred to as categories. (Even if you had continuous values to represent on the x axis, however, for the bar chart to make sense, their range on the x axis should be divided into intervals or bins. The frequency of these values at each interval is represented by the height of the bar on the y axis, and the result is a histogram.)

Listing 4-10. Ch4_01.html

```
...
var yAxis = d3.svg.axis()
    .scale(y)
    .orient("left")
    .tickFormat(formatPercent);

var yGrid = d3.svg.axis()
    .scale(y)
    .orient("left")
    .ticks(5)
    .tickSize(-w, 0, 0)
    .tickFormat("");

var svg = d3.select("body").append("svg")
    .attr("width", w + margin.left + margin.right)
    .attr("height", h + margin.top + margin.bottom)
    .append("g")
    .attr("transform", "translate(" + margin.left + ", " + margin.top + ")");

d3.csv("data_04.csv", function(error, data) {
    ...
    svg.append("g")
        .attr("class", "y axis")
        .call(yAxis);

    svg.append("g")
        .attr("class", "grid")
        .call(yGrid);
});
```

Since the grid lies only on the y axis, the same thing applies for the corresponding axis label. In order to separate the components of the chart between them in some way, it is good practice to define a variable for each SVG element <g> which identifies a chart component, generally with the same name you use to identify the class of the component. Thus, just as you define a `labels` variable, you also define a `title` variable. And so on, for all the other components that you intend to add.

Unlike jqPlot, it is not necessary to include a specific plug-in to rotate the axis label; rather, use one of the possible transformations which SVG provides you with, more specifically a rotation. The only thing you need to do is to pass the angle (in degrees) at which you want to rotate the SVG element. The rotation is clockwise if the passed value is positive. If, as in your case, you want to align the axis label to the y axis, then you will need to rotate it 90 degrees counterclockwise: so specify `rotate(-90)` as a transformation (see Listing 4-11). Regarding the `title` element, you place it at the top of your chart, in a central position.

Listing 4-11. Ch4_01.html

```
d3.csv("data_04.csv", function(error, data) {
    ...

    svg.append("g")
        .attr("class", "grid")
        .call(yGrid);

    var labels = svg.append("g")
        .attr("class", "labels");

    labels.append("text")
            .attr("transform", "rotate(-90)")
            .attr("y", 6)
            .attr("dy", ".71em")
            .style("text-anchor", "end")
            .text("Income [%]");

    var title = svg.append("g")
        .attr("class", "title");

    title.append("text")
            .attr("x", (w / 2))
            .attr("y", -30 )
            .attr("text-anchor", "middle")
            .style("font-size", "22px")
            .text("My first bar chart");

});
```

Once you have defined all of the SVG components, you must not forget to specify the attributes of the CSS classes in Listing 4-12.

Listing 4-12. Ch4_01.html

```
<style>
body {
    font: 14px sans-serif;
}

.axis path,
.axis line {
    fill: none;
    stroke: #000;
    shape-rendering: crispEdges;
}
.grid .tick {
    stroke: lightgrey;
    opacity: 0.7;
}
```

```
.grid path {
    stroke-width: 0;
}

.x.axis path {
    display: none;
}
</style>
```

At the end, add the SVG elements which make up your bars. Since you want to draw a bar for each set of data, here you have to take advantage of the iterative function(error,data) function within the d3.csv() function. As shown in Listing 4-13, you therefore add the data(data) and enter() functions within the function chain. Moreover, defining the function(d) within each attr() function, you can assign data values iteratively, one after the other, to the corresponding attribute. In this way, you can assign a different value (one for each row in the CSV file) to the attributes x, y, height, and fill, which affect the position, color, and size of each bar. With this mechanism each .bar element will reflect the data contained in one of the rows in the CSV file.

Listing 4-13. Ch4_01.html

```
d3.csv("data_04.csv", function(error, data) {
    ...

    title.append("text")
        .attr("x", (w / 2))
        .attr("y", -30 )
        .attr("text-anchor", "middle")
        .style("font-size", "22px")
        .text("My first bar chart");

    svg.selectAll(".bar")
        .data(data)
        .enter().append("rect")
        .attr("class", "bar")
        .attr("x", function(d) { return x(d.country); })
        .attr("width", x.rangeBand())
        .attr("y", function(d) { return y(d.income/sum); })
        .attr("height", function(d) { return h - y(d.income/sum); })
        .attr("fill", function(d) { return color(d.country); });
});
```

At the end, all your efforts will be rewarded with the beautiful bar chart shown in Figure 4-1.

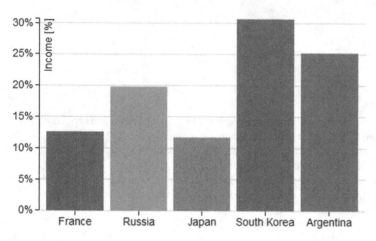

Figure 4-1. *A simple bar chart*

Drawing a Stacked Bar Chart

You have introduced the bar chart with the simplest case where you had a number of groups represented per country and a corresponding value (income). Very often, you need to represent data which are a bit more complex, for example, data in which you want to divide the total income sector by sector. In this case, you will have the income for each country divided into various portions, each of which represents the income of a sector of production. For our example, we will use a CSV file in a way that is very similar to that used in the previous example (see Listing 4-1), but with multiple values for each country, so that you may work with multiseries bar charts. Therefore, write the data in Listing 4-14 with a text editor and save it as data_05.csv.

Listing 4-14. data_05.csv

```
Country,Electronics,Software,Mechanics
Germany,12,14,18
Italy,8,12,10
Spain,6,4,5
France,10,14,9
UK,7,11,9
```

Looking at the content of the file, you may notice that the columns are now four. The first column still contains the names of the nations, but now the incomes are three, each corresponding to a different sector of production: electronics, software, and mechanics. These titles are listed in the headers.

Start with the code of the previous example, making some changes and deleting some rows, until you get the code shown in Listing 4-15. The pieces of code in bold are the ones that need to be changed (the title and the CSV file) m while those that are not present must be deleted. Those of you who are starting directly from this section can easily copy the contents shown in Listing 4-15.

Listing 4-15. Ch4_02.html

```html
<!DOCTYPE html>
<html>
<head>
<meta charset="utf-8">
<script src="http://d3js.org/d3.v3.js"></script>
<style>
body {
    font: 14px sans-serif;
}
.axis path,
.axis line {
    fill: none;
    stroke: #000;
    shape-rendering: crispEdges;
}
.x.axis path {
    display: none;
}
</style>
</head>
<body>
<script type="text/javascript">
var color = d3.scale.category10();

var margin = {top: 70, right: 20, bottom: 30, left: 40},
    w = 500 - margin.left - margin.right,
    h = 350 - margin.top - margin.bottom;

var x = d3.scale.ordinal()
    .rangeRoundBands([0, w], .1);

var y = d3.scale.linear()
    .range([h, 0]);

var formatPercent = d3.format(".0%");

var xAxis = d3.svg.axis()
    .scale(x)
    .orient("bottom");

var yAxis = d3.svg.axis()
    .scale(y)
    .orient("left")
    .tickFormat(formatPercent);
```

```
var yGrid = d3.svg.axis()
    .scale(y)
    .orient("left")
    .ticks(5)
    .tickSize(-w, 0, 0)
    .tickFormat("");

var svg = d3.select("body").append("svg")
    .attr("width", w + margin.left + margin.right)
    .attr("height", h + margin.top + margin.bottom)
    .append("g")
    .attr("transform", "translate(" + margin.left + ", " + margin.top + ")");

d3.csv("data_05.csv", function(error, data) {

    svg.append("g")
        .attr("class", "x axis")
        .attr("transform", "translate(0, " + h + ")")
        .call(xAxis);

    svg.append("g")
        .attr("class", "y axis")
        .call(yAxis);

    svg.append("g")
        .attr("class", "grid")
        .call(yGrid);
});
var labels = svg.append("g")
    .attr("class", "labels");

labels.append("text")
        .attr("transform", "rotate(-90)")
        .attr("x", 50)
        .attr("y", -20)
        .attr("dy", ".71em")
        .style("text-anchor", "end")
        .text("Income [%]");

var title = svg.append("g")
    .attr("class", "title")

title.append("text")
    .attr("x", (w / 2))
    .attr("y", -30 )
    .attr("text-anchor", "middle")
    .style("font-size", "22px")
    .text("A stacked bar chart");
</script>
</body>
</html>
```

Now think of the colors and the domain you want to set. In the previous case, you drew each bar (country) with a different color. In fact, you could even give all the bars of the same color. Your approach was an optional choice, mainly due to aesthetic factors. In this case, however, using a set of different colors is necessary to distinguish the various portions that compose each bar. Thus, you will have a series of identical colors for each bar, where each color will correspond to a sector of production. A small tip: when you need a legend to identify various representations of data, you need to use a sequence of colors, and vice versa. You define the domain of colors relying on the headers of the file and deleting the first item, "Country," through a filter (see Listing 4-16).

Listing 4-16. Ch4_02.html

```
d3.csv("data_05.csv", function(error, data) {

    color.domain(d3.keys(data[0]).filter(function(key) {
    return key !== "Country"; }));

    svg.append("g")
        .attr("class", "x axis")
        .attr("transform", "translate(0, " + h + ")")
        .call(xAxis);
```

. . .

On the y axis you must not plot the values of the income, but their percentage of the total. In order to do this, you need to know the sum of all values of income, so with an iteration of all the data read from the file, you may obtain the sum. Again, in order to make it clear to D3 that the values in the three columns (Electronics, Mechanics, and Software) are numeric values, you must specify them explicitly in the iteration in this way:

```
values = +values;
```

In Listing 4-17, you see how the forEach() function iterates the values of the file and, at the same time, calculates the sum you need to obtain your percentages.

Listing 4-17. Ch4_02.html

```
d3.csv("data_05.csv", function(error, data) {

    color.domain(d3.keys(data[0]).filter(function(key) {
    return key !== "Country"; }));

    var sum = 0;

    data.forEach(function(d){
        d.Electronics = +d.Electronics;
        d.Mechanics = +d.Mechanics;
        d.Software = +d.Software;
        sum = sum +d.Electronics +d.Mechanics +d.Software;
    });

    svg.append("g")
        .attr("class", "x axis")
        .attr("transform", "translate(0, " + h + ")")
        .call(xAxis);
```

. . .

Now you need to create a data structure which can serve your purpose. Build an array of objects for each bar in which each object corresponds to one of the portions in which the total income is divided. Name this array "countries" and create it through an iterative function (see Listing 4-18).

Listing 4-18. Ch4_02.html

```
d3.csv("data_05.csv", function(error, data) {
    ...
    data.forEach(function(d){
        d.Electronics = +d.Electronics;
        d.Mechanics = +d.Mechanics;
        d.Software = +d.Software;
        sum = sum +d.Electronics +d.Mechanics +d.Software;
    });

    data.forEach(function(d) {
        var y0 = 0;
        d.countries = color.domain().map(function(name) {
        return {name: name, y0: y0/sum, y1: (y0 += +d[name])/sum }; });
        d.total = d.countries[d.countries.length - 1].y1;
    });

    svg.append("g")
        .attr("class", "x axis")
        .attr("transform", "translate(0, " + h + ")")
        .call(xAxis);
```

...

Using the Firebug console (see the section "Firebug and DevTool" in Chapter 1), you can directly see the internal structure of this array. Thus, add (temporarily) the call to the console to the code passing the **countries** array as an argument, as shown in Listing 4-19.

Listing 4-19. Ch4_02.html

```
data.forEach(function(d) {
    var y0 = 0;
    d.countries = color.domain().map(function(name) {
    return {name: name, y0: y0/sum, y1: (y0 += +d[name])/sum }; });
    d.total = d.countries[d.countries.length - 1].y1;
    console.log(d.countries);
});
```

Figure 4-2 shows the internal structure of the countries array along with all its content how it is displayed by the Firebug console.

```
[ Object { name="Electronics", y0=0, y1=0.08053691275167785 }, Object {
name="Software", y0=0.08053691275167785, y1=0.174496644295302 }, Object {
name="Mechanics", y0=0.174496644295302, y1=0.2953020134228188 } ]
[ Object { name="Electronics", y0=0, y1=0.06711409395973154 }, Object {
name="Software", y0=0.06711409395973154, y1=0.1610738255033557 }, Object {
name="Mechanics", y0=0.1610738255033557, y1=0.2214765100671141 } ]
[ Object { name="Electronics", y0=0, y1=0.053691275167785234 }, Object {
name="Software", y0=0.053691275167785234, y1=0.1342281879194631 }, Object {
name="Mechanics", y0=0.1342281879194631, y1=0.20134228187919462 } ]
[ Object { name="Electronics", y0=0, y1=0.04697986577181208 }, Object {
name="Software", y0=0.04697986577181208, y1=0.12080536912751678 }, Object {
name="Mechanics", y0=0.12080536912751678, y1=0.18120805369127516 } ]
```

Figure 4-2. *The Firebug console shows the content and the structure of the countries array*

If you analyze in detail the first element of the array:

```
[Object {name="Electronics", y0=0, y1=0.08053691275167785},
 Object {name="Software", y0=0.08053691275167785, y1=0.174496644295302},
 Object {name="Mechanics", y0=0.174496644295302, y1=0.2953020134228188}]
```

You may notice that each element of the array is, in turn, an array containing three objects. These three objects represent the three categories (the three series of the multiseries bar chart) into which you want to split the data. The values of y0 and y1 are the percentages of the beginning and the end of each portion in the bar, respectively.

After you have arranged all the data you need, you can include it in the domain of x and y, as shown in Listing 4-20.

Listing 4-20. Ch4_02.html

```
d3.csv("data_05.csv", function(error, data) {
  ...
  data.forEach(function(d) {
  ...
  console.log(d.countries);
  });

    x.domain(data.map(function(d) { return d.Country; }));
    y.domain([0, d3.max(data, function(d) { return d.total; })]);

    svg.append("g")
        .attr("class", "x axis")
        .attr("transform", "translate(0, " + h + ")")
        .call(xAxis);

...
```

And then, in Listing 4-21 you start to define the rect elements which will constitute the bars of your chart.

Listing 4-21. Ch4_02.html

```
d3.csv("data_05.csv", function(error, data) {
    ...
    svg.append("g")
        .attr("class", "grid")
        .call(yGrid);

    var country = svg.selectAll(".country")
        .data(data)
        .enter().append("g")
        .attr("class", "country")
        .attr("transform", function(d) {
        return "translate(" + x(d.Country) + ",0)"; });

    country.selectAll("rect")
            .data(function(d) { return d.countries; })
            .enter().append("rect")
            .attr("width", x.rangeBand())
            .attr("y", function(d) { return y(d.y1); })
            .attr("height", function(d) { return (y(d.y0) - y(d.y1)); })
            .style("fill", function(d) { return color(d.name); });
});
```

You have seen the internal structure of the array with the library, and since D3 always starts with basic graphics, the most complex part lies in translating the data structure into a hierarchical structure of SVG elements. The <g> tag comes to your aid to build proper hierarchical groupings. In this regard, you have to define an element <g> for each country. First, you need to use the data read from the CSV file iteratively. This can be done by passing the data array (the original data array, not the countries array you have just defined) as argument to the data() function. When all this is done, you have five new group items <g>, as five are the countries which are listed in the CSV file and five are also the bars which will be drawn. The position on the x axis of each bar should also be managed. You do not need to do any calculations to pass the right x values to translate(x,0) function. In fact, as shown in Figure 4-3, these values are automatically generated by D3, exploiting the fact that you have defined an ordinal scale on the x axis.

```
⊞ <g class="country" transform="translate(9,0)">
⊞ <g class="country" transform="translate(95,0)">
⊞ <g class="country" transform="translate(181,0)">
⊞ <g class="country" transform="translate(267,0)">
⊞ <g class="country" transform="translate(353,0)">
```

Figure 4-3. *Firebug shows the different translation values on the x axis that are automatically generated by the D3 library*

Within each of the group elements <g>, you must now create the <rect> elements, which will generate the colored rectangles for each portion. Furthermore, it will be necessary to ensure that the correct values are assigned to the y and height attributes, in order to properly place the rectangles one above the other, avoiding them from overlapping, and thus to obtain a single stacked bar for each country.

This time, it is the countries array which will be used, passing it as an argument to the data() function. Since it is necessary to make a further iteration for each element <g> that you have created, you will pass the iterative function(d) to the data() function as an argument. In this way, you create an iteration in another iteration: the first scans the values in data (countries); the second, inner one scans the values in the countries array (sectors of production).

Thus, you assign the final percentages (y1) to the y attributes, and you assign the difference between the initial and final percentage (y0–y1) to the height attributes. The values y0 and y1 have been calculated previously when you have defined the objects contained within the countries array one by one (see Figure 4-4).

```
<g class="country" transform="translate(9,0)">
    <rect width="77" y="182" height="68" style="fill: rgb(31, 119, 180);">
    <rect width="77" y="102" height="80" style="fill: rgb(255, 127, 14);">
    <rect width="77" y="0" height="102" style="fill: rgb(44, 160, 44);">
</g>
```

Figure 4-4. *Firebug shows the different height values attributed to each rect element*

At the, end you can admire your stacked bar chart in Figure 4-5.

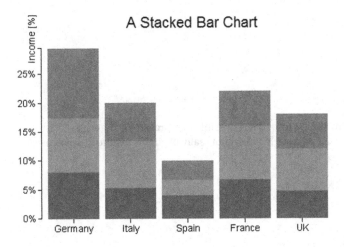

Figure 4-5. *A stacked bar chart*

Looking at your stacked bar chart, you immediately notice that something is missing. How do you recognize the sector of production, and what are their reference colors? Why not add a legend?

As you did for the other chart components, you may prefer to define a legend variable for this new component. Once you have created the group element <g>, an iteration is required also for the legend (see Listing 4-22). The iteration has to be done on the sectors of production. For each item, you need to acquire the name of the sector and the corresponding color. For this purpose, this time you will exploit the color domain which you have defined earlier: for the text element, you will use the headers in the CSV file, whereas for the color you directly assign the value of the domain.

Listing 4-22. Ch4_02.html

```
d3.csv("data_05.csv", function(error, data) {
    ...
    country.selectAll("rect")
        .data(function(d) { return d.countries; })
        .enter().append("rect")
        .attr("width", x.rangeBand())
        .attr("y", function(d) { return y(d.y1); })
        .attr("height", function(d) { return (y(d.y0) - y(d.y1)); })
        .style("fill", function(d) { return color(d.name); });
```

```
var legend = svg.selectAll(".legend")
    .data(color.domain().slice().reverse())
    .enter().append("g")
    .attr("class", "legend")
    .attr("transform", function(d, i) {
    return "translate(0, " + i * 20 + ")"; });

legend.append("rect")
        .attr("x", w - 18)
        .attr("y", 4)
        .attr("width", 10)
        .attr("height", 10)
        .style("fill", color);

legend.append("text")
        .attr("x", w - 24)
        .attr("y", 9)
        .attr("dy", ".35em")
        .style("text-anchor", "end")
        .text(function(d) { return d; });
});
```

Just to complete the topic of stack bar charts, using the D3 library it is possible to represent the bars in descending order, by adding the single line in Listing 4-23. Although you do not really need this feature in your case, it could be useful in certain other particular cases.

Listing 4-23. Ch4_02.html

```
d3.csv("data_05.csv", function(error, data) {
    ...
    data.forEach(function(d) {
        ...
        console.log(d.countries);
    });

    data.sort(function(a, b) { return b.total - a.total; });

    x.domain(data.map(function(d) { return d.Country; }));
    ...
});
```

Figure 4-6 shows your stacked bars represented along the x axis in descending order.

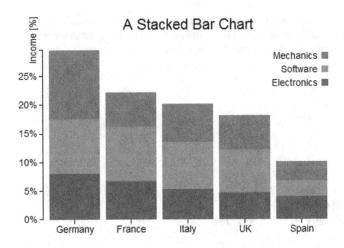

Figure 4-6. *A sorted stacked bar chart with a legend*

A Normalized Stacked Bar Chart

In this section, you will see how to convert the preceding chart in a normalized chart. By "normalized," we mean that the range of values to be displayed in the chart is converted into another target range, which often goes from 0 to 1, or 0 to 100 if you are talking about percentages (a very similar concept was treated in relation to the "Ranges, Domains, and Scales" section in Chapter 2). Therefore, if you want to compare different series covering ranges of values that are very different from each other, you need to carry out a normalization, reporting all of these intervals in percentage values between 0 and 100 (or between 0 and 1). In fact, having to compare multiple series of data, we are often interested in their relative characteristics. In our example, for instance, you might be interested in how the mechanical sector affects the economic income of a nation (normalization), and also in comparing how this influence differs from country to country (comparison between normalized values). So, in order to respond to such a demand, you can represent your stacked chart in a normalized format.

You have already reported the percentage values on the y axis; however, the percentages of each sector of production were calculated with respect to the total amount of the income of all countries. This time, the percentages will be calculated with respect to the income of each country. Thus, in this case you do not care how each individual portion partakes (in percentage) of the global income (referring to all five countries), but you care only about the percentage of income which each single sector produces in the respective country. In this case, therefore, each country will be represented by a bar at 100%. Now, there is no information about which country produces more income than others, but you are interested only in the information internal to each individual country.

All of this reasoning is important for you to understand that, although starting from the same data, you will need to choose a different type of chart depending on what you want to focus the attention of those who would be looking at the chart.

For this example, you are going to use the same file data_05.csv (refer to Listing 4-14); as we have just said, the incoming information is the same, but it is its interpretation which is different. In order to normalize the previous stacked bar chart, you need to effect some changes to the code. Start by extending the left and the right margins by just a few pixels as shown in Listing 4-24.

Listing 4-24. Ch4_03.html

```
var margin = {top: 70, right: 70, bottom: 30, left: 50},
    w = 500 - margin.left - margin.right,
    h = 350 - margin.top - margin.bottom;
```

In Listing 4-25, inside the d3.csv() function you must eliminate the iterations for calculating the sum of the total income, which is no longer needed. Instead, you add a new iteration which takes the percentages referred to each country into account. Then, you must eliminate the definition of the y domain, leaving only the x domain.

Listing 4-25. Ch4_03.html

```
d3.csv("data_05.csv", function(error, data) {
    color.domain(d3.keys(data[0]).filter(function(key) {
    return key !== "Country"; }));

    data.forEach(function(d) {
      var y0 = 0;
      d.countries = color.domain().map(function(name) {
      return {name: name, y0: y0, y1: y0 += +d[name]}; });
      d.countries.forEach(function(d) { d.y0 /= y0; d.y1 /= y0; });
    });

    x.domain(data.map(function(d) { return d.Country; }));

    var country = svg.selectAll(".country")
...
```

With this new type of chart, the y label would be covered by the bars. You must therefore delete or comment out the rotate() function in order to make it visible again as shown in Listing 4-26.

Listing 4-26. Ch4_03.html

```
labels.append("text")
    //.attr("transform", "rotate(-90)")
      .attr("x", 50)
      .attr("y", -20)
      .attr("dy", ".71em")
      .style("text-anchor", "end")
      .text("Income [%]");
```

While you're at it, why not take the opportunity to change the title to your chart? Thus, modify the title as shown in Listing 4-27.

Listing 4-27. Ch4_03.html

```
title.append("text")
      .attr("x", (w / 2))
      .attr("y", -30 )
      .attr("text-anchor", "middle")
      .style("font-size", "22px")
      .text("A normalized stacked bar chart");
```

Even the legend is no longer required. In fact, you will replace it with another type of graphic representation which has very similar functions. Thus, you can delete the lines which define the legend in Listing 4-28 from the code.

Listing 4-28. Ch4_03.html

```
var legend = svg.selectAll(".legend")
    .data(color.domain().slice().reverse())
    .enter().append("g")
    .attr("class", "legend")
    .attr("transform", function(d, i) {
        return "translate(0, " + i * 20 + ")"; });

  legend.append("rect")
        .attr("x", w - 18)
        .attr("y", 4)
        .attr("width", 10)
        .attr("height", 10)
        .style("fill", color);

  legend.append("text")
        .attr("x", w - 24)
        .attr("y", 9)
        .attr("dy", ".35em")
        .style("text-anchor", "end")
        .text(function(d) { return d; });
```

Now that you have removed the legend and made the right changes, if you load the web page you get the normalized stacked bar chart in Figure 4-7.

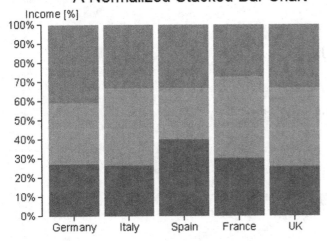

Figure 4-7. *A normalized stacked bar chart*

Without the legend, you must once again know, in some way, what the colors in the bars refer to; you are going to label the last bar on the right with labels reporting the names of the groups.

Start by adding a new style class in Listing 4-29.

Listing 4-29. ch4_03.html

```
<style>
...
.x.axis path {
    display: none;
}
.legend line {
    stroke: #000;
    shape-rendering: crispEdges;
}
</style>
```

Hence, in place of the code that you have just removed, as shown in Listing 4-28, you add the code in Listing 4-30.

Listing 4-30. ch4_03.html

```
country.selectAll("rect")
        .data(function(d) { return d.countries; })
        .enter().append("rect")
        .attr("width", x.rangeBand())
        .attr("y", function(d) { return y(d.y1); })
        .attr("height", function(d) { return (y(d.y0) - y(d.y1)); })
        .style("fill", function(d) { return color(d.name); });

var legend = svg.select(".country:last-child")
        .data(data);

legend.selectAll(".legend")
        .data(function(d) { return d.countries; })
        .enter().append("g")
        .attr("class", "legend")
        .attr("transform", function(d) {
            return "translate(" + x.rangeBand()*0.9 + ", " +
            y((d.y0 + d.y1) / 2) + ")";
});

legend.selectAll(".legend")
        .append("line")
        .attr("x2", 10);

legend.selectAll(".legend")
        .append("text")
        .attr("x", 13)
        .attr("dy", ".35em")
        .text(function(d) { return d.name; });
});
```

As you add the labels to the last bar, the SVG elements which define them must belong to the group corresponding to the last country. So, you use the .country: last-child selector to get the last element of the selection containing all the bars. So, the new chart will look like Figure 4-8.

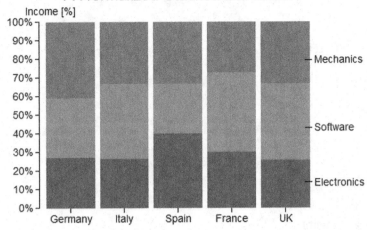

Figure 4-8. *A normalized stacked bar chart with labels as legend*

Drawing a Grouped Bar Chart

Always using the same data contained in data_05.csv, you can obtain another representation: a grouped bar chart. This representation is most appropriate when you want to focus on the individual income for each sector of production. In this case, you do not care in what measure the sectors partake of the total income. Thus, the percentages disappear and are replaced by y values written in the CSV file.

Listing 4-31 shows the part of code that is almost comparable to that present in other previous examples, so we will not discuss it in detail. In fact, you will use it as a starting point upon which to add other code snippets.

Listing 4-31. Ch4_04.html

```
<!DOCTYPE html>
<html>
<head>
<meta charset="utf-8">
<script src="../src/d3.v3.js"></script>
<style>
body {
    font: 14px sans-serif;
}
.axis path,
.axis line {
    fill: none;
    stroke: #000;
shape-rendering: crispEdges;
}
.x.axis path {
    display: none;
}
</style>
</head>
```

```
<body>
<script type="text/javascript">
var color = d3.scale.category10();

var margin = {top: 70, right: 70, bottom: 30, left: 50},
    w = 500 - margin.left - margin.right,
    h = 350 - margin.top - margin.bottom;

var yGrid = d3.svg.axis()
    .scale(y)
    .orient("left")
    .ticks(5)
    .tickSize(-w, 0, 0)
    .tickFormat("")

var svg = d3.select("body").append("svg")
    .attr("width", w + margin.left + margin.right)
    .attr("height", h + margin.top + margin.bottom)
    .append("g")
    .attr("transform", "translate(" + margin.left + ", " + margin.top + ")");

d3.csv("data_05.csv", function(error, data) {

    svg.append("g")
        .attr("class", "x axis")
        .attr("transform", "translate(0, " + h + ")")
        .call(xAxis);

    svg.append("g")
        .attr("class", "y axis")
        .call(yAxis);

    svg.append("g")
        .attr("class", "grid")
        .call(yGrid);
});
</script>
</body>
</html>
```

For this specific purpose, you need to define two different variables on the x axis: x0 and x1, both following an ordinal scale as shown in Listing 4-32. The x0 identifies the ordinal scale of all the groups of bars, representing a country, while x1 is the ordinal scale of each single bar within each group, representing a sector of production.

Listing 4-32. Ch4_04.html

```
var margin = {top: 70, right: 70, bottom: 30, left: 50},
    w = 500 - margin.left - margin.right,
    h = 350 - margin.top - margin.bottom;

var x0 = d3.scale.ordinal()
    .rangeRoundBands([0, w], .1);
var x1 = d3.scale.ordinal();
var y = d3.scale.linear()
    .range([h, 0]);

...
```

Consequently, in the definition of the axes, you assign the *x0* to the x axis, and the y to the y axis (see Listing 4-33). Instead, the variable x1 will be used later only as a reference for the representation of the individual bar.

Listing 4-33. Ch4_04.html

```
...
var y = d3.scale.linear()
    .range([h, 0]);

var xAxis = d3.svg.axis()
    .scale(x0)
    .orient("bottom");

var yAxis = d3.svg.axis()
    .scale(y)
    .orient("left");
...
```

Inside the d3.csv() function, you extract all the names of the sectors of production with the keys() function and exclude the "country" header by filtering it out from the array with the filter() function as shown in Listing 4-34. Here, too, you build an array of objects for each country, but the structure is slightly different. The new array looks like this:

```
[Object {name="Electronics", value=12},
 Object {name="Software", value=14},
 Object {name="Mechanics", value=18}]
```

Listing 4-34. Ch4_04.html

```
...
d3.csv("data_05.csv", function(error, data) {
  var sectorNames = d3.keys(data[0]).filter(function(key) {
    return key !== "Country"; });
  data.forEach(function(d) {
    d.countries = sectorNames.map(function(name) {
      return {name: name, value: +d[name]
    };
  });
  ...
});
```

Once you define the data structure, you can define the new domains as shown in Listing 4-35.

Listing 4-35. Ch4_04.html

```
d3.csv("data_05.csv", function(error, data) {
    ...
    data.forEach(function(d) {
    ...
});

x0.domain(data.map(function(d) { return d.Country; }));
x1.domain(sectorNames).rangeRoundBands([0, x0.rangeBand()]);
y.domain([0, d3.max(data, function(d) {
    return d3.max(d.countries, function(d) { return d.value; });
})]);

svg.append("g")
    .attr("class", "x axis")
    .attr("transform", "translate(0, " + h + ")")
    .call(xAxis);
...
```

As mentioned before, with x0 you specify the ordinal domain with the names of each country. Instead, in x1 the names of the various sectors make up the domain. Finally, in y the domain is defined by numerical values. Update the values passed in the iterations with the new domains (see Listing 4-36).

Listing 4-36. Ch4_04.html

```
d3.csv("data_05.csv", function(error, data) {
    ...
    svg.append("g")
        .attr("class", "grid")
        .call(yGrid);

    var country = svg.selectAll(".country")
        .data(data)
        .enter().append("g")
        .attr("class", "country")
        .attr("transform", function(d) {
            return "translate(" + x0(d.Country) + ",0)";
        });

    country.selectAll("rect")
        .data(function(d) { return d.countries; })
        .enter().append("rect")
        .attr("width", x1.rangeBand())
        .attr("x", function(d) { return x1(d.name); })
        .attr("y", function(d) { return y(d.value); })
        .attr("height", function(d) { return h - y(d.value); })
        .style("fill", function(d) { return color(d.name); });
});
```

Then, externally to the csv() function you can define the SVG element which will represent the axis label on the y axis, as shown in Listing 4-37. It does not need to be defined within the csv() function, since it is independent from the data contained in the CSV file.

Listing 4-37. Ch4_04.html

```
d3.csv("data_05.csv", function(error, data) {
    ...
});

var labels = svg.append("g")
    .attr("class", "labels")

labels.append("text")
        .attr("transform", "rotate(-90)")
        .attr("y", 5)
        .attr("dy", ".71em")
        .style("text-anchor", "end")
        .text("Income");
</script>
```

One last thing... you need to add an appropriate title to the chart as shown in Listing 4-38.

Listing 4-38. Ch4_04.html

```
labels.append("text")
    ...
    .text("Income");

var title = svg.append("g")
    .attr("class", "title")

title.append("text")
        .attr("x", (w / 2))
        .attr("y", -30 )
        .attr("text-anchor", "middle")
        .style("font-size", "22px")
        .text("A grouped bar chart");
</script>
```

And Figure 4-9 is the result.

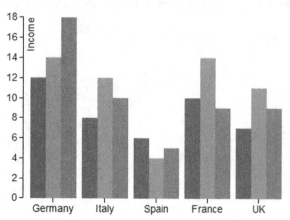

Figure 4-9. *A grouped bar chart*

In the previous case, with the normalized bar chart, you looked at an alternative way to represent a legend. You have built this legend by putting some labels which report the series name on the last bar (refer to Figure 4-8). Actually you made use of point labels. These labels can contain any text and are directly connected to a single value in the chart. At this point, introduce point labels. You will place them at the top of each bar, showing the numerical value expressed by that bar. This greatly increases the readability of each type of chart.

As you have done for any other chart component, having defined the *PointLabels* variable, you use it in order to assign the chain of functions applied to the corresponding selection. Also, for this type of component, which has specific values for individual data, you make use of an iteration for the data contained in the CSV file. The data on which you want to iterate are the same data you used for the bars. You therefore pass the same iterative function(d) to the data() function as argument (see Listing 4-39). In order to draw the data on top of the bars, you will apply a translate() transformation for each *PointLabel*.

Listing 4-39. Ch4_04.html

```
d3.csv("data_05.csv", function(error, data) {
    ...
    country.selectAll("rect")
    ...
        .attr("height", function(d) { return h - y(d.value); })
        .style("fill", function(d) { return color(d.name); });

    var pointlabels = country.selectAll(".pointlabels")
        .data(function(d) { return d.countries; })
        .enter().append("g")
        .attr("class", "pointlabels")
        .attr("transform", function(d) {
            return "translate(" + x1(d.name) + ", " + y(d.value) + ")";
        })
```

```
        .append("text")
        .attr("dy", "-0.3em")
        .attr("x", x1.rangeBand()/2)
        .attr("text-anchor", "middle")
        .text(function(d) { return d.value; });
...
});
```

And finally, there is nothing left to do but to add a legend, grouped in the classic format, to the chart (see Listing 4-40).

Listing 4-40. ch4_04.html

```
d3.csv("data_05.csv", function(error, data) {
    ...
    pointlabels.append("text")
    ...
        .text(function(d) { return d.value; });

    var legend = svg.selectAll(".legend")
        .data(color.domain().slice().reverse())
        .enter().append("g")
        .attr("class", "legend")
        .attr("transform", function(d, i) {
            return "translate(0, " + i * 20 + ")";
        });

    legend.append("rect")
            .attr("x", w - 18)
            .attr("y", 4)
            .attr("width", 10)
            .attr("height", 10)
            .style("fill", color);

    legend.append("text")
            .attr("x", w - 24)
            .attr("y", 9)
            .attr("dy", ".35em")
            .style("text-anchor", "end")
            .text(function(d) { return d; });
});
```

Figure 4-10 shows the new chart with point labels and a segments legend.

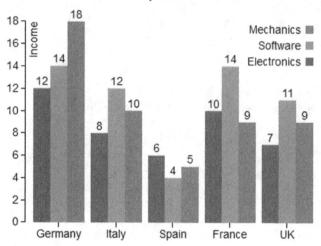

Figure 4-10. *A grouped bar chart reporting the values above each bar*

Horizontal Bar Chart with Negative Values

So far you have used only positive values, but what if you have both positive and negative values? How can you represent them in a bar chart? Take, for example, this sequence of values containing both positive and negative values (see Listing 4-41).

Listing 4-41. Ch4_05.html

```
var data = [4, 3, 1, -7, -10, -7, 1, 5, 7, -3, -5, -12, -7, -11, 3, 7, 8, -1];
```

Before analyzing the data to be displayed, start adding margins to your charts as shown in Listing 4-42.

Listing 4-42. Ch4_05.html

```
var data = [4, 3, 1, -7, -10, -7, 1, 5, 7, -3, -5, -12, -7, -11, 3, 7, 8, -1];

var margin = {top: 30, right: 10, bottom: 10, left: 30},
    w = 700 - margin.left - margin.right,
    h = 400 - margin.top - margin.bottom;
```

In this particular case, you will make use of horizontal bars where the values in the input array will be represented on the x axis, with the value 0 in the middle. In order to achieve this, it is first necessary to find the maximum value in absolute terms (both negative and positive). You then create the x variable on a linear scale, while the y variable is assigned to an ordinal scale containing the sequence in which data are placed in the input array (see Listing 4-43).

Listing 4-43. Ch4_05.html

```
...
var margin = {top: 30, right: 10, bottom: 10, left: 30},
    w = 700 - margin.left - margin.right,
    h = 400 - margin.top - margin.bottom;

var xMax = Math.max(-d3.min(data), d3.max(data));

var x = d3.scale.linear()
    .domain([-xMax, xMax])
    .range([0, w])
    .nice();

var y = d3.scale.ordinal()
    .domain(d3.range(data.length))
    .rangeRoundBands([0, h], .2);
```

In Listing 4-44, you assign the two scales to the corresponding x axis and y axis. This time, the x axis will be drawn in the upper part of the chart while the y axis will be oriented downwards (the y values are growing downwards).

Listing 4-44. Ch4_05.html

```
var y = d3.scale.ordinal()
    .domain(d3.range(data.length))
    .rangeRoundBands([0, h], .2);

var xAxis = d3.svg.axis()
    .scale(x)
    .orient("top");

var yAxis = d3.svg.axis()
    .scale(y)
    .orient("left");
```

At this point, there is nothing left to do but to begin to implement the drawing area. Create the root <svg> element, assigning the margins that have been previously defined. Then, you define the x axis and y axis (see Listing 4-45).

Listing 4-45. Ch4_05.html

```
var yAxis = d3.svg.axis()
    .scale(y)
    .orient("left")

var svg = d3.select("body").append("svg")
    .attr("width", w + margin.left + margin.right)
    .attr("height", h + margin.top + margin.bottom)
    .append("g")
    .attr("transform", "translate(" + margin.left + ", " + margin.top + ")");
```

```
svg.append("g")
   .attr("class", "x axis")
   .call(xAxis);

svg.append("g")
   .attr("class", "y axis")
   .attr("transform", "translate("+x(0)+",0)")
   .call(yAxis);
```

Finally, you need to insert a <rect> element for each bar to be represented, being careful to divide the bars into two distinct groups: negative bars and positive bars (see Listing 4-46). These two categories must be distinguished in order to set their attributes separately, with a CSS style class (e.g., color).

Listing 4-46. Ch4_05.html

```
svg.append("g")
   .attr("class", "y axis")
   .attr("transform", "translate("+x(0)+",0)")
   .call(yAxis);

svg.selectAll(".bar")
   .data(data)
   .enter().append("rect")
   .attr("class", function(d) {
      return d <0 ? "bar negative" : "bar positive";
   })
   .attr("x", function(d) { return x(Math.min(0, d)); })
   .attr("y", function(d, i) { return y(i); })
   .attr("width", function(d) { return Math.abs(x(d) - x(0)); })
   .attr("height", y.rangeBand());
```

In fact, if you analyze the structure with Firebug in Figure 4-11, you will see that the iteration has created two different types of bars within the same group, recognizable by the characterization of the class name "bar positive" and "bar negative." Through these two different names, you apply two different CSS styles in order to distinguish the bars with negative values from those with positive values.

```
⊞ <g class="y axis" transform="translate(330,0)">
   <rect class="bar positive" x="330" y="11" width="110" height="15">
   <rect class="bar positive" x="330" y="30" width="82.5" height="15">
   <rect class="bar positive" x="330" y="49" width="27.5" height="15">
   <rect class="bar negative" x="137.5" y="68" width="192.5" height="15">
   <rect class="bar negative" x="55" y="87" width="275" height="15">
   <rect class="bar negative" x="137.5" y="106" width="192.5" height="15">
   <rect class="bar positive" x="330" y="125" width="27.5" height="15">
   <rect class="bar positive" x="330" y="144" width="137.49999999999994" height="15">
```

Figure 4-11. *Firebug shows how it is possible to distinguish the positive from the negative bars, indicating the distinction in the class of each rect element*

According to what we have just said, you set the style class attributes for negative and positive bars as in Listing 4-47.

Listing 4-47. Ch4_05.html

```
<style>
.bar.positive {
    fill: red;
    stroke: darkred;
}
.bar.negative {
    fill: lightblue;
    stroke: blue;
}
.axis path,
.axis line {
    fill: none;
    stroke: #000;
  }
body {
  font: 14px sans-serif;
}
</style>
```

At the end, you get the chart in Figure 4-12 with red bars for positive values and blue bars for negative values.

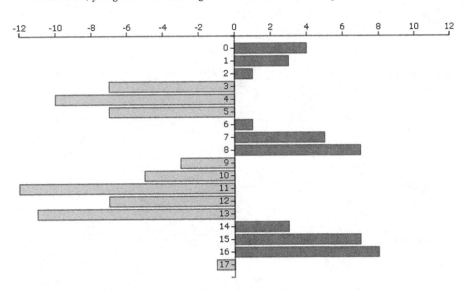

Figure 4-12. *A horizontal bar chart*

Summary

In this chapter, you have covered almost all of the fundamental aspects related to the implementation of a bar chart, the same type of chart which was developed in the first section of the book using the jqPlot library. Here, you made use of the D3 library. Thus, you saw how you can realize a simple bar chart element by element; then you moved on to the various cases of stacked bar charts and grouped bar charts, to finally look at a most peculiar case: a horizontal bar chart which portrays negative values.

In the next chapter, you will continue with the same approach: you will learn how to implement pie charts in a way similar to that used when working with jqPlot, but this time you will be using the D3 library.

CHAPTER 5

■ ■ ■

Pie Charts with D3

In the previous chapter, you have just seen how bar charts represent a certain category of data. You have also seen that starting from the same data structure, depending on your intentions you could choose one type of chart rather than another in order to accentuate particular aspects of the data. For instance, in choosing a normalized stacked bar chart, you wanted to focus on the percentage of income that each sector produces in its country.

Very often, such data represented by bar charts can also be represented using pie charts. In this chapter, you will learn how to create even this type of chart using the D3 library. Given that this library does not provide the graphics which are already implemented, as jqPlot does, but requires the user to build them using basic scalar vector graphics (SVG) elements, you will start by looking at how to build arcs and circular sectors. In fact, as with rectangles for bar charts and lines for line charts, these shapes are of fundamental importance if you are to realize pie charts (using circular sectors) or donut charts (using arcs). After you have implemented a classic example of a pie chart, we will deepen the topic further, by creating some variations. In the second part of the chapter, you will tackle donut charts, managing multiple series of data that are read from a comma-separated values (CSV) file.

Finally, we will close the chapter with a chart that we have not dealt with yet: the polar area diagram. This type of chart is a further evolution of a pie chart, in which the slices are no longer enclosed in a circle, but all have different radii. With polar area diagram, the information will no longer be expressed only by the angle that a slice occupies but also by its radius.

The Basic Pie Charts

To better highlight the parallels between bar charts and pie charts, in this example you will use the same CSV file that you used to create a basic bar chart (see the "Drawing a bar chart" section in Chapter 4). Thus, in this section, your purpose will be to implement the corresponding pie chart using the same data. In order to do this, before you start "baking" pies and donuts, you must first obtain "baking trays" of the right shape. The D3 library also allows you to represent curved shapes such as arches and circular sectors, although there actually are no such SVG elements. In fact, as you will soon see, thanks to some of its methods D3 can handle arcs and sectors as it handles other real SVG elements (rectangles, circles, lines, etc.). Once you are confident with the realization of these elements, your work in the creation of a basic pie chart will be almost complete. In the second part of this section, you will produce some variations on the theme, playing mainly with shape borders and colors in general.

Drawing a Basic Pie Chart

Turn your attention again to data contained in the CSV file named data_04.csv (see Listing 5-1).

Listing 5-1. data_04.csv

```
country,income
France,14
Russia,22
Japan,13
South Korea,34
Argentina,28
```

Now, we will demonstrate how these data fit well in a pie chart representation. First, in Listing 5-2, the drawing area and margins are defined.

Listing 5-2. Ch5_01a.html

```
var margin = {top: 70, right: 20, bottom: 30, left: 40},
    w = 500 - margin.left - margin.right,
    h = 400 - margin.top - margin.bottom;
```

Even for pie charts, you need to use a sequence of colors to differentiate the slices between them. Generally, it is usual to use the category10() function to create a domain of colors, and that is what you have done so far. You could do the same thing in this example, but this is not always required. We thus take advantage of this example to see how it is possible to pass a sequence of custom colors. Create a customized example by defining the colors to your liking, one by one, as shown in Listing 5-3.

Listing 5-3. Ch5_01a.html

```
var margin = {top: 70, right: 20, bottom: 30, left: 40},
    w = 500 - margin.left - margin.right,
    h = 400 - margin.top - margin.bottom;

var color = d3.scale.ordinal()
    .range(["#ffc87c", "#ffeba8", "#f3b080", "#916800", "#dda66b"]);
```

Whereas previously you had bars built with rect elements, now you have to deal with the sections of a circle. Thus, you are dealing with circles, angles, arches, radii, etc. In D3 there is a whole set of tools which allow you to work with these kinds of objects, making your work with pie charts easier.

To express the slices of a pie chart (circle sectors), D3 provides you with a function: d3.svg.arc(). This function actually defines the arches. By the term "arc," we mean a particular geometric surface bound by an angle and by two circles, one with a smaller radius (inner radius) and the other with a larger radius (outer radius). The circular sector, i.e., the slice of a pie chart, is nothing more than an arc with an inner radius equal to 0 (see Figure 5-1).

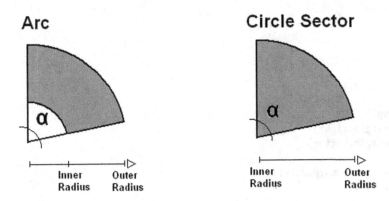

Figure 5-1. *By increasing the inner radius, it is possible to switch from a circle sector to an arc*

First, you calculate a radius which is concordant to the size of the drawing area. Then, according to this range, you delimit the outer radius and inner radius, which in this case is 0 (see Listing 5-4).

Listing 5-4. Ch5_01a.html

```
...
var color = d3.scale.ordinal()
    .range(["#ffc87c", "#ffeba8", "#f3b080", "#916800", "#dda66b"]);

var radius = Math.min(w, h) / 2;
var arc = d3.svg.arc()
    .outerRadius(radius)
    .innerRadius(0);
```

D3 also provides a function to define the pie chart: the d3.layout.pie() function. This function builds a layout that allows you to compute the start and end angles of an arc in a very easy way. It is not mandatory to use such a function, but the pie layout automatically converts an array of data into an array of objects. Thus, define a pie with an iterative function on income values as shown in Listing 5-5.

Listing 5-5. Ch5_01a.html

```
...
var arc = d3.svg.arc()
    .outerRadius(radius)
    .innerRadius(0);

var pie = d3.layout.pie()
    .sort(null)
    .value(function(d) { return d.income; });
```

Now, as seen in Listing 5-6, you insert the root element <svg>, assigning the correct dimensions and the appropriate translate() transformation.

Listing 5-6. Ch5_01a.html

```
...
var pie = d3.layout.pie()
    .sort(null)
    .value(function(d) { return d.income; });

var svg = d3.select("body").append("svg")
    .attr("width", w + margin.left + margin.right)
    .attr("height", h + margin.top + margin.bottom)
    .append("g")
    .attr("transform", "translate(" +(w / 2 + margin.left) +
            "," + (h / 2 + margin.top) + ")");
```

Next, for the reading of data in CSV files, you use the d3.csv() function, as always. Here too you must ensure that the income is interpreted in numeric values and not as strings. Then, you write the iteration with the forEach() function and assign the values of income with the sign '+' beside them, as shown in Listing 5-7.

Listing 5-7. Ch5_01a.html

```
...
    .append("g")
    .attr("transform", "translate(" +(w/2+margin.left)+
            "," +(h/2+margin.top)+ ")");

d3.csv("data_04.csv", function(error, data) {

    data.forEach(function(d) {
        d.income = +d.income;
    });

});
```

It is now time to add an <arc> item, but this element does not exist as an SVG element. In fact, what you use here really is a <path> element which describes the shape of the arc. It is D3 itself which builds the corresponding path thanks to the pie() and arc() functions. This spares you a job which is really too complex. You are left only with the task of defining these elements as if they were <arc> elements (see Listing 5-8).

Listing 5-8. Ch5_01a.html

```
d3.csv("data_04.csv", function(error, data) {

    data.forEach(function(d) {
        d.income = +d.income;
    });

    var g = svg.selectAll(".arc")
        .data(pie(data))
        .enter().append("g")
        .attr("class", "arc");
```

```
    g.append("path")
        .attr("d", arc)
        .style("fill", function(d) { return color(d.data.country); });

});
```

If you analyze the SVG structure with Firebug, you can see in Figure 5-2 that the arc paths are created automatically, and that you have a <g> element for each slice.

```
⊞ <script type="text/javascript">
⊟ <svg width="500" height="400">
    ⊟ <g transform="translate(260,220)">
        ⊟ <g class="arc">
                <path d="M8.572527594031473e-15,-140A14
                <text transform="translate(27.016469129
            </g>
        ⊞ <g class="arc">
        ⊞ <g class="arc">
        ⊞ <g class="arc">
        ⊞ <g class="arc">
    </g>
```

Figure 5-2. With Firebug, you can see how the D3 library automatically builds the arc element

Moreover, it is necessary to add an indicative label to each slice so that you can understand which country it relates to, as shown in Listing 5-9. Notice the arc.centroid() function. This function computes the centroid of the arc. The centroid is defined as the midpoint between the inner and outer radius and the start and end angle. Thus, the label text appears perfectly in the middle of every slice.

Listing 5-9. Ch5_01a.html

```
d3.csv("data_04.csv", function(error, data) {
    ...
    g.append("path")
        .attr("d", arc)
        .style("fill", function(d) { return color(d.data.country); });

    g.append("text")
        .attr("transform", function(d) {
            return "translate(" + arc.centroid(d) + ")"; })
        .style("text-anchor", "middle")
        .text(function(d) { return d.data.country; });

});
```

Even for pie charts, it is good practice to add a title at the top and in a central position (see Listing 5-10).

Listing 5-10. Ch5_01a.html

```
d3.csv("data_04.csv", function(error, data) {
    ...
    g.append("text")
        .attr("transform", function(d) {
            return "translate(" + arc.centroid(d) + ")"; })
        .style("text-anchor", "middle")
        .text(function(d) { return d.data.country; });

    var title = d3.select("svg").append("g")
        .attr("transform", "translate(" +margin.left+ ", " +margin.top+ ")")
        .attr("class", "title")

    title.append("text")
        .attr("x", (w / 2))
        .attr("y", -30 )
        .attr("text-anchor", "middle")
        .style("font-size", "22px")
        .text("My first pie chart");
});
```

As for the CSS class attributes, you can add the definitions in Listing 5-11.

Listing 5-11. Ch5_01a.html

```
<style>
body {
    font: 16px sans-serif;
}

.arc path {
    stroke: #000;
}
</style>
```

At the end, you get your first pie chart using the D3 library, as shown in Figure 5-3.

My first pie chart

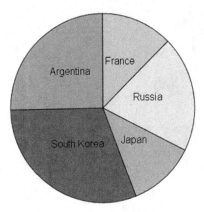

Figure 5-3. *A simple pie chart*

Some Variations on Pie Charts

Now, you will effect some changes to the basic pie chart that you have just created, illustrating some of the infinite possibilities of variations on the theme that you can obtain:

- working on color sequences;
- sorting the slices in a pie chart;
- adding spaces between the slices;
- representing the slices only with outlines;
- combining all of the above.

Working on Color Sequences

In the previous example, we defined the colors in the scale, and in the preceding examples we used the category10() function. There are other already defined categorical color scales: category20(), category20b(), and category20c(). Apply them to your pie chart, just to see how they affect its appearance. Listing 5-12 shows a case in which you use the category10() function. For the other categories, you only need to replace this function with others.

Listing 5-12. Ch5_01b.html

```
var color = d3.scale.category10();
```

Figure 5-4 shows the color variations among the scales (reflected in different grayscale tones in print). The category10() and category20() functions generate a scale with alternating colors; instead, category20b() and category 20c() generate a scale with a slow gradation of colors.

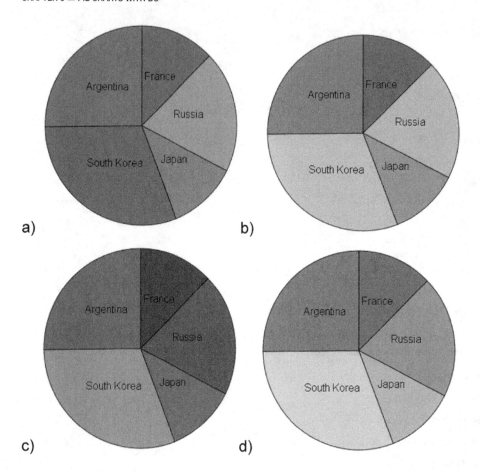

Figure 5-4. *Different color sequences: a) category10, b) category20, c) category20b, d) category20c*

Sorting the Slices in a Pie Chart

Another thing to notice is that, by default, the pie chart in D3 undergoes an implicit sorting. Thus, in case you had not made the request explicitly by passing null to the sort() function, as shown in Listing 5-13.

Listing 5-13. Ch5_01c.html

```
var pie = d3.layout.pie()
    //.sort(null)
    .value(function(d) { return d.income; });
```

Then, the pie chart would have had looked different, as shown in Figure 5-5.

My first pie chart

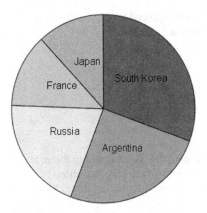

Figure 5-5. *A simple pie chart with sorted slices*

In a pie chart, the first slice is the greatest, and then the other slices are gradually added in descending order.

Adding Spaces Between the Slices

Often, the slices are shown spaced out between them, and this can be achieved very easily. You just need to make some changes to the CSS style class for the path elements as shown in Listing 5-14.

Listing 5-14. Ch5_01d.html

```
.arc path {
    stroke: #fff;
    stroke-width: 4;
}
```

Figure 5-6 shows how the pie chart assumes a more pleasing appearance when the slices are spaced apart by a white gap.

My first pie chart

Figure 5-6. *The slices are separated by a white space*

137

Representing the Slices Only with Outlines

It is a little more complex to draw your pie chart with slices which are bounded only by colored borders and empty inside. You have seen similar cases with jqPlot. Change the CSS style class, as shown in Listing 5-15.

Listing 5-15. Ch5_01e.html

```
.arc path {
    fill: none;
    stroke-width: 6;
}
```

In fact, this time you do not want to fill the slices with specific colors, but you want the edges, defining them, to be colored with specific colors. So you need to replace the `fill` with the `stroke` attribute in the style definition of the SVG element. Now it is the line which is colored with the indicative color. But you need to make another change, which is a little bit more complex to understand.

You are using the borders of every slice to specify the colored part, but they are actually overlapped. So, the following color covers the previous one partially and it is not so neat to have all the slices attached. It would be better to add a small gap. This could be done very easily, simply by applying a translation for each slice. Every slice should be driven off the center by a small distance, in a centrifugal direction. Thus, the translation is different for each slice and here you exploit the capabilities of the centroid() function, which gives you the direction (x and y coordinates) of the translation (see Listing 5-16).

Listing 5-16. Ch5_01e.html

```
var g = svg.selectAll(".arc")
    .data(pie(data))
    .enter().append("g")
    .attr("class", "arc")
    .attr("transform", function(d) {
        a = arc.centroid(d)[0]/6;
        b = arc.centroid(d)[1]/6;
        return "translate(" + a +", "+b + ")";
    })

g.append("path")
    .attr("d", arc)
    .style("stroke", function(d) { return color(d.data.country); });
```

Figure 5-7 illustrates how these changes affect the pie chart.

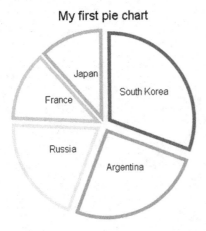

Figure 5-7. *A pie chart with unfilled slices*

Mixing All of This

But it does not end here. You can create a middle solution between these last two pie charts: get the slices with more intensely colored edges and fill them with a lighter color. It is enough to define two identical but differently colored paths, as shown in Listing 5-17. The first will have a uniform color which is slightly faint, while the second will have only colored edges and the inside will be white.

Listing 5-17. Ch5_01f.html

```
var g = svg.selectAll(".arc")
    .data(pie(data))
    .enter().append("g")
    .attr("class", "arc")
    .attr("transform", function(d) {
        a = arc.centroid(d)[0]/6;
        b = arc.centroid(d)[1]/6;
        return "translate(" + a +", "+b + ")";
    })

g.append("path")
    .attr("d", arc)
    .style("fill", function(d) { return color(d.data.country); })
    .attr('opacity', 0.5);

g.append("path")
    .attr("d", arc)
    .style("stroke", function(d) { return color(d.data.country); });
```

Figure 5-8 shows the spaced pie chart with two paths that color the slices and their borders.

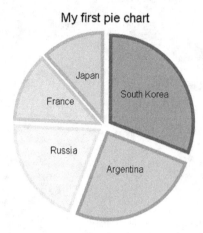

Figure 5-8. *A different way to color the slices in a pie chart*

Donut Charts

As the pie chart is to the bar chart, so the donut chart is to the multiseries bar chart. In fact, when you have multiple sets of values, you would have to represent them with a pie chart for each series. If you use donuts charts instead, you can represent them all together and also compare them in a single chart (see Figure 5-9).

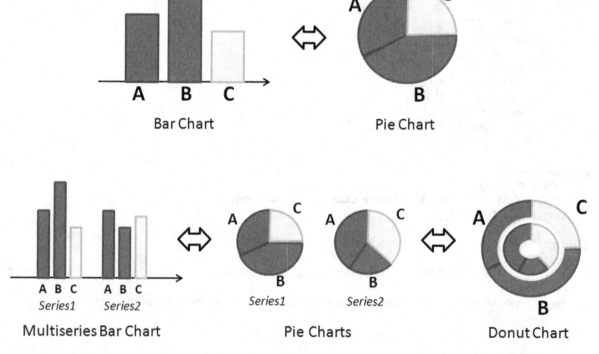

Figure 5-9. *A diagram representing the parallelism between pie charts and bar charts both with one and with multiple series of data*

Begin by writing the code in Listing 5-18; we will not provide any explanation because it is identical to the previous example.

Listing 5-18. Ch5_02.html

```
<!DOCTYPE html>
<html>
<head>
<meta charset="utf-8">
<script src="http://d3js.org/d3.v3.js"></script>
<style>
body {
    font: 16px sans-serif;
}
.arc path {
    stroke: #000;
}
</style>
</head>
<body>
<script type="text/javascript">
var margin = {top: 70, right: 20, bottom: 30, left: 40},
    w = 500 - margin.left - margin.right,
    h = 400 - margin.top - margin.bottom;

var color = d3.scale.ordinal()
    .range(["#ffc87c", "#ffeba8", "#f3b080", "#916800", "#dda66b"]);

var radius = Math.min(w, h) / 2;

var svg = d3.select("body").append("svg")
    .attr("width", w + margin.left + margin.right)
    .attr("height", h + margin.top + margin.bottom)
    .append("g")
    .attr("transform", "translate(" +(w/2+margin.left)+
        "," +(h/2+margin.top)+ ")");

var title = d3.select("svg").append("g")
    .attr("transform", "translate(" +margin.left+ ", " +margin.top+ ")")
    .attr("class", "title");

title.append("text")
    .attr("x", (w / 2))
    .attr("y", -30 )
    .attr("text-anchor", "middle")
    .style("font-size", "22px")
    .text("A donut chart");
</script>
</body>
</html>
```

For an example of multiseries data, you will add another column of data representing the expense to the file data_04.csv as shown in Listing 5-19, and you will save this new version as data_06.csv.

Listing 5-19. data_06.csv

```
country,income,expense
France,14,10
Russia,22,19
Japan,13,6
South Korea,34,12
Argentina,28,26
```

You have added a new set of data. Differently from the previous example, you must, therefore, create a new arc for this series. Then, in addition to the second arc, you add a third one. This arc is not going to draw the slices of a series, but you are going to use it in order to distribute labels circularly. These labels show the names of the countries, providing an alternative to a legend. Thus, divide the radius into three parts, leaving a gap in between to separate the series as shown in Listing 5-20.

Listing 5-20. Ch5_02.html

```
var arc1 = d3.svg.arc()
    .outerRadius(0.4 * radius)
    .innerRadius(0.2 * radius);
var arc2 = d3.svg.arc()
    .outerRadius(0.7 * radius )
    .innerRadius(0.5 * radius );
var arc3 = d3.svg.arc()
    .outerRadius(radius)
    .innerRadius(0.8 * radius);
```

You have just created two arcs to manage the two series, and consequently it is now necessary to create two pies, one for the values of income and the other for the values of expenses (see Listing 5-21).

Listing 5-21. Ch5_02.html

```
var pie = d3.layout.pie()
    .sort(null)
    .value(function(d) { return d.income; });
var pie2 = d3.layout.pie()
    .sort(null)
    .value(function(d) { return d.expense; });
```

You use the d3.csv() function to read the data within the file as shown in Listing 5-22. You do the usual iteration of data with forEach() for the interpretation of income and expense as numerical values.

Listing 5-22. Ch5_02.html

```
d3.csv("data_06.csv", function(data) {

    data.forEach(function(d) {
        d.income = +d.income;
        d.expense = +d.expense;
    });

});
```

In Listing 5-23, you create the path elements which draw the various sectors of the two donuts, corresponding to the two series. With the functions data(), you bind the data of the two pie layouts to the two representations. Both the donuts must follow the same sequence of colors. Once the path element is defined, you connect it with a text element in which the corresponding numeric value is reported. Thus, you have added some labels which make it easier to read the chart.

Listing 5-23. Ch5_02.html

```
var g = svg.selectAll(".arc1")
    .data(pie(data))
    .enter().append("g")
    .attr("class", "arc1");

g.append("path")
    .attr("d", arc1)
    .style("fill", function(d) { return color(d.data.country); });

g.append("text")
    .attr("transform", function(d) {
        return "translate(" + arc1.centroid(d) + ")"; })
    .attr("dy", ".35em")
    .style("text-anchor", "middle")
    .text(function(d) { return d.data.income; });

var g = svg.selectAll(".arc2")
    .data(pie2(data))
    .enter().append("g")
    .attr("class", "arc2");

g.append("path")
    .attr("d", arc2)
    .style("fill", function(d) { return color(d.data.country); });

g.append("text")
    .attr("transform", function(d) {
        return "translate(" + arc2.centroid(d) + ")"; })
    .attr("dy", ".35em")
    .style("text-anchor", "middle")
    .text(function(d) { return d.data.expense; });
```

Now, all that remains to do is to add the external labels carrying out the functions of the legend as shown in Listing 5-24.

Listing 5-24. Ch5_02.html

```
g.append("text")
    .attr("transform", function(d) {
        return "translate(" + arc3.centroid(d) + ")"; })
    .style("text-anchor", "middle")
    .text(function(d) { return d.data.country; });
```

And so you get the donut chart shown in Figure 5-10.

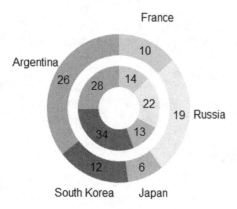

Figure 5-10. *A donut chart*

Polar Area Diagrams

Polar area diagrams are very similar to pie charts, but they differ in how far each sector extends from the center of the circle, giving the possibility to represent a further value. The extent of every slice is proportional to this new added value (see Figure 5-11).

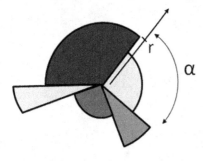

Figure 5-11. *In a polar area diagram, each slice is characterized by a radius r and an angle*

Consider the data in the file data_04.csv again and add an additional column which shows the growth of the corresponding country as shown in Listing 5-25. Save it as data_07.csv.

Listing 5-25. data_07.csvl

```
country,income,growth
France,14,10
Russia,22,19
Japan,13,9
South Korea,34,12
Argentina,28,16
```

Start writing the code in Listing 5-26; again, we will not explain this part because it is identical to the previous examples.

Listing 5-26. Ch5_03.html

```
<!DOCTYPE html>
<html>
<head>
<meta charset="utf-8">
<script src="http://d3js.org/d3.v3.js"></script>
<style>
body {
    font: 16px sans-serif;
}
.arc path {
    stroke: #000;
}
</style>
</head>
<body>
<script type="text/javascript">
var margin = {top: 70, right: 20, bottom: 30, left: 40},
    w = 500 - margin.left - margin.right,
    h = 400 - margin.top - margin.bottom;

var color = d3.scale.ordinal()
    .range(["#ffc87c", "#ffeba8", "#f3b080", "#916800", "#dda66b"]);

var radius = Math.min(w, h) / 2;

var pie = d3.layout.pie()
    .sort(null)
    .value(function(d) { return d.income; });

var svg = d3.select("body").append("svg")
    .attr("width", w + margin.left + margin.right)
    .attr("height", h + margin.top + margin.bottom)
    .append("g")
    .attr("transform", "translate(" +(w/2-margin.left)+
      "," +(h/2+margin.top)+ ")");
```

```
var title = d3.select("svg").append("g")
    .attr("transform", "translate(" +margin.left+ ", " +margin.top+ ")")
    .attr("class", "title");

title.append("text")
    .attr("x", (w / 2))
    .attr("y", -30 )
    .attr("text-anchor", "middle")
    .style("font-size", "22px")
    .text("A polar area diagram");
</script>
</body>
</html>
```

In Listing 5-27, you read the data in the data_07.csv file with the d3.csv() function and make sure that the values of income and growth are interpreted as numeric values.

Listing 5-27. Ch5_03.html

```
d3.csv("data_07.csv", function(error, data) {

    data.forEach(function(d) {
        d.income = +d.income;
        d.growth = +d.growth;
    });
});
```

Differently to the previous examples, here you define not only an arc, but an arc which will vary with the variation of data being read; we will call it arcs, since the outerRadius is no longer constant but is proportional to the growth values in the file. In order to do this, you need to apply a general iterative function, and then the arcs must be declared within the d3.csv() function (see Listing 5-28).

Listing 5-28. Ch5_03.html

```
d3.csv("data_07.csv", function(error, data) {

    data.forEach(function(d) {
        d.income = +d.income;
        d.growth = +d.growth;
    });

    arcs = d3.svg.arc()
        .innerRadius( 0 )
        .outerRadius( function(d,i) { return 8*d.data.growth; });
});
```

Now, you just have to add the SVG elements which draw the slices with labels containing the values of growth and income (see Listing 5-29). The labels reporting income values will be drawn inside the slices, right at the value returned by the centroid() function. Instead, as regards the labels reporting the growth values, these will be drawn just outside the slices. To obtain this effect, you can use the x and y values returned by centroid() and multiply them by a value greater than 2. You must recall that the centroid is at the very center of the angle and in the middle between innerRadius and outerRadius. Therefore, multiplying them by 2, you get the point at the center of the outer edge of the slice. If you multiply them by a value greater than 2, then you will find x and y positions outside the slice, right where you want to draw the label with the value of growth.

Listing 5-29. Ch5_03.html

```
var g = svg.selectAll(".arc")
    .data(pie(data))
    .enter().append("g")
    .attr("class", "arc");

g.append("path")
    .attr("d", arcs)
    .style("fill", function(d) { return color(d.data.country); });

g.append("text")
    .attr("class", "growth")
    .attr("transform", function(d) {
       a = arcs.centroid(d)[0]*2.2;
       b = arcs.centroid(d)[1]*2.2;
       return "translate(" +a+", "+b+ ")"; })
    .attr("dy", ".35em")
    .style("text-anchor", "middle")
    .text(function(d) { return d.data.growth; });

g.append("text")
    .attr("class", "income")
    .attr("transform", function(d) {
       return "translate(" +arcs.centroid(d)+ ")"; })
    .attr("dy", ".35em")
    .style("text-anchor", "middle")
    .text(function(d) { return d.data.income; });
```

One thing you have not yet done to the pie chart is adding a legend. In Listing 5-30, we define, outside the d3.csv() function, an element <g> in which to insert the table of the legend, and inside the function we define all the elements related to the countries, since defining them requires access to the values written in the file.

Listing 5-30. Ch5_03.html

```
var legendTable = d3.select("svg").append("g")
    .attr("transform", "translate(" +margin.left+ ", "+margin.top+")")
    .attr("class", "legendTable");

d3.csv("data_07.csv", function(error, data) {
...
var legend = legendTable.selectAll(".legend")
    .data(pie(data))
    .enter().append("g")
    .attr("class", "legend")
    .attr("transform", function(d, i) {
       return "translate(0, " + i * 20 + ")"; });
```

```
legend.append("rect")
      .attr("x", w - 18)
      .attr("y", 4)
      .attr("width", 10)
      .attr("height", 10)
      .style("fill", function(d) { return color(d.data.country); });

legend.append("text")
      .attr("x", w - 24)
      .attr("y", 9)
      .attr("dy", ".35em")
      .style("text-anchor", "end")
      .text(function(d) { return d.data.country; });
});
```

Finally, you can make some adjustments to the CSS style classes as shown in Listing 5-31.

Listing 5-31. Ch5_03.html

```
<style>
body {
    font: 16px sans-serif;
}
.arc path {
    stroke: #fff;
    stroke-width: 4;
}
.arc .income {
    font: 12px Arial;
    color: #fff;
}
</style>
```

And here is the polar area diagram (see Figure 5-12).

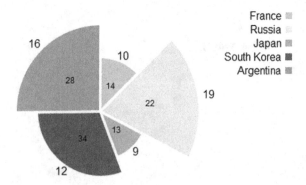

Figure 5-12. *A polar area diagram*

Summary

In this chapter, you learned how to implement pie charts and donut charts using the D3 library, following almost the same guidelines as those provided in the previous chapters. Furthermore, at the end of the chapter you learned how to make a polar area diagram, a type of chart which you had not met before and which the D3 library allows you to implement easily.

In the next chapter, you will implement the two types of Candlestick chart which you had already discussed in the first part of the book covering the jqPlot library, only this time you will be using the D3 library.

CHAPTER 6

■ ■ ■

Candlestick Charts with D3

In this short but nonetheless important chapter, you will look at candlestick charts. This type of chart is based on a particular data format (OHLC, or open-high-low-close). Thus, you will need to implement a parser to read OHLC data from an external file. Moreover, another nontrivial aspect that you need to solve is how to deal with date and time data.

Although this sounds complex, in this chapter you will discover how the D3 library provides you with tools which make things easy and immediate for you.

You will first begin with building a simple OHLC chart, in order to focus particularly on the reading of the OHLC data. Then you will look in detail at how D3 handles date and time data, and finally you will represent the OHLC chart using only scalar vector graphics (SVG) elements such as lines.

In the last part, you will convert your OHLC chart in a more complete candlestick chart by means of only a few modifications.

Creating an OHLC Chart

Because of the capability of D3 to build new graphical structures from small graphical components, you can also create candlestick charts such as those generated with jqPlot. You have already seen that a candlestick chart requires a well-defined data structure: a timeline of data which consists of a date and the four OHLC values. You copy the data from Listing 6-1 into a file and save it as data_08.csv.

Listing 6-1. data_08.csv

```
date,open,min,max,close,
08/08/2012,1.238485,1.2327,1.240245,1.2372,
08/09/2012,1.23721,1.22671,1.23873,1.229295,
08/10/2012,1.2293,1.22417,1.23168,1.228975,
08/12/2012,1.229075,1.22747,1.22921,1.22747,
08/13/2012,1.227505,1.22608,1.23737,1.23262,
08/14/2012,1.23262,1.23167,1.238555,1.232385,
08/15/2012,1.232385,1.22641,1.234355,1.228865,
08/16/2012,1.22887,1.225625,1.237305,1.23573,
08/17/2012,1.23574,1.22891,1.23824,1.2333,
08/19/2012,1.23522,1.23291,1.235275,1.23323,
08/20/2012,1.233215,1.22954,1.236885,1.2351,
08/21/2012,1.23513,1.23465,1.248785,1.247655,
08/22/2012,1.247655,1.24315,1.254415,1.25338,
08/23/2012,1.25339,1.252465,1.258965,1.255995,
08/24/2012,1.255995,1.248175,1.256665,1.2512,
08/26/2012,1.25133,1.25042,1.252415,1.25054,
```

```
08/27/2012,1.25058,1.249025,1.25356,1.25012,
08/28/2012,1.250115,1.24656,1.257695,1.2571,
08/29/2012,1.25709,1.251895,1.25736,1.253065,
08/30/2012,1.253075,1.248785,1.25639,1.25097,
08/31/2012,1.25096,1.249375,1.263785,1.25795,
09/02/2012,1.257195,1.256845,1.258705,1.257355,
09/03/2012,1.25734,1.25604,1.261095,1.258635,
09/04/2012,1.25865,1.25264,1.262795,1.25339,
09/05/2012,1.2534,1.250195,1.26245,1.26005,
09/06/2012,1.26006,1.256165,1.26513,1.26309,
09/07/2012,1.26309,1.262655,1.281765,1.281625,
09/09/2012,1.28096,1.27915,1.281295,1.279565,
09/10/2012,1.27957,1.27552,1.28036,1.27617,
09/11/2012,1.27617,1.2759,1.28712,1.28515,
09/12/2012,1.28516,1.281625,1.29368,1.290235,
```

In what by now has become almost a habit, you begin by writing the code which is common to almost all charts and does not require further explanations (see Listing 6-2).

Listing 6-2. Ch6_01.html

```
<!DOCTYPE html>
<html>
<head>
<meta charset="utf-8">
<script src="http://d3js.org/d3.v3.js"></script>
<style>
body {
    font: 16px sans-serif;
}
</style>
</head>
<body>
<script type="text/javascript">
var margin = {top: 70, right: 20, bottom: 30, left: 40},
    w = 500 - margin.left - margin.right,
    h = 400 - margin.top - margin.bottom;

var svg = d3.select("body").append("svg")
    .attr("width", w + margin.left + margin.right)
    .attr("height", h + margin.top + margin.bottom)
    .append("g")
    .attr("transform", "translate(" +margin.left+ ", " +margin.top+ ")");

var title = d3.select("svg").append("g")
    .attr("transform", "translate(" +margin.left+ ", " +margin.top+ ")")
    .attr("class", "title");
```

```
title.append("text")
    .attr("x", (w / 2))
    .attr("y", -30 )
    .attr("text-anchor", "middle")
    .style("font-size", "22px")
    .text("My candlestick chart");
</script>
</body>
</html>
```

Since in the first column of the file there are values of date type, you need to define a parser to set their format (see Listing 6-3).

Listing 6-3. Ch6_01.html

```
...
    w = 500 - margin.left - margin.right,
    h = 400 - margin.top - margin.bottom;

var parseDate = d3.time.format("%m/%d/%Y").parse;
...
```

A candlestick chart is a type of data representation which is generally temporal, i.e., the four OHLC data are related to a single time unit and their variations over time are visible along the x axis. You will therefore have an x axis on which you will have to handle time values, whereas on the y axis you will assign a linear scale. In defining the x axis, you make sure that the dates are reported showing only day and month, which will be indicated by the first three initial characters (see Listing 6-4).

Listing 6-4. Ch6_01.html

```
var parseDate = d3.time.format("%m/%d/%Y").parse;

var x = d3.time.scale()
    .range([0, w]);

var y = d3.scale.linear()
    .range([h, 0]);

var xAxis = d3.svg.axis()
    .scale(x)
    .orient("bottom")
    .tickFormat(d3.time.format("%d-%b"))
    .ticks(5);

var yAxis = d3.svg.axis()
    .scale(y)
    .orient("left");

...
```

Now observing what is inside the data file (Listing 6-1), you can see five columns of data, of which the last four are numbers. The first column contains dates which must be submitted to the parser, while the other four are to be interpreted as numeric values. Moreover, you need to figure out which are the maximum and minimum values among all of the OHLC data. Manage all these aspects within the iterative function forEach() as shown in Listing 6-5.

Listing 6-5. Ch6_01.html

```
...
var svg = d3.select("body").append("svg")
    .attr("width", w + margin.left + margin.right)
    .attr("height", h + margin.top + margin.bottom)
    .append("g")
    .attr("transform", "translate(" +margin.left+ ", " +margin.top+ ")");

d3.csv("data_08.csv", function(error, data) {
    var maxVal = -1000;
    var minVal = 1000;
    data.forEach(function(d) {
        d.date = parseDate(d.date);
        d.open = +d.open;
        d.close = +d.close;
        d.max = +d.max;
        d.min = +d.min;
        if (d.max > maxVal)
            maxVal = d.max;
        if (d.min < minVal)
            minVal = d.min;
    });
});
...
```

Next, in Listing 6-6, you create the domains of x and y. While on the x axis, the domain will handle dates, the y domain will have an extension which will cover all the values between the minimum and maximum values that have just been found (minVal and maxVal).

Listing 6-6. Ch6_01.html

```
d3.csv("data_08.csv", function(error, data) {

    data.forEach(function(d) {
        ...
    });

    x.domain(d3.extent(data, function(d) { return d.date; }));
    y.domain([minVal,maxVal]);
});
```

Once the domains are well defined you can draw the two axes x and y with the SVG elements along with their labels as shown in Listing 6-7.

Listing 6-7. Ch6_01.html

```
d3.csv("data_08.csv", function(error, data) {
    ...
    y.domain([minVal,maxVal]);

    svg.append("g")
        .attr("class", "x axis")
        .attr("transform", "translate(0, " + h + ")")
        .call(xAxis)

    svg.append("text")
        .attr("class", "label")
        .attr("x", w)
        .attr("y", -6)
        .style("text-anchor", "end");

  svg.append("g")
    .attr("class", "y axis")
    .call(yAxis);

    svg.append("text")
        .attr("class", "label")
        .attr("transform", "rotate(-90)")
        .attr("y", 6)
        .attr("dy", ".71em")
        .style("text-anchor", "end")
        .text("Dollar [$]");
});
```

And you use the SVG element <line> to plot the data on the OHLC chart (see Listing 6-8). The ext line is the vertical line which defines the range between the *high* and *low* values. The close and open lines are two horizontal lines corresponding to *open* and *close* values.

Listing 6-8. Ch6_01.html

```
d3.csv("data_08.csv", function(error, data) {
    ...
    svg.append("text")
        .attr("class", "label")
        .attr("transform", "rotate(-90)")
        .attr("y", 6)
        .attr("dy", ".71em")
        .style("text-anchor", "end")
        .text("Dollar [$]")
```

```
svg.selectAll("line.ext")
    .data(data)
    .enter().append("svg:line")
    .attr("class", "ext")
    .attr("x1", function(d) { return x(d.date)})
    .attr("x2", function(d) { return x(d.date)})
    .attr("y1", function(d) { return y(d.min);})
    .attr("y2", function(d) { return y(d.max); });

svg.selectAll("line.close")
    .data(data)
    .enter().append("svg:line")
    .attr("class", "close")
    .attr("x1", function(d) { return x(d.date)+5})
    .attr("x2", function(d) { return x(d.date)-1})
    .attr("y1", function(d) { return y(d.close);})
    .attr("y2", function(d) { return y(d.close); });

svg.selectAll("line.open")
    .data(data)
    .enter().append("svg:line")
    .attr("class", "open")
    .attr("x1", function(d) { return x(d.date)+1})
    .attr("x2", function(d) { return x(d.date)-5})
    .attr("y1", function(d) { return y(d.open);})
    .attr("y2", function(d) { return y(d.open); });
});
```

Thanks to the way in which you have defined the classes of the newly generated elements, you can define attributes to the CSS styles for all of the three lines together, by using the line class, or defining them individually using the line.open, line.close, and line.ext classes (see Listing 6-9).

Listing 6-9. Ch6_01.html

```
<style>
body {
    font: 16px sans-serif;
}
.axis path,
.axis line {
    fill: none;
    stroke: #000;
    shape-rendering: crispEdges;
}
line.open, line.close, line.ext {
    stroke: blue;
    stroke-width: 2;
    shape-rendering: crispEdges;
}
</style>
```

At the end, you get the candlestick chart shown in Figure 6-1.

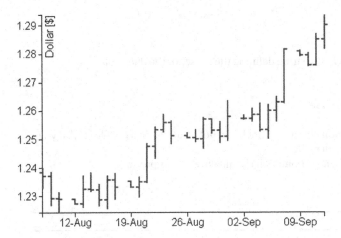

Figure 6-1. *An OHLC chart*

Date Format

Having to deal with this class of charts which makes use of OHLC data, you will always deal with time and date values along the x axis. Therefore taking a cue from this observation, analyze how the D3 library handles this type of data.

What would have happened if in the previous example you did not have the dates of the days and months zero-padded, or the year was reported with only two digits (e.g., "8/9/12")? Inside the d3.csv() function, D3 would not have been able to read dates with this format, and consequently, the candlestick chart would not have appeared. Actually, what you need to do is very simple, i.e., guess the correct sequence of formatters to insert in the parser. By formatter, we mean a set of characters with the "%" sign before, which according to the specific (case-sensitive) character expresses a unit of time written in a certain way.

```
var parseDate = d3.time.format("%m/%e/%y").parse;
```

Even dates expressed literally can be handled in the same way. You have already seen this format of dates:

```
08-Aug-12,1.238485,1.2327,1.240245,1.2372,
```

It can be handled with this parser:

```
var parseDate = d3.time.format("%d-%b-%y").parse;
```

But there are much more complex cases, such as the following:

```
Monday 16 April 2012,1.238485,1.2327,1.240245,1.2372,
```

And it can be handled with this parser:

```
var parseDate = d3.time.format("%A %e %B %Y").parse;
```

All separation characters (including spaces) between the different values should be reported in the same position in the parser. Thus, if the dates are defined in this way…

```
'8 Aug-12',1.238485,1.2327,1.240245,1.2372,
```

You have to insert both the space and the quotes in the string defining the parser or the date would not be recognized.

```
var parseDate = d3.time.format("'%d %b-%y'").parse;
```

You must also keep in mind that the only separation character which can not be added in a csv file is " , ". If you must insert it, you have to use a TSV (tab-separated values) file.

Table 6-1 includes all the available formatters. Their combination should cover any input size.

Table 6-1. *D3 Date and Time Formatters*

Formatter	Description
%a	Abbreviated weekday name
%A	Full weekday name
%b	Abbreviated month name
%B	Full month name
%c	Date and time, as "%a %b %e %H:%M:%S %Y"
%d	Zero-padded day of the month as a decimal number [01,31]
%e	Space-padded day of the month as a decimal number [1,31]
%H	Hour (24-hour clock) as a decimal number [00,23]
%I	Hour (12-hour clock) as a decimal number [01,12]
%j	Day of the year as a decimal number [001,366]
%m	Month as a decimal number [01,12]
%M	Minute as a decimal number [00,59]
%p	Either AM or PM
%S	Second as a decimal number [00,61]
%U	Week number of the year (Sunday as the first day of the week) as a decimal number [00,53]
%w	Weekday as a decimal number [0(Sunday),6]
%W	Week number of the year (Monday as the first day of the week) as a decimal number [00,53]
%x	Date, as "%m/%d/%y"
%X	Time, as "%H:%M:%S"
%y	Year without century as a decimal number [00,99]
%Y	Year with century as a decimal number
%Z	Time zone offset, such as "-0700"
%%	A literal "%" character

Box Representation in Candlestick Charts

With jqPlot, you also saw other ways to display OHLC data. For example, often such data are represented by a vertical line and a vertical box covering it for a certain length. The vertical line is the same representation as the previous candlestick, it lies between the *high* and *low* value of the OHLC. Instead, the box represents the range between the *open* and *close* values. Moreover, if the *open* value is greater than the *close* value, the box will be of a given color, but if the opposite happens, of another color.

You use the same data contained in the data_08.csv file, and starting from the code in the previous example, you will look at the changes to be made.

Replace the ext, open, and close lines with these three new lines: ext, ext1, and ext2 (see Listing 6-10). Then you have to add the rectangle representing the box. The lines should be black, whereas the boxes should be red when the *open* values are greater than *close* values, or else, in the opposite case, the boxes will be green.

Listing 6-10. Ch6_02.html

```
svg.selectAll("line.ext")
   .data(data)
   .enter().append("svg:line")
   .attr("class", "ext")
   .attr("x1", function(d) { return x(d.date)})
   .attr("x2", function(d) { return x(d.date)})
   .attr("y1", function(d) { return y(d.min);})
   .attr("y2", function(d) { return y(d.max);});

svg.selectAll("line.ext1")
   .data(data)
   .enter().append("svg:line")
   .attr("class", "ext")
   .attr("x1", function(d) { return x(d.date)+3})
   .attr("x2", function(d) { return x(d.date)-3})
   .attr("y1", function(d) { return y(d.min);})
   .attr("y2", function(d) { return y(d.min); });

svg.selectAll("line.ext2")
   .data(data)
   .enter().append("svg:line")
   .attr("class", "ext")
   .attr("x1", function(d) { return x(d.date)+3})
   .attr("x2", function(d) { return x(d.date)-3})
   .attr("y1", function(d) { return y(d.max);})
   .attr("y2", function(d) { return y(d.max); });

svg.selectAll("rect")
   .data(data)
   .enter().append("svg:rect")
   .attr("x", function(d) { return x(d.date)-3; })
   .attr("y", function(d) { return y(Math.max(d.open, d.close));})
   .attr("height", function(d) {
   return y(Math.min(d.open, d.close))-y(Math.max(d.open, d.close));})
   .attr("width", 6)
   .attr("fill", function(d) {
   return d.open > d.close ? "darkred" : "darkgreen" ;});
});
```

The last thing is to set the CSS style classes in Listing 6-11.

Listing 6-11. Ch6_02.html

```
<style>
body {
    font: 16px sans-serif;
}
.axis path,
.axis line {
    fill: none;
    stroke: #000;
    shape-rendering: crispEdges;
}
line.ext, line.ext1, line.ext2 {
    stroke: #000;
    stroke-width: 1;
    shape-rendering: crispEdges;
}
</style>
```

And the chart in Figure 6-2 is the result.

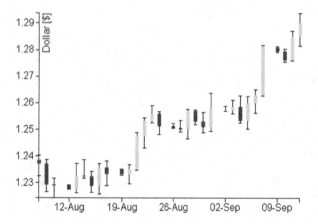

Figure 6-2. *A candlestick chart*

Summary

In this chapter, you have seen the types of **candlestick chart** already discussed in the first part of the book dedicated to the jqPlot library, but this time you used D3. You have seen how you can easily get similar results while keeping full control over every single graphic element. In addition, since this kind of chart uses time data, here you have delved deeper into how the D3 library manages this type of data and the various ways to manage format.

Continuing to follow the parallelism between the jqPlot library and the D3 library regarding the implementation of the various types of chart, in the next chapter you will learn about **scatter plots** and **bubble charts** and how to implement them with the D3 library.

CHAPTER 7

Scatterplot and Bubble Charts with D3

In this chapter, you will learn about scatterplot charts. Whenever you have a set of data pairs [x, y] and you want to analyze their distribution in the xy plane, you will refer to this type of chart. Thus, you will see first how to make this type of chart using the D3 library. In the first example, you will begin reading a TSV (tab-separated values) file containing more than one series of data, and through them, you will see how to achieve a scatterplot.

Once the scatterplot is completed, you will see how to represent the data points using markers with particular shapes, either choosing them from a predefined set or by creating original.

This class of charts is very important. It is a fundamental tool for analyzing data distributions; in fact, from these diagrams you can find particular trends (trendlines) and groupings (clusters). In this chapter, two simple examples will show you how you can represent trendlines and clusters.

Moreover, you will see how to add the highlighting functionality to your charts by the event handling and how the D3 library manages it.

Finally, the chapter will close with a final example in which you will need to represent data with three parameters [x, y, z]. Therefore, properly modifying the scatterplot, you will discover how you can get a bubble chart, which is a scatterplot modified to be able to represent an additional parameter.

Scatterplot

Thanks to the D3 library, there is no limit to the graphic representations which you can generate, combining graphical elements as if they were bricks. The creation of scatterplots is no exception.

You begin with a collection of data (see Listing 7-1), this time in a tabulated form (therefore a TSV file) which you will copy and save as a file named data_09.tsv. (See the following Note.)

■ **Note**   Notice that the values in a TSV file are TAB separated, so when you write or copy Listing 7-1, remember to check that there is only a TAB character between each value.

Listing 7-1. data_09.tsv

time	intensity	group
10	171.11	Exp1
14	180.31	Exp1
17	178.32	Exp1
42	173.22	Exp3
30	145.22	Exp2
30	155.68	Exp3

```
23      200.56      Exp2
15      192.33      Exp1
24      173.22      Exp2
20      203.78      Exp2
18      187.88      Exp1
45      180.00      Exp3
27      181.33      Exp2
16      198.03      Exp1
47      179.11      Exp3
27      175.33      Exp2
28      162.55      Exp2
24      208.97      Exp1
23      200.47      Exp1
43      165.08      Exp3
27      168.77      Exp2
23      193.55      Exp2
19      188.04      Exp1
40      170.36      Exp3
21      184.98      Exp2
15      197.33      Exp1
50      188.45      Exp3
23      207.33      Exp1
28      158.60      Exp2
29      151.31      Exp2
26      172.01      Exp2
23      191.33      Exp1
25      226.11      Exp1
60      198.33      Exp3
```

Suppose that the data contained in the file belong to three different experiments (labeled as Exp1, Exp2, and Exp3), each applied to a different object (for example, three luminescent substances), in which you want to measure how their emission intensity varies over time. The readings are done repeatedly and at different times. Your aim will be to represent these values in the xy plane in order to analyze their distribution and eventual properties.

Observing the data, you can see that they are composed of three columns: time, intensity, and group membership. This is a typical data structure which can be displayed in the form of a scatterplot. You will put the time scale on the x axis, put the intensity values on the y axis, and finally identify groups by the shape or by the color of the markers which will mark the position of the point in the scatterplot.

As it has become customary, you begin by writing the code in Listing 7-2. This code represents your starting code, and since it is common to almost all charts you have seen in the previous example, it does not require further explanation.

Listing 7-2. Ch7_01.html

```html
<!DOCTYPE html>
<html>
<head>
<meta charset="utf-8">
<script src="http://d3js.org/d3.v3.js"></script>
<style>
body {
    font: 16px sans-serif;
}
```

```
.axis path,
.axis line {
    fill: none;
    stroke: #000;
    shape-rendering: crispEdges;
}
</style>
</head>
<body>
<script type="text/javascript">
var margin = {top: 70, right: 20, bottom: 40, left: 40},
    w = 500 - margin.left - margin.right,
    h = 400 - margin.top - margin.bottom;

var color = d3.scale.category10();

var x = d3.scale.linear()
    .range([0, w]);

var y = d3.scale.linear()
    .range([h, 0]);

var xAxis = d3.svg.axis()
    .scale(x)
    .orient("bottom");

var yAxis = d3.svg.axis()
    .scale(y)
    .orient("left");

var svg = d3.select("body").append("svg")
    .attr("width", w + margin.left + margin.right)
    .attr("height", h + margin.top + margin.bottom)
    .append("g")
    .attr("transform", "translate(" + margin.left+ "," +margin.top+ ")");

var title = d3.select("svg").append("g")
    .attr("transform", "translate(" + margin.left+ "," +margin.top+ ")")
    .attr("class","title");

title.append("text")
    .attr("x", (w / 2))
    .attr("y", -30 )
    .attr("text-anchor", "middle")
    .style("font-size", "22px")
    .text("My Scatterplot");
</script>
</body>
</html>
```

In Listing 7-3, you read the tabulated data from the TSV file with the d3.tsv() function, making sure that the numerical values will be read as such. Here, even if you have times on the first column, these do not require parsing since they are seconds and can thus be considered on a linear scale.

Listing 7-3. Ch7_01.html

```
...
var svg = d3.select("body").append("svg")
    .attr("width", w + margin.left + margin.right)
    .attr("height", h + margin.top + margin.bottom)
    .append("g")
    .attr("transform", "translate(" + margin.left+ "," +margin.top+ ")");

d3.tsv("data_09.tsv", function(error, data) {
    data.forEach(function(d) {
        d.time = +d.time;
        d.intensity = +d.intensity;
    });
});

var title = d3.select("svg").append("g")
    .attr("transform", "translate(" + margin.left+ "," +margin.top+ ")")
    .attr("class","title");
...
```

Also with regard to the domains, the assignment is very simple, as shown in Listing 7-4. Furthermore, you will use the nice() function, which rounds off the values of the domain.

Listing 7-4. Ch7_01.html

```
d3.tsv("data_09.tsv", function(error, data) {
    data.forEach(function(d) {
        d.time = +d.time;
        d.intensity = +d.intensity;
    });

    x.domain(d3.extent(data, function(d) { return d.time; })).nice();
    y.domain(d3.extent(data, function(d) { return d.intensity; })).nice();
});
```

You add also the axis label, bringing "Time [s]" on the x axis and "Intensity" on the y axis, as shown in Listing 7-5.

Listing 7-5. Ch7_01.html

```
d3.tsv("data_09.tsv", function(error, data) {
    ...
    x.domain(d3.extent(data, function(d) { return d.time; })).nice();
    y.domain(d3.extent(data, function(d) { return d.intensity; })).nice();

    svg.append("g")
        .attr("class", "x axis")
        .attr("transform", "translate(0," + h + ")")
        .call(xAxis);
```

```
svg.append("text")
    .attr("class", "label")
    .attr("x", w)
    .attr("y", h + margin.bottom - 5)
    .style("text-anchor", "end")
    .text("Time [s]");

svg.append("g")
    .attr("class", "y axis")
    .call(yAxis);

svg.append("text")
    .attr("class", "label")
    .attr("transform", "rotate(-90)")
    .attr("y", 6)
    .attr("dy", ".71em")
    .style("text-anchor", "end")
    .text("Intensity");
});
```

Finally, you have to draw the markers directly on the graph. These can be represented by the SVG element
<circle>. The data points to be represented on the ` will therefore be of small dots of radius 3.5 pixels
(see Listing 7-6). To define their representation of different groups, the markers are drawn in different colors.

Listing 7-6. Ch7_01.html

```
d3.tsv("data_09.tsv", function(error, data) {
    ...
    svg.append("text")
      .attr("class", "label")
      .attr("transform", "rotate(-90)")
      .attr("y", 6)
      .attr("dy", ".71em")
      .style("text-anchor", "end")
      .text("Intensity");

    svg.selectAll(".dot")
      .data(data)
      .enter().append("circle")
      .attr("class", "dot")
      .attr("r", 3.5)
      .attr("cx", function(d) { return x(d.time); })
      .attr("cy", function(d) { return y(d.intensity); })
      .style("fill", function(d) { return color(d.group); });
});
```

Now you have so many colored markers on the scatterplot, but no reference to their color and the group to which
they belong. Therefore, it is necessary to add a legend showing the names of the various groups associated with the
different colors (see Listing 7-7).

Listing 7-7. Ch7_01.html

```
d3.tsv("data_09.tsv", function(error, data) {
    ...
    svg.selectAll(".dot")
       .data(data)
       .enter().append("circle")
       .attr("class", "dot")
       .attr("r", 3.5)
       .attr("cx", function(d) { return x(d.time); })
       .attr("cy", function(d) { return y(d.intensity); })
       .style("fill", function(d) { return color(d.group); });

    var legend = svg.selectAll(".legend")
       .data(color.domain())
       .enter().append("g")
       .attr("class", "legend")
       .attr("transform", function(d, i) {
          return "translate(0," + (i * 20) + ")"; });

    legend.append("rect")
       .attr("x", w - 18)
       .attr("width", 18)
       .attr("height", 18)
       .style("fill", color);

    legend.append("text")
       .attr("x", w - 24)
       .attr("y", 9)
       .attr("dy", ".35em")
       .style("text-anchor", "end")
       .text(function(d) { return d; });
});
```

After all the work is complete, you get the scatterplot shown in Figure 7-1.

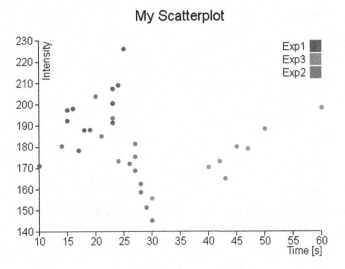

Figure 7-1. *A scatterplot showing the data distribution*

Markers and Symbols

When you want to represent a scatterplot, an aspect not to be underestimated is the shape of the marker with which you want to represent the data points. Not surprisingly, the D3 library provides you with a number of methods that manage the marker representation by symbols. In this chapter, you will learn about this topic since it is well suited to this kind of chart (scatterplots), but does not alter its application to other types of chart (e.g., line charts).

Using Symbols as Markers

D3 library provides a set of symbols that can be used directly as a marker. In Table 7-1, you can see a list reporting various predefined symbols.

Table 7-1. *Predefined Symbols in D3 Library*

Symbol	Description
Circle	A circle
Cross	A Greek cross (or plus sign)
Diamond	A rhombus
Square	An axis-aligned square
Triangle-down	A downward-pointing equilateral triangle
Triangle-up	An upward-pointing equilateral triangle

Continuing with the previous example, you replace the dots in the scatterplot chart with different symbols used as markers. These symbols will vary depending on the series of membership of the data (Exp1, Exp2, or Exp3). So this time, to characterize the series to which data belong, it will be both the color and the shape of the marker.

First, you need to assign each series to a symbol within the groupMarker object, as shown in Listing 7-8.

167

Listing 7-8. Ch7_01b.html

```
var margin = {top: 70, right: 20, bottom: 40, left: 40},
    w = 500 - margin.left - margin.right,
    h = 400 - margin.top - margin.bottom;

var groupMarker = {
    Exp1: "cross",
    Exp2: "diamond",
    Exp3: "triangle-down"
};

var color = d3.scale.category10();
```

Then, you delete from the code the lines concerning the representation of the dots (see Listing 7-9). These lines will be replaced with others generating the markers (see Listing 7-10).

Listing 7-9. Ch7_01b.html

```
svg.selectAll(".dot")
    .data(data)
    .enter().append("circle")
    .attr("class", "dot")
    .attr("r", 3.5)
    .attr("cx", function(d) { return x(d.time); })
    .attr("cy", function(d) { return y(d.intensity); })
    .style("fill", function(d) { return color(d.group); });
```

Actually, you are going to generate symbols that are nothing more than the predefined SVG paths. You may guess this from the fact that in Listing 7-10 the addition of the symbols is performed through the use of the append("path") function. Concerning instead the generation of the symbol as such, the D3 library provides a specific function: d3. svg.symbol(). The symbol to be displayed is passed as argument through the type() function, for example if you want to use the symbols to cross utilize type("cross").

In this case, however, the symbols to be represented are three and they depend on the series of each point. So, you have to implement an iteration on all data by function (d) applied to groupMarker, which will return the string corresponding to the "cross", "diamond", and "triangle-down" symbols.

Finally, being constituted by a SVG path, the symbol can also be changed by adjusting the Cascading Style Sheets (CSS) styles. In this example, you can choose to represent only the outlines of the symbols by setting the fill attribute to white.

Listing 7-10. Ch7_01b.html

```
d3.tsv("data_09.tsv", function(error, data) {
    ...
    svg.append("text")
        .attr("class", "label")
        .attr("transform", "rotate(-90)")
        .attr("y", 6)
        .attr("dy", ".71em")
        .style("text-anchor", "end")
        .text("Intensity");
```

```
svg.selectAll("path")
    .data(data)
    .enter().append("path")
    .attr("transform", function(d) {
        return "translate(" + x(d.time) + "," + y(d.intensity) + ")";
    })
    .attr("d", d3.svg.symbol().type( function(d) {
        return groupMarker[d.group];
    }))
    .style("fill", "white")
    .style("stroke", function(d) { return color(d.group); })
    .style("stroke-width", "1.5px");

var legend = svg.selectAll(".legend")
...
});
```

Figure 7-2 shows the scatterplot using various symbols in place of dots.

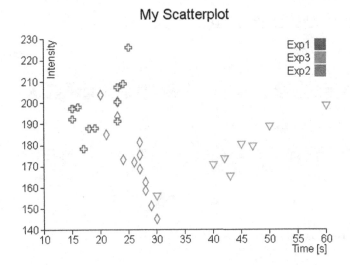

Figure 7-2. *In a scatterplot, the series could be represented by different symbols*

Using Customized Markers

You have just seen that the markers with the D3 library are nothing more than SVG paths. You could use this to your advantage by customizing your chart with the creation of other symbols that will be added to those already defined.

On the Internet, you can find a huge number of SVG symbols; once you have decided what symbol to use, you get its path in order to add it in your web page. More enterprising readers can also decide to edit SVG symbols with a SVG editor. I suggest you to use the Inkscape editor (see Figure 7-3); you can download it from its official site: http://inkscape.org. Or, more simply, you can start from an already designed SVG symbol and then modify it according to your taste. To do this, I recommend using the SVG Tryit page at this link: www.w3schools.com/svg/tryit.asp?filename=trysvg_path (see Figure 7-4).

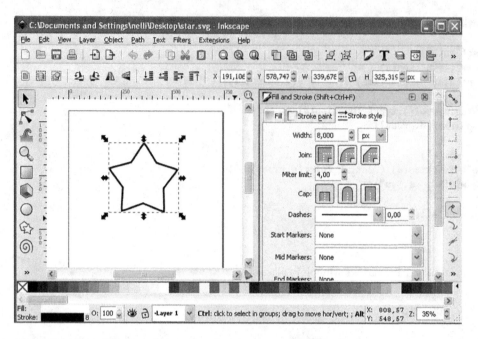

Figure 7-3. *Inkscape: a good SVG editor for generating symbols*

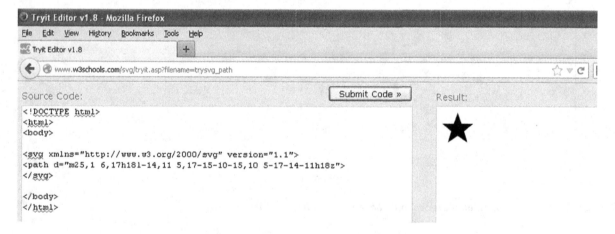

Figure 7-4. *Tryit is a useful tool to preview SVG symbols in real time inserting the path*

Therefore, choose three new symbols (e.g., a crescent moon, a star, and the Mars symbol) that go to replace the default ones. You extract their path and then insert into the definition of a new object, which you call `markers`, as shown in Listing 7-11.

Listing 7-11. Ch7_01c.html

```
var margin = {top: 70, right: 20, bottom: 40, left: 40},
    w = 500 - margin.left - margin.right,
    h = 400 - margin.top - margin.bottom;

var markers = {
    mars: "m15,7 a 7,7 0 1,0 2,2 z l 1,1 7-7m-7,0 h 7 v 7",
    moon: "m15,3 a 8.5,8.5 0 1,0 0,13 a 6.5,6.5 0 0,1 0,-13",
    star: "m11,1 3,9h9l-7,5.5 2.5,8.5-7.5-5-7.5,5 2.5-8.5-7-6.5h9z"
};

var groupMarker = {
    ...
```

Now you have to update the associations between symbols and groups that you defined within the groupMarker variable, as shown in Listing 7-12.

Listing 7-12. Ch7_01c.html

```
var groupMarker = {
    Exp1: markers.star,
    Exp2: markers.moon,
    Exp3: markers.mars
};
```

The last thing you can do is to change the definition of the path when you are creating the SVG elements (see Listing 7-13).

Listing 7-13. Ch7_01c.html

```
svg.selectAll("path")
    .data(data)
    .enter().append("path")
    .attr("transform", function(d) {
        return "translate(" + x(d.time) + "," + y(d.intensity) + ")";
    })
    .attr("d", function(d) { return groupMarker[d.group]; })
    .style("fill", "white")
    .style("stroke", function(d) { return color(d.group); })
    .style("stroke-width", "1.5px");
```

At the end, you obtain a scatterplot reporting the symbols that you have personally created or downloaded from the Internet (see Figure 7-5).

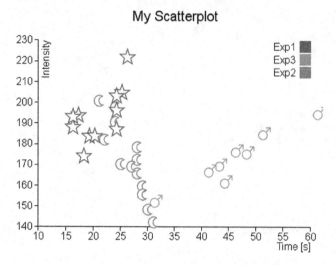

Figure 7-5. *A scatterplot with a customized set of markers*

Adding More Functionalities

Now that you have learned how to represent a distribution of data using scatterplots, it is time to introduce the trendline and clusters. Very often, analyzing in detail some sets of points in the data distribution, you can see that they follow a particular trend or tend to congregate in clusters. Therefore, it will be very useful to highlight this graphically. In this section, you will see a first example of how to calculate and represent linear trendlines. Then, you will see a second example which will illustrate a possibility of how to highlight some clusters present in the xy plane.

Trendlines

For reasons of simplicity, you will calculate the trendline of a set of points (a series) following a linear trend. To do this, you use the method of *least squares*. This method ensures that you find, given a set of data, the line that best fits the trend of the points, as much as possible by minimizing the error (the sum of the squares of the errors).

■ **Note** For further information, I suggest you visit the Wolfram MathWorld article at http://mathworld.wolfram.com/ LeastSquaresFitting.html.

For this example, you will continue working with the code of the scatterplot, but excluding all the changes made with the insertion of symbols. To avoid unnecessary mistakes and more repetition, Listing 7-14 shows the code you need to use as the starting point for this example.

Listing 7-14. Ch7_02.html

```html
<!DOCTYPE html>
<html>
<head>
<meta charset="utf-8">
<script src="http://d3js.org/d3.v3.js"></script>
<style>
body {
    font: 16px sans-serif;
}
.axis path, .axis line {
    fill: none;
    stroke: #000;
    shape-rendering: crispEdges;
}
</style>
</head>
<body>
<script type="text/javascript">
var margin = {top: 70, right: 20, bottom: 40, left: 40},
    w = 500 - margin.left - margin.right,
    h = 400 - margin.top - margin.bottom;
var color = d3.scale.category10();
var x = d3.scale.linear()
    .range([0, w]);
var y = d3.scale.linear()
    .range([h, 0]);
var xAxis = d3.svg.axis()
    .scale(x)
    .orient("bottom");
var yAxis = d3.svg.axis()
    .scale(y)
    .orient("left");
var svg = d3.select("body").append("svg")
    .attr("width", w + margin.left + margin.right)
    .attr("height", h + margin.top + margin.bottom)
    .append("g")
    .attr("transform", "translate(" +margin.left+ "," +margin.top+ ")");
d3.tsv("data_09.tsv", function(error, data) {
    data.forEach(function(d) {
        d.time = +d.time;
        d.intensity = +d.intensity;
    });
    x.domain(d3.extent(data, function(d) { return d.time; })).nice();
    y.domain(d3.extent(data, function(d) { return d.intensity; })).nice();
    svg.append("g")
        .attr("class", "x axis")
        .attr("transform", "translate(0," + h + ")")
        .call(xAxis);
    svg.append("text")
        .attr("class", "label")
```

```
        .attr("x", w)
        .attr("y", h + margin.bottom - 5)
        .style("text-anchor", "end")
        .text("Time [s]");
    svg.append("g")
        .attr("class", "y axis")
        .call(yAxis);
    svg.append("text")
        .attr("class", "label")
        .attr("transform", "rotate(-90)")
        .attr("y", 6)
        .attr("dy", ".71em")
        .style("text-anchor", "end")
        .text("Intensity");
    svg.selectAll(".dot")
        .data(data)
        .enter().append("circle")
        .attr("class", "dot")
        .attr("r", 3.5)
        .attr("cx", function(d) { return x(d.time); })
        .attr("cy", function(d) { return y(d.intensity); })
        .style("fill", function(d) { return color(d.group); });
    var legend = svg.selectAll(".legend")
        .data(color.domain())
        .enter().append("g")
        .attr("class", "legend")
        .attr("transform", function(d, i) {
            return "translate(0," + (i * 20) + ")";
        });
    legend.append("rect")
        .attr("x", w - 18)
        .attr("width", 18)
        .attr("height", 18)
        .style("fill", color);
    legend.append("text")
        .attr("x", w - 24)
        .attr("y", 9)
        .attr("dy", ".35em")
        .style("text-anchor", "end")
        .text(function(d) { return d; });
});
var title = d3.select("svg").append("g")
    .attr("transform", "translate(" + margin.left + "," + margin.top + ")")
    .attr("class","title");
title.append("text")
    .attr("x", (w / 2))
    .attr("y", -30)
    .attr("text-anchor", "middle")
    .style("font-size", "22px")
    .text("My Scatterplot");
</script>
</body></html>
```

First, you define all the variables that will serve for the method of least squares within the `tsv()` function, as shown in Listing 7-15. For each variable you define an array of size 3, since there are three series to be represented in your chart.

Listing 7-15. Ch7_02.html

```
d3.tsv("data_09.tsv", function(error, data) {

    sumx = [0,0,0];
    sumy = [0,0,0];
    sumxy = [0,0,0];
    sumx2 = [0,0,0];
    n = [0,0,0];
    a = [0,0,0];
    b = [0,0,0];
    y1 = [0,0,0];
    y2 = [0,0,0];
    x1 = [9999,9999,9999];
    x2 = [0,0,0];
    colors = ["","",""];

    data.forEach(function(d) {
    ...
});
```

Now you exploit the iteration of data performed during the parsing of data, to calculate simultaneously all the summations necessary for the method of least squares (see Listing 7-16). Moreover, it is convenient for the representation of a straight line to determine the maximum and minimum x values in each series.

Listing 7-16. Ch7_02.html

```
d3.tsv("data_09.tsv", function(error, data) {
    ...
    data.forEach(function(d) {
        d.time = +d.time;
        d.intensity = +d.intensity;
        for(var i = 0; i < 3; i=i+1)
        {
            if(d.group == "Exp"+(i+1)){
                colors[i] = color(d.group);
                sumx[i] = sumx[i] + d.time;
                sumy[i] = sumy[i] + d.intensity;
                sumxy[i] = sumxy[i] + (d.time * d.intensity);
                sumx2[i] = sumx2[i] + (d.time * d.time);
                n[i] = n[i] +1;
                if(d.time < x1[i])
                    x1[i] = d.time;
                if(d.time > x2[i])
                    x2[i] = d.time;
            }
        }
    });

    x.domain(d3.extent(data, function(d) { return d.time; })).nice();
    ...
});
```

Once you have calculated all the summations, it is time to make the calculation of the least squares in Listing 7-17. Since the series are three, you will repeat the calculation for three times within a for() loop. Furthermore, within each loop you directly insert the creation of the SVG element for drawing the line corresponding to the result of each calculation.

Listing 7-17. Ch7_02.html

```
d3.tsv("data_09.tsv", function(error, data) {
    ...
    x.domain(d3.extent(data, function(d) { return d.time; })).nice();
    y.domain(d3.extent(data, function(d) { return d.intensity; })).nice();

    for(var i = 0; i < 3; i = i + 1){
        b[i] = (sumxy[i] - sumx[i] * sumy[i] / n[i]) /
            (sumx2[i] - sumx[i] * sumx[i] / n[i]);
        a[i] = sumy[i] / n[i] - b[i] * sumx[i] / n[i];
        y1[i] = b[i] * x1[i] + a[i];
        y2[i] = b[i] * x2[i] + a[i];
        svg.append("svg:line")
            .attr("class","trendline")
            .attr("x1", x(x1[i]))
            .attr("y1", y(y1[i]))
            .attr("x2", x(x2[i]))
            .attr("y2", y(y2[i]))
            .style("stroke", colors[i])
            .style("stroke-width", 4);
    }
```

Now that you have completed the whole, you can see the representation of the three trendlines within the scatterplot, as shown in Figure 7-6.

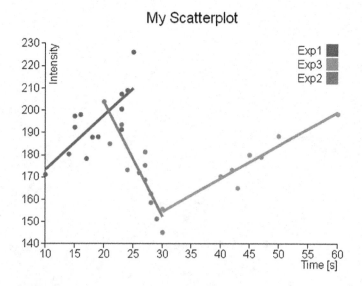

Figure 7-6. *Each group shows its trendline*

Clusters

When you work with the scatterplot, you may need to perform a clustering analysis. On the Internet, there are many analysis methods and algorithms that allow you to perform various operations of identification and research of clusters.

The cluster analysis is a classification technique that has the aim to identify data groups (clusters precisely) within a distribution of data (in this case, the scatterplot on the xy plane). The assignment of the various data points to these clusters is not defined a priori, but it is the task of cluster analysis to determine the criteria for selection and grouping. These clusters should be differentiated as much as possible, and in this case, as the grouping criterion, the cluster analysis will be based on the exaxt distances between the various data points and a point representative of the cluster called centroid (see Figure 7-7).

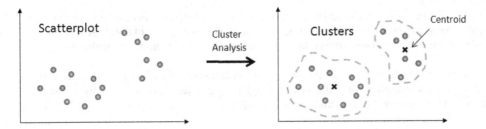

Figure 7-7. *The cluster analysis groups a set of data points around a centroid for each cluster*

Thus, the aim of this analysis is primarily to identify possible similarities within a data distribution, and in this regard there is nothing more appropriate of a scatterplot chart in which you can highlight these similarities through the different colors of the different points depending on the cluster membership.

In this section, you will see how to implement a cluster analysis algorithm and then how it is possible to integrate it into a scatterplot.

K-Mean Algorithm

Given the complexity of the cluster analysis, this chapter will not go into this topic in detail. You are interested only in highlighting the various points of the scatterplot in a different way from that of the series to which they belong (Exp1, Exp2, and Exp3). In this example, you want to color the data points depending on the cluster to which they belong. In order to do this, you will use a simple case of cluster analysis: the K-means algorithm. You define first the number of clusters into which you want to divide all the data, and then for each cluster, a representative point (centroid) is chosen. The distance between each data point and the three centroids is considered as a criterion for membership.

There are some examples available on the Internet in which the K-means method is applied, and it is totally implemented in JavaScript; among them I choose one developed by Heather Arthur (https://github.com/harthur/clusterfck), but you can replace it with any other.

For the example in question, I have taken the liberty to modify the code to make it as easy as possible. Starting from the data points contained within the TSV file, and representing them in a scatterplot, you are practically analyzing how these points are distributed in space xy. Now you are interested to recognize in this distribution, for example, three different clusters.

To do so you will apply the following algorithm:

1. Make a random choice of three data points as cluster centroids.

2. Iterate over all the data points in the file, assigning each of them to the cluster that has the closest centroid. At the end, you have all the data points divided into three clusters.

3. Within each cluster, a new centroid is calculated, which this time will not correspond to any given point but will be the "midpoint" interposed between all points in the cluster.

4. Recalculate steps 2 and 3 until the new centroids correspond to the previous ones (that is, the coordinates of the centroids in the xy plane remain unchanged).

Once the algorithm is completed, you will have the points in the scatterplot with three different colors corresponding to three different clusters.

Please note that in this algorithm there is no optimization, and thus the result will always be different every time you upload the page in your browser. In fact, what you get every time is a possible solution, not the "best solution."

Now to keep some of modularity, you will write the code of the analysis of clusters in an external file which you will call kmeans.js.

First, you will implement the randomCentroids() function, which will choose k points (in this example, k = 3) among those contained in the file (here passed within the points array) to assign them as centroids of the k clusters (see Listing 7-18). This function corresponds to the point 1 of the algorithm.

Listing 7-18. kmeans.js

```
function randomCentroids(points, k) {
    var centroids = points.slice(0);
    centroids.sort(function() {
        return (Math.round(Math.random()) - 0.5);
    });
    return centroids.slice(0, k);
}:
```

Now you have to assign all the points contained in the file to the three different clusters. To do this, you need to calculate the distance between each data point and the centroid in question, and thus you need to implement a specific function that calculates the distance between two points. In Listing 7-19, it is defined the distance() function, which returns the distance between v1 and v2 generic points.

Listing 7-19. kmeans.js

```
function distance(v1, v2) {
    var total = 0;
    for (var i = 0; i < v1.length; i++) {
        total += Math.pow((v2[i] - v1[i]), 2);
    }
    return Math.sqrt(total);
};
```

Now that you know how to calculate the distance between two points, you can implement a function that is able to decide which is the cluster assignment of each data point, calculating its distance with all centroids and choosing the smaller one. Thus, you can add the closestCentroid() function to the code, as shown in Listing 7-20.

Listing 7-20. kmeans.js

```
function closestCentroid(point, centroids) {
    var min = Infinity;
    var index = 0;
    for (var i = 0; i < centroids.length; i++) {
        var dist = distance(point, centroids[i]);
        if (dist < min) {
            min = dist;
            index = i;
        }
    }
    return index;
};
```

Now you can write the function that expresses the algorithm first exposed in its entirety. This function requires two arguments, the input data points (points) and the number of clusters into which they will be divided (k) (see Listing 7-21). Within it, you then choose the centroids using the newly implemented randomCentroids() function (point 1 of the algorithm).

Listing 7-21. kmeans.js

```
function kmeans(points, k) {
    var centroids = randomCentroids(points, k);
};
```

Once you have chosen the three centroids, you can assign all data points (contained in the points array) to the three clusters, defining the assignment array as shown in Listing 7-22 (point 2 of the algorithm). This array has the same length of the points array and is constructed in such a way that the order of its elements corresponds to the order of data points. Every element contains the number of the cluster to which they belong. If, for example, in the third element of the assignment array you have a value of 2, then it will mean that the third data point belongs to the third cluster (clusters are 0, 1, and 2).

Listing 7-22. kmeans.js

```
function kmeans(points, k) {
    var centroids = randomCentroids(points, k);
    var assignment = new Array(points.length);
    var clusters = new Array(k);
    var movement = true;
    while (movement) {
        for (var i = 0; i < points.length; i++) {
            assignment[i] = closestCentroid(points[i], centroids);
        }
        movement = false;
    }
    return clusters;
};
```

Finally, by selecting a cluster at a time, you will recalculate the centroids and with these repeat the whole process until you get always the same values. First, as you can see in Listing 7-23, you make an iteration through the iterator j to analyze a cluster at a time. Inside of it, based on the contents of the assignment array, you fill the assigned array with all data points belonging to the cluster. These values serve you for the calculation of the new centroid defined in the newCentroid variable. To determine its new coordinates [x, y], you sum all x and y values, respectively, of all points of the cluster. These amounts are then divided by the number of points, so the x and y values of the new centroid are nothing more than the averages of all the coordinates.

To do all this, you need to implement a double iteration (two for() loops) with the g and i iterators. The iteration on g allows you to work on a coordinate at a time (first x, then y, and so on), while the iteration on i allows you to sum point after point in order to make the summation.

If the new centroids differ from the previous ones, then the assignment of the various data points to clusters repeats again, and the cycle begins again (steps 3 and 4 of the algorithm).

Listing 7-23. kmeans.js

```
function kmeans(points, k) {
    ...
    while (movement) {
        for (var i = 0; i < points.length; i++) {
            assignment[i] = closestCentroid(points[i], centroids);
        }
        movement = false;
        for (var j = 0; j < k; j++) {
            var assigned = [];
            for (var i = 0; i < assignment.length; i++) {
                if (assignment[i] == j) {
                    assigned.push(points[i]);
                }
            }
            if (!assigned.length) {
                continue;
            }
            var centroid = centroids[j];
            var newCentroid = new Array(centroid.length);
            for (var g = 0; g < centroid.length; g++) {
                var sum = 0;
                for (var i = 0; i < assigned.length; i++) {
                    sum += assigned[i][g];
                }
                newCentroid[g] = sum / assigned.length;
                if (newCentroid[g] != centroid[g]) {
                    movement = true;
                }
            }
            centroids[j] = newCentroid;
            clusters[j] = assigned;
        }
    }
    return clusters;
};
```

Applying the Cluster Analysis to the Scatterplot

Having concluded the JavaScript code for the clustering analysis, it is time to come back to the web page. As you did for the example of the trendlines, you will use the code of the scatterplot as shown in Listing 7-24. This is the starting point on which you make the various changes and additions needed to integrate the cluster analysis.

Listing 7-24. Ch7_03.html

```
<!DOCTYPE html>
<html>
<head>
<meta charset="utf-8">
<script src="http://d3js.org/d3.v3.js"></script>
<style>
body {
    font: 16px sans-serif;
}
.axis path, .axis line {
    fill: none;
    stroke: #000;
    shape-rendering: crispEdges;
}
</style>
</head>
<body>
<script type="text/javascript">
var margin = {top: 70, right: 20, bottom: 40, left: 40},
    w = 500 - margin.left - margin.right,
    h = 400 - margin.top - margin.bottom;
var color = d3.scale.category10();
var x = d3.scale.linear()
    .range([0, w]);
var y = d3.scale.linear()
    .range([h, 0]);
var xAxis = d3.svg.axis()
    .scale(x)
    .orient("bottom");
var yAxis = d3.svg.axis()
    .scale(y)
    .orient("left");
var svg = d3.select("body").append("svg")
    .attr("width", w + margin.left + margin.right)
    .attr("height", h + margin.top + margin.bottom)
    .append("g")
    .attr("transform", "translate(" +margin.left+ "," +margin.top+ ")");
d3.tsv("data_09.tsv", function(error, data) {
    data.forEach(function(d) {
        d.time = +d.time;
        d.intensity = +d.intensity;
    });
    x.domain(d3.extent(data, function(d) { return d.time; })).nice();
    y.domain(d3.extent(data, function(d) { return d.intensity; })).nice();
```

```
    svg.append("g")
        .attr("class", "x axis")
        .attr("transform", "translate(0," + h + ")")
        .call(xAxis);
    svg.append("text")
        .attr("class", "label")
        .attr("x", w)
        .attr("y", h + margin.bottom - 5)
        .style("text-anchor", "end")
        .text("Time [s]");
    svg.append("g")
        .attr("class", "y axis")
        .call(yAxis);
    svg.append("text")
        .attr("class", "label")
        .attr("transform", "rotate(-90)")
        .attr("y", 6)
        .attr("dy", ".71em")
        .style("text-anchor", "end")
        .text("Intensity");
    var legend = svg.selectAll(".legend")
        .data(color.domain())
        .enter().append("g")
        .attr("class", "legend")
        .attr("transform", function(d, i) {
            return "translate(0," + (i * 20) + ")";
        });
    legend.append("rect")
        .attr("x", w - 18)
        .attr("width", 18)
        .attr("height", 18)
        .style("fill", color);
    legend.append("text")
        .attr("x", w - 24)
        .attr("y", 9)
        .attr("dy", ".35em")
        .style("text-anchor", "end")
        .text(function(d) { return d; });
});
var title = d3.select("svg").append("g")
    .attr("transform", "translate(" + margin.left + "," + margin.top + ")")
    .attr("class","title");
title.append("text")
    .attr("x", (w / 2))
    .attr("y", -30)
    .attr("text-anchor", "middle")
    .style("font-size", "22px")
    .text("My Scatterplot");
</script>
</body>
</html>
```

First, you need to include the file kmeans.js you have just created in order to use the functions defined within (see Listing 7-25).

Listing 7-25. Ch7_03.html

```
...
<meta charset="utf-8">
<script src="http://d3js.org/d3.v3.js"></script>
<script src="./kmeans.js"></script>
<style>
body {
    ...
```

Prepare an array which will hold the data to be analyzed and call it myPoints. Once this is done, you can finally add the call to the kmean() function, as shown in Listing 7-26.

Listing 7-26. Ch7_03.html

```
d3.tsv("data_09.tsv", function(error, data) {
    var myPoints = [];
    data.forEach(function(d) {
        d.time = +d.time;
        d.intensity = +d.intensity;
        myPoints.push([d.time, d.intensity]);
    });
    var clusters = kmeans(myPoints, 3);
    x.domain(d3.extent(data, function(d) { return d.time; })).nice();
    y.domain(d3.extent(data, function(d) { return d.intensity; })).nice();
    ...
};
```

Finally, you modify the definition of the circle SVG elements so that these are represented in the basis of the results returned by the kmeans() function, as shown in Listing 7-27.

Listing 7-27. Ch7_03.html

```
d3.tsv("data_09.tsv", function(error, data) {
    ...
    svg.append("text")
      .attr("class", "label")
      .attr("transform", "rotate(-90)")
      .attr("y", 6)
      .attr("dy", ".71em")
      .style("text-anchor", "end")
      .text("Intensity");

    for(var i = 0; i < 3; i = i + 1){
        svg.selectAll(".dot" + i)
          .data(clusters[i])
          .enter().append("circle")
          .attr("class", "dot")
          .attr("r", 5)
```

```
        .attr("cx", function(d) { return x(d[0]); })
        .attr("cy", function(d) { return y(d[1]); })
        .style("fill", function(d) { return color(i); });
    }

    var legend = svg.selectAll(".legend")
        .data(color.domain())
        .enter().append("g")
    ...
};
```

In Figure 7-8, you can see the representation of one of the possible results which could be obtained after a clustering analysis.

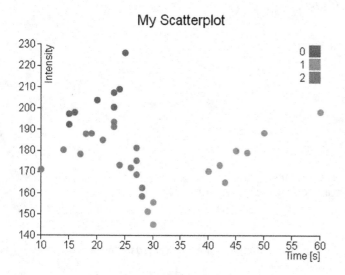

Figure 7-8. *The scatterplot shows one possible solution of the clustering analysis applied to the data in the TSV file*

Highlighting Data Points

Another functionality that you have not yet covered with the library D3, but you have seen with the jqPlot library (see Chapter 10) is **highlighting** and the events related to it. The D3 library even allows you to add this functionality to your charts and handle events in a way that is very similar to that seen with the jqPlot library.

The D3 library provides a particular function to activate or remove event listeners: the on() function. This function is applied directly to a selection by chaining method and generally requires two arguments: the *type* and the *listener*.

```
selection.on(type, listener);
```

The first argument is the type of event that you want to activate, and it is expressed as a string containing the event name (such as mouseover, submit, etc.). The second argument is typically made up of a function which acts as a listener and makes an operation when the event is triggered.

Based on all this, if you want to add the highlighting functionality, you need to manage two particular events: one is when the user hovers the mouse over a data point by highlighting it, and the other is when the user moves out the mouse from above the data point, restoring it to its normal state. These two events are defined in the D3 library as mouseover and mouseout. Now you have to join these events to two different actions. With mouseover, you will enlarge the volume of data points and you will increase the vividness of its color to further contrast it with the others. Instead, you will do the complete opposite with mouseout, restoring the color and size of the original data points.

Listing 7-28 shows the highlight functionality applied to the scatterplot code.

Listing 7-28. Ch7_04.html

```
<!DOCTYPE html>
<html>
<head>
<meta charset="utf-8">
<script src="http://d3js.org/d3.v3.js"></script>
<style>
body {
    font: 16px sans-serif;
}
.axis path, .axis line {
    fill: none;
    stroke: #000;
    shape-rendering: crispEdges;
}
</style>
</head>
<body>
<script type="text/javascript">
var margin = {top: 70, right: 20, bottom: 40, left: 40},
    w = 500 - margin.left - margin.right,
    h = 400 - margin.top - margin.bottom;
var color = d3.scale.category10();
var x = d3.scale.linear()
    .range([0, w]);
var y = d3.scale.linear()
    .range([h, 0]);
var xAxis = d3.svg.axis()
    .scale(x)
    .orient("bottom");
var yAxis = d3.svg.axis()
    .scale(y)
    .orient("left");
var svg = d3.select("body").append("svg")
    .attr("width", w + margin.left + margin.right)
    .attr("height", h + margin.top + margin.bottom)
    .append("g")
    .attr("transform", "translate(" +margin.left+ "," +margin.top+ ")");
d3.tsv("data_09.tsv", function(error, data) {
    data.forEach(function(d) {
        d.time = +d.time;
        d.intensity = +d.intensity;
    });
```

```
x.domain(d3.extent(data, function(d) { return d.time; })).nice();
y.domain(d3.extent(data, function(d) { return d.intensity; })).nice();
svg.append("g")
    .attr("class", "x axis")
    .attr("transform", "translate(0," + h + ")")
    .call(xAxis);
svg.append("text")
    .attr("class", "label")
    .attr("x", w)
    .attr("y", h + margin.bottom - 5)
    .style("text-anchor", "end")
    .text("Time [s]");
svg.append("g")
    .attr("class", "y axis")
    .call(yAxis);
svg.append("text")
    .attr("class", "label")
    .attr("transform", "rotate(-90)")
    .attr("y", 6)
    .attr("dy", ".71em")
    .style("text-anchor", "end")
    .text("Intensity");

var dots = svg.selectAll(".dot")
  .data(data)
  .enter().append("circle")
  .attr("class", "dot")
  .attr("r", 5)
  .attr("cx", function(d) { return x(d.time); })
  .attr("cy", function(d) { return y(d.intensity); })
  .style("fill", function(d) { return color(d.group); })
  .on("mouseover", function() { d3.select(this)
     .style("opacity",1.0)
     .attr("r", 15);
  })
  .on("mouseout", function() { d3.select(this)
     .style("opacity",0.6)
     .attr("r", 5);
  }) ;

var legend = svg.selectAll(".legend")
   .data(color.domain())
   .enter().append("g")
   .attr("class", "legend")
   .attr("transform", function(d, i) {
      return "translate(0," + (i * 20) + ")";
   });
legend.append("rect")
   .attr("x", w - 18)
   .attr("width", 18)
   .attr("height", 18)
```

```
            .style("fill", color);
        legend.append("text")
            .attr("x", w - 24)
            .attr("y", 9)
            .attr("dy", ".35em")
            .style("text-anchor", "end")
            .text(function(d) { return d; });
});
var title = d3.select("svg").append("g")
        .attr("transform", "translate(" + margin.left + "," + margin.top + ")")
        .attr("class","title");
title.append("text")
        .attr("x", (w / 2))
        .attr("y", -30)
        .attr("text-anchor", "middle")
        .style("font-size", "22px")
        .text("My Scatterplot");
</script>
</body>
</html>
```

Before loading the web page to see the result, you need to dull all the colors of the data points by setting the opacity attribute in the CSS styles, as shown in Listing 7-29.

Listing 7-29. Ch7_04.html

```
<style>
body {
    font: 16px sans-serif;
}
.axis path,
.axis line {
    fill: none;
    stroke: #000;
    shape-rendering: crispEdges;
}
.dot {
    stroke: #000;
    opacity: 0.6;
}
</style>
```

Figure 7-9 shows one of many data points in the bubble chart in two different states. On the left you can see the data point in its normal state, while on the right it is highlighted.

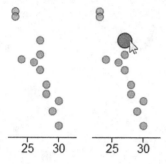

Figure 7-9. *A bubble assumes two states: normal on the left and highlighted when moused over on the right*

Bubble Chart

It is very easy to build a bubble chart by effecting only a few changes to the previous scatterplot example. First of all, you need to add a new column to your data. In this case (see Listing 7-30), you add bandwidth values as the last column to the data_09.tsv and you save it as data_10.tsv.

Listing 7-30. data_10.tsv

time	intensity	group	bandwidth
10	171.11	Exp1	20
14	180.31	Exp1	30
17	178.32	Exp1	10
42	173.22	Exp3	40
30	145.22	Exp2	35
30	155.68	Exp3	80
23	200.56	Exp2	10
15	192.33	Exp1	30
24	173.22	Exp2	10
20	203.78	Exp2	20
18	187.88	Exp1	60
45	180.00	Exp3	10
27	181.33	Exp2	40
16	198.03	Exp1	30
47	179.11	Exp3	20
27	175.33	Exp2	30
28	162.55	Exp2	10
24	208.97	Exp1	10
23	200.47	Exp1	10
43	165.08	Exp3	10
27	168.77	Exp2	20
23	193.55	Exp2	50
19	188.04	Exp1	10
40	170.36	Exp3	40
21	184.98	Exp2	20
15	197.33	Exp1	30
50	188.45	Exp3	10
23	207.33	Exp1	10
28	158.60	Exp2	10

29	151.31	Exp2	30
26	172.01	Exp2	20
23	191.33	Exp1	10
25	226.11	Exp1	10
60	198.33	Exp3	10

Now you have a third parameter in the list of data corresponding to the new column bandwidth. This value is expressed by a number, and in order to read it as such you need to add the bandwidth variable to the parsing of data, as shown in Listing 7-31. You must not forget to replace the name of the TSV file with data_10.tsv in the tsv() function.

Listing 7-31. Ch7_05.html

```
d3.tsv("data_10.tsv", function(error, data) {
    var myPoints = [];
    data.forEach(function(d) {
        d.time = +d.time;
        d.intensity = +d.intensity;
        d.bandwidth = +d.bandwidth;
        myPoints.push([d.time, d.intensity]);
    });
    ...
});
```

Now you can turn all the dots into circular areas just by increasing their radius, since they are already set as SVG element <circle> as shown in Listing 7-32. The radii of these circles must be proportional to the bandwidth value, which therefore can be directly assigned to the r attribute. The 0.4 value is a correction factor which fits the bandwidth values to be very well represented in the bubble chart (in other cases, you will need to use other values as a factor).

Listing 7-32. Ch7_05.html

```
d3.tsv("data_10.tsv", function(error, data) {
    ...
  svg.append("text")
      .attr("class", "label")
      .attr("transform", "rotate(-90)")
      .attr("y", 6)
      .attr("dy", ".71em")
      .style("text-anchor", "end")
      .text("Intensity");

    svg.selectAll(".dot")
      .data(data)
      .enter().append("circle")
      .attr("class", "dot")
      .attr("r", function(d) { return d.bandwidth * 0.4 })
      .attr("cx", function(d) { return x(d.time); })
      .attr("cy", function(d) { return y(d.intensity); })
      .style("fill", function(d) { return color(d.group); })
      .on("mouseover", function() { d3.select(this)
          .style("opacity",1.0)
          .attr("r", function(d) { return d.bandwidth * 0.5 });
```

```
    })
    .on("mouseout", function() { d3.select(this)
        .style("opacity",0.6)
        .attr("r", function(d) { return d.bandwidth * 0.4 });
    });

var legend = svg.selectAll(".legend")
    ...
});
```

Last but not least, you need to update the title of the new chart as shown in Listing 7-33.

Listing 7-33. Ch7_05.html

```
title.append("text")
    .attr("x", (w / 2))
    .attr("y", -30 )
    .attr("text-anchor", "middle")
    .style("font-size", "22px")
    .text("My Bubble Chart");
```

And Figure 7-10 will be the result.

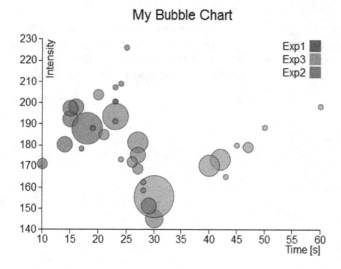

Figure 7-10. *A bubble chart*

Summary

In this chapter, you briefly saw how to generate **bubble charts** and **scatterplots** with the D3 library. Even here, you carried out the same type of charts which you saw in the second part of the book with the jqPlot library. Thus, you can get an idea of these two different libraries and of the respective approaches in the implementation of the same type of charts.

In the next chapter, you will implement a type of chart with which you still have not dealt with in the book: **radar charts**. This example of representation is not feasible with jqPlot, but it is possible to implement it thanks to D3 graphic elements. Thus, the next chapter will be a good example of how to use the potentialities of the D3 library to develop other types of charts which differ from those most commonly encountered.

■ ■ ■

CHAPTER 8

Radar Charts with D3

This chapter covers a type of chart that you have not yet read about: the radar chart. First you will get to know what it is, including its basic features, and how to create one using the SVG elements provided by the D3 library.

You'll start by reading a small handful of representative data from a CSV file. Then, making reference to the data, you'll see how it is possible to implement all the components of a radar chart, step by step. In the second part of the chapter, you'll use the same code to read data from more complex file, in which both the number of series and the amount of data to be processed are greater. This approach is a fairly common practice when you need to represent a new type of chart from scratch. You begin by working with a simple but complete example, and then, once you've implemented the basic example, you'll extend it with more complex and real data.

Radar Chart

Radar charts are also known as web or spider charts, for the typical web structure they assume (see Figure 8-1). They are two-dimensional charts that enable you to represent three or more quantitative variables. They consist of a sequence of spokes, all having the same angle, with each spoke representing one of the variables. A point is represented on every spoke and the point's distance from the center is proportional to the magnitude of the given variable. Then a line connects the point reported on each spoke, thus giving the plot a web-like appearance. Without this connecting line, the chart would look more like a scanning radar.

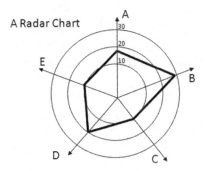

Figure 8-1. A radar chart looks like a spider web

Building Auto Scaling Axes

Copy the following data and save it in a file as data_11.csv (see Listing 8-1).

Listing 8-1. data_11.csv

```
section,set1,set2,
A,1,6,
B,2,7,
C,3,8,
D,4,9,
E,5,8,
F,4,7,
G,3,6,
H,2,5,
```

In Listing 8-2, you define the drawing area and the margins. You then create a color sequence with the category10() function.

Listing 8-2. Ch8_01.html

```
var margin = {top: 70, right: 20, bottom: 40, left: 40},
    w = 500 - margin.left - margin.right,
    h = 400 - margin.top - margin.bottom;

var color = d3.scale.category20();
```

In the drawing area you just defined, you also have to define a specific area that can accommodate a circular shape, which in this case is the radar chart. Once you have defined this area, you define the radius like a Cartesian axis. In fact, each spoke on a radar chart is considered an axis upon which you place a variable. You therefore define a linear scale on the radius, as shown in Listing 8-3.

Listing 8-3. ch8_01.html

```
var circleConstraint = d3.min([h, w]);
var radius = d3.scale.linear()
    .range([0, (circleConstraint / 2)]);
```

You need to find the center of the drawing area. This is the center of the radar chart, and the point from which all the spokes radiate (see Listing 8-4).

Listing 8-4. Ch8_01.html

```
var centerXPos = w / 2 + margin.left;
var centerYPos = h / 2 + margin.top;
```

Begin to draw the root element <svg>, as shown in Listing 8-5.

Listing 8-5. Ch8_01.html

```
var svg = d3.select("body").append("svg")
    .attr("width", w + margin.left + margin.right)
    .attr("height", h + margin.top + margin.bottom)
    .append("g")
    .attr("transform", "translate(" + centerXPos + ", " + centerYPos + ")");
```

Now, as shown in Listing 8-6, you read the contents of the file with the d3.csv() function. You need to verify that the read values set1 and set2 are interpreted as numeric values. You also want to know which is the maximum value among all these, in order to define a scale that extends according to its value.

Listing 8-6. ch8_01.html

```
d3.csv("data_11.csv", function(error, data) {
    var maxValue =0;
    data.forEach(function(d) {
        d.set1 = +d.set1;
        d.set2 = +d.set2;
        if(d.set1 > maxValue)
            maxValue = d.set1;
        if(d.set2 > maxValue)
            maxValue = d.set2;
    });
});
```

Once you know the maximum value of the input data, you set the full scale value equal to this maximum value multiplied by one and a half. In this case, instead of using the automatic generation of ticks on the axes, you have to define them manually. In fact, these ticks have a spherical shape and consequently, quite particular features. This example divides the range of the radius axis into five ticks. Once the values of the ticks are defined, you can assign a domain to the radius axis (see Listing 8-7).

Listing 8-7. Ch8_01.html

```
d3.csv("data_11.csv", function(error, data) {
    ...
    data.forEach(function(d) {
    ...
    });

    var topValue =1.5 * maxValue;
    var ticks = [];
    for(i =0; i <5;i += 1){
        ticks[i] = topValue * i / 5;
    }
  radius.domain([0,topValue]);
});
```

Now that you have all of the numerical values, we can embed some <svg> elements in order to design a radar grid that will vary in shape and value depending on the data entered (see Listing 8-8).

Listing 8-8. Ch8_01.html

```
d3.csv("data_11.csv", function(error, data) {
    ...
    radius.domain([0, topValue]);

    var circleAxes = svg.selectAll(".circle-ticks")
        .data(ticks)
        .enter().append("g")
        .attr("class", "circle-ticks");
```

```
circleAxes.append("svg:circle")
    .attr("r", function(d) {return radius(d);})
    .attr("class", "circle")
    .style("stroke", "#CCC")
    .style("fill", "none");

circleAxes.append("svg:text")
    .attr("text-anchor", "middle")
    .attr("dy", function(d) {return radius(d)})
    .text(String);
});
```

You have created a structure of five <g> tags named `circle-ticks`, as you can see in Figure 8-2, each containing a <circle> element (which draws the grid) and a <text> element (which shows the corresponding numeric value).

```
☐ <g transform="translate(260, 215)">
    ☐ <g class="circle-ticks">
        <circle class="circle" r="0" style="stroke: rgb(204, 204, 204); fill: none;">
        <text text-anchor="middle" dy="0">0</text>
    </g>
    ⊞ <g class="circle-ticks">
    ⊞ <g class="circle-ticks">
    ⊞ <g class="circle-ticks">
    ⊞ <g class="circle-ticks">
</g>
```

Figure 8-2. *FireBug shows how the* `circle-ticks` *are structured*

All of this code generates the circular grid shown in Figure 8-3.

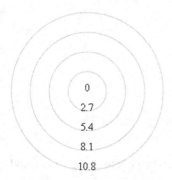

Figure 8-3. *The circular grid of a radar chart*

As you can see, the values reported on the tick will vary depending on the maximum value contained in the data.

Now is the time to draw the spokes, as many rays as there are lines in the `data_11.csv` file. Each of these lines corresponds to a variable, the name of which is entered in the first column of the file (see Listing 8-9).

Listing 8-9. Ch8_01.html

```
d3.csv("data_11.csv", function(error, data) {
    ...
    circleAxes.append("svg:text")
        .attr("text-anchor", "middle")
        .attr("dy", function(d) {return radius(d)})
        .text(String);

    lineAxes = svg.selectAll('.line-ticks')
        .data(data)
        .enter().append('svg:g')
        .attr("transform", function (d, i) {
            return "rotate(" + ((i / data.length * 360) - 90) +
            ")translate(" + radius(topValue) + ")";
        })
        .attr("class", "line-ticks");

    lineAxes.append('svg:line')
        .attr("x2", -1 * radius(topValue))
        .style("stroke", "#CCC")
        .style("fill", "none");

    lineAxes.append('svg:text')
        .text(function(d) { return d.section; })
        .attr("text-anchor", "middle")
        .attr("transform", function (d, i) {
            return "rotate("+(90 - (i * 360 / data.length)) + ")";
        });
});
```

You now have spokes represented in the chart, as shown in Figure 8-4.

Figure 8-4. *The radial axes of a radar chart*

Adding Data to the Radar Chart

It is now time to consider the numeric columns in the file. Each column can be considered a series and each series must be assigned a color. You can define the series by taking the headers from the file and removing the first column. Then you can create the domain of colors according to the sequence of the series and then define the lines that draw them (see Listing 8-10).

Listing 8-10. Ch8_01.html

```
d3.csv("data_11.csv", function(error, data) {
    ...
    lineAxes.append('svg:text')
        .text(function(d) { return d.section; })
        .attr("text-anchor", "middle")
        .attr("transform", function (d, i) {
            return "rotate("+(90-(i*360/data.length))+")";
        });

    var series = d3.keys(data[0])
        .filter(function(key) { return key !== "section"; })
        .filter(function(key) { return key !== ""; });

    color.domain(series);

    var lines = color.domain().map(function(name){
        return (data.concat(data[0])).map(function(d){
            return +d[name];
        });
    });
});
```

This is the content of the series arrays:

```
["set1", "set2"]
```

And this is the content of the lines arrays:

```
[[1,2,3,...],[6,7,8,...]]
```

These lines will help you create the corresponding path elements and enable you to draw the trend of the series on the radar chart. Each series will pass through the values assumed in the various spokes (see Listing 8-11).

Listing 8-11. Ch8_01.html

```
d3.csv("data_11.csv", function(error, data) {
    ...
    var lines = color.domain().map(function(name){
        return (data.concat(data[0])).map(function(d){
            return +d[name];
        });
    });
});
```

```
var sets = svg.selectAll(".series")
    .data(series)
    .enter().append("g")
    .attr("class", "series");

sets.append('svg:path')
    .data(lines)
    .attr("class", "line")
    .attr("d", d3.svg.line.radial()
    .radius(function (d) {
      return radius(d);
    })
    .angle(function (d, i) {
        if (i == data.length) {
            i =0;
        } //close the line
        return (i / data.length) * 2 * Math.PI;
    }))
    .data(series)
    .style("stroke-width", 3)
    .style("fill", "none")
    .style("stroke", function(d,i){
        return color(i);
    });
});
```

You can also add a legend showing the names of the series (which are, actually, the headers of the columns) and a title placed on top in the drawing area, as shown in Listing 8-12.

Listing 8-12. Ch8_01.html

```
d3.csv("data_11.csv", function(error, data) {
    ...
        .data(series)
        .style("stroke-width", 3)
        .style("fill", "none")
        .style("stroke", function(d,i){
            return color(i);
        });

    var legend = svg.selectAll(".legend")
        .data(series)
        .enter().append("g")
        .attr("class", "legend")
        .attr("transform", function(d, i) {
            return "translate(0," + i * 20 + ")";
        });
```

```
  legend.append("rect")
    .attr("x", w/2 -18)
    .attr("y", h/2 - 60)
    .attr("width", 18)
    .attr("height", 18)
    .style("fill", function(d,i){ return color(i);});

  legend.append("text")
    .attr("x", w/2 -24)
    .attr("y", h/2 - 60)
    .attr("dy","1.2em")
    .style("text-anchor", "end")
    .text(function(d) { return d; });
});
var title = d3.select("svg").append("g")
  .attr("transform", "translate(" +margin.left+ "," +margin.top+ ")")
  .attr("class","title");

title.append("text")
  .attr("x", (w / 2))
  .attr("y", -30 )
  .attr("text-anchor", "middle")
  .style("font-size", "22px")
  .text("My Radar Chart");
```

Last but not least, you can add a CSS style class to rule the text style, as shown in Listing 8-13.

Listing 8-13. Ch8_01.html

```
<style>
body {
  font: 16px sans-serif;
}
</style>
```

Figure 8-5 shows the resulting radar chart.

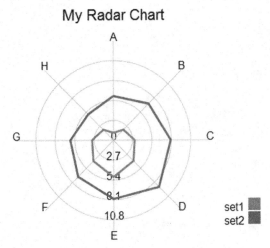

Figure 8-5. *A radar chart with two series*

Improving Your Radar Chart

If you followed along in the previous example, you should not have any problem adding more columns and rows to the radar chart. Open the last input data file, called data_11.csv, and add two more columns and rows. Save the file as data_12.csv, as shown in Listing 8-14.

Listing 8-14. data_12.csv

```
section,set1,set2,set3,set4,
A,1,6,2,10,
B,2,7,2,14,
C,3,8,1,10,
D,4,9,4,1,
E,5,8,7,2,
F,4,7,11,1,
G,3,6,14,2,
H,2,5,2,1,
I,3,4,5,2,
L,1,5,1,2,
```

You now have to replace the call to the data11.csv file with the data12.csv file in the d3.csv() function, as shown in Listing 8-15.

Listing 8-15. Ch8_02.html

```
d3.csv("data_12.csv", function(error, data) {
...});
```

Figure 8-6 shows the result.

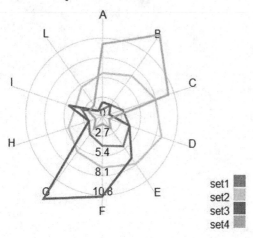

Figure 8-6. *A radar chart with four series*

Wow, it works! Ready to add yet another feature? So far, you've traced a line that runs through the various spokes to return circularly to the starting point; the trend now describes a specific area. You'll often be more interested in the areas of a radar chart that are delimited by the different lines than in the lines themselves. If you want to make this small conversion to your radar chart in order to show the areas, you need to add just one more path, as shown in Listing 8-16. This path is virtually identical to the one already present, only instead of drawing the line representing the series, this new path colors the area enclosed inside. In this example, you'll use the colors of the corresponding lines, but adding a bit of transparency, so as not to cover the underlying series.

Listing 8-16. Ch8_02.html

```
d3.csv("data_12.csv", function(error, data) {
    ...
    var sets = svg.selectAll(".series")
        .data(series)
        .enter().append("g")
        .attr("class", "series");

    sets.append('svg:path')
        .data(lines)
        .attr("class", "line")
        .attr("d", d3.svg.line.radial()
        .radius(function (d) {
            return radius(d);
        })
        .angle(function (d, i) {
            if (i == data.length) {
                i =0;
            }
            return (i / data.length) * 2 * Math.PI;
        }))
```

```
        .data(series)
        .style("stroke-width", 3)
        .style("opacity", 0.4)
        .style("fill", function(d,i){
            return color(i);
        })
        .style("stroke", function(d,i){
            return color(i);
        });

    sets.append('svg:path')
        .data(lines)
        .attr("class", "line")
        .attr("d", d3.svg.line.radial())
        ...
});
```

As you can see in Figure 8-7, you now have a radar chart with semi-transparent areas.

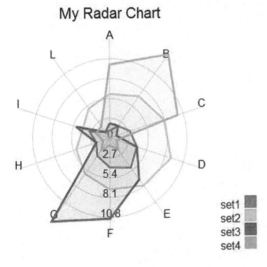

Figure 8-7. *A radar chart with color filled areas*

Summary

This chapter explained how to implement **radar charts**. This type of chart is not so common but it is especially useful to highlight the potential of the D3 library. It shows an example that helps you to understand how you can develop other charts that differ from the most commonly encountered types.

The next chapter concludes the book by considering two different cases. These cases are intended to propose, in a simplified way, the classic situations that developers have to face when they deal with real data. In the first example, you'll see how, using D3, it is possible to represent data that are generated or acquired in real time. You'll create a chart that's constantly being updated, always showing the current situation. In the second example, you'll use the D3 library to read the data contained in a database.

■ ■ ■

CHAPTER 9

Handling Live Data with D3

In this chapter you will see how to develop real-time charts using the D3 library. Indeed, you will create a line chart that displays the real-time values generated from a function that simulates an external source of data. The data will be generated continuously, and therefore the line chart will vary accordingly, always showing the latest situation.

In the second part of this chapter you will develop a chart that is slightly more complex. This time, you will be using an example in which the data source is a real database. First, you will implement a line chart that will read the data contained in an external file. Later, you will learn how to use the example to read the same data, but this time from the table of a database.

Real-Time Charts

You have a data source that simulates a function that returns random variations on the performance of a variable. These values are stored in an array that has the functions of a buffer, in which you want to contain only the ten most recent values. For each input value that is generated or acquired, the oldest one is replaced with the new one. The data contained in this array are displayed as a line chart that updates every 3 seconds. Everything is activated by clicking a button.

Let us start setting the bases to represent a line chart (to review developing line charts with the D3 library, see Chapter 3). First, you write the HTML structure on which you will build your chart, as shown in Listing 9-1.

Listing 9-1. Ch9_01.html

```
<!DOCTYPE html>
<html>
<head>
<meta charset="utf-8">
<script src="http://d3js.org/d3.v3.js"></script>
<style>
    //add the CSS styles here
</style>
<body>
<script type="text/javascript">
    // add the JavaScript code here
</script>
</body>
</html>
```

Now, you start to define the variables that will help you during the writing of the code, beginning with the management of the input data. As previously stated, the data that you are going to represent on the chart come from a function that generates random variations, either positive or negative, from a starting value. You decide to start from 10.

So, starting from this value, you receive from the random function a sequence of values to be collected within an array, which you will call data (see Listing 9-2). For now, you assign to it only inside the starting value (10). Given this array, to receive the values in real time, you will need to set a maximum limit, which, in this example, is eleven elements (0–10). Once filled, you will manage the array as a queue, in which the oldest item will be removed to make room for the new one.

Listing 9-2. Ch9_01.html

```
<script type="text/javascript">
var data = [10];
  w = 400;
  h = 300;
  margin_x = 32;
  margin_y = 20;
  ymax = 20;
  ymin = 0;
  y = d3.scale.linear().domain([ymin, ymax]).range([0 + margin_y, h - margin_y]);
  x = d3.scale.linear().domain([0, 10]).range([0 + margin_x, w - margin_x]);
</script>
```

The values contained within the data array will be represented along the y axis, so it is necessary to establish the range of values that the tick labels will have to cover. Starting from the value of 10, you can decide, for example, that this range covers the values from 0 to 20 (later, you will ensure that the ticks correspond to a range of multiples of 5, i.e., 0, 5, 10, 15, and 20). Because the values to display are randomly generated, they will gradually assume values even higher than 20, and, if so, you will see the disappearance of the line over the top edge of the chart. What to do?

Because the main goal is to create a chart that redraws itself after acquiring new data, you will ensure that even the tick labels are adjusted according to the range covered by the values contained within the data array. To accomplish this, you need to define the y range with the ymax and ymin variables, with the x range covering the static range [0–10].

The w and h variables (width and height) define the size of the drawing area on which you will draw the line chart, whereas margin_x and margin_y allow you to adjust the margins.

Now, let us create the scalar vector graphics (SVG) elements that will represent the various parts of your chart. You start by creating the <svg> root and then define the x and y axes, as shown in Listing 9-3.

Listing 9-3. Ch9_01.html

```
<script type="text/javascript">
...
y = d3.scale.linear().domain([ymin, ymax]).range([0 + margin_y, h - margin_y]);
x = d3.scale.linear().domain([0, 10]).range([0 + margin_x, w - margin_x]);

var svg = d3.select("body")
    .append("svg:svg")
    .attr("width", w)
    .attr("height", h);

var g = svg.append("svg:g")
    .attr("transform", "translate(0, " + h + ")");
```

```
// draw the x axis
g.append("svg:line")
    .attr("x1", x(0))
    .attr("y1", -y(0))
    .attr("x2", x(w))
    .attr("y2", -y(0));

// draw the y axis
g.append("svg:line")
    .attr("x1", x(0))
    .attr("y1", -y(0))
    .attr("x2", x(0))
    .attr("y2", -y(25));
</script>
```

Next, you add the ticks and the corresponding labels on both axes and then the grid. Finally, you draw the line on the chart with the line() function (see Listing 9-4).

Listing 9-4. Ch9_01.html

```
<script type="text/javascript">
...
g.append("svg:line")
    .attr("x1", x(0))
    .attr("y1", -y(0))
    .attr("x2", x(0))
    .attr("y2", -y(25));

// draw the xLabels
g.selectAll(".xLabel")
    .data(x.ticks(5))
    .enter().append("svg:text")
    .attr("class", "xLabel")
    .text(String)
    .attr("x", function(d) { return x(d) })
    .attr("y", 0)
    .attr("text-anchor", "middle");

// draw the yLabels
g.selectAll(".yLabel")
    .data(y.ticks(5))
    .enter().append("svg:text")
    .attr("class", "yLabel")
    .text(String)
    .attr("x", 25)
    .attr("y", function(d) { return -y(d) })
    .attr("text-anchor", "end");
```

```
// draw the x ticks
g.selectAll(".xTicks")
    .data(x.ticks(5))
    .enter().append("svg:line")
    .attr("class", "xTicks")
    .attr("x1", function(d) { return x(d); })
    .attr("y1", -y(0))
    .attr("x2", function(d) { return x(d); })
    .attr("y2", -y(0) - 5);

// draw the y ticks
g.selectAll(".yTicks")
    .data(y.ticks(5))
    .enter().append("svg:line")
    .attr("class", "yTicks")
    .attr("y1", function(d) { return -1 * y(d); })
    .attr("x1", x(0) +5)
    .attr("y2", function(d) { return -1 * y(d); })
    .attr("x2", x(0))

// draw the x grid
g.selectAll(".xGrids")
    .data(x.ticks(5))
    .enter().append("svg:line")
    .attr("class", "xGrids")
    .attr("x1", function(d) { return x(d); })
    .attr("y1", -y(0))
    .attr("x2", function(d) { return x(d); })
    .attr("y2", -y(25));

// draw the y grid
g.selectAll(".yGrids")
    .data(y.ticks(5))
    .enter().append("svg:line")
    .attr("class", "yGrids")
    .attr("y1", function(d) { return -1 * y(d); })
    .attr("x1", x(w))
    .attr("y2", function(d) { return -y(d); })
    .attr("x2", x(0));

var line = d3.svg.line()
    .x(function(d,i) { return x(i); })
    .y(function(d) { return -y(d); })

</script>
```

To give a pleasing aspect to your chart, it is also necessary to define the Cascading Style Sheets (CSS) styles, as demonstrated in Listing 9-5.

Listing 9-5. Ch9_01.html

```
<style>
path {
    stroke: steelblue;
    stroke-width: 3;
    fill: none;
}
line {
    stroke: black;
}
.xGrids {
    stroke: lightgray;
}
.yGrids {
    stroke: lightgray;
}
text {
    font-family: Verdana;
    font-size: 9pt;
}
</style>
```

Now, you add a button above the chart, ensuring that the updateData() function is activated when a user clicks it, as presented in Listing 9-6.

Listing 9-6. Ch9_01.html

```
< body>
<div id="option">
    <input name="updateButton"
        type="button"
        value="Update"
        onclick="updateData()" />
</div>
```

Then, you implement the getRandomInt() function, which generates a random integer value between the minimum and maximum values (see Listing 9-7).

Listing 9-7. Ch9_01.html

```
function getRandomInt (min, max) {
    return Math.floor(Math.random() * (max - min +1)) + min;
};
```

Listing 9-8 shows the updateData() function, in which the value generated by the getRandomInt() function is added to the most recent value of the array to simulate variations on the trend. This new value is stored in the array, while the oldest value is removed; thus, the size of the array always remains the same.

Listing 9-8. Ch9_01.html

```
function updateData() {
    var last = data[data.length-1];
    if(data.length >10){
        data.shift();
    }
    var newlast = last + getRandomInt(-3,3);
    if(newlast <0)
        newlast = 0;
    data.push(newlast);
};
```

If the new value returned by the getRandomInt() function is greater or less than the range represented on the y axis, you will see the line of data extending over the edges of the chart. To prevent this from occurring, you must change the interval on the y axis by varying the ymin and ymax variables and updating the y range with these new values, as shown in Listing 9-9.

Listing 9-9. Ch9_01.html

```
function updateData() {
    ...
    if(newlast <0)
        newlast = 0;
    data.push(newlast);

    if(newlast > ymax){
        ymin = ymin + (newlast - ymax);
        ymax = newlast;
        y = d3.scale.linear().domain([ymin, ymax])
            .range([0 + margin_y, h - margin_y]);
    }

    if(newlast < ymin){
        ymax = ymax - (ymin - newlast);
        ymin = newlast;
        y = d3.scale.linear().domain([ymin, ymax])
            .range([0 + margin_y, h - margin_y]);
    }
};
```

Because the new data acquired must then be redrawn, you will need to delete the invalid SVG elements and replace them with new ones. Let us do both with the tick labels and with the line of data (see Listing 9-10). Finally, it is necessary to repeat the refresh of the chart at a fixed time. Thus, using the requestAnimFrame() function, you can repeat the execution of the content of the UpdateData() function.

Listing 9-10. Ch9_01.html

```
function updateData() {
    ...
    if(newlast < ymin){
        ymax = ymax - (ymin - newlast);
        ymin = newlast;
        y = d3.scale.linear().domain([ymin, ymax]).range([0 + margin_y, h - margin_y]);
    }
    var svg = d3.select("body").transition();
    g.selectAll(".yLabel").remove();
    g.selectAll(".yLabel")
        .data(y.ticks(5))
        .enter().append("svg:text")
        .attr("class", "yLabel")
        .text(String)
        .attr("x", 25)
        .attr("y", function(d) { return -y(d) })
        .attr("text-anchor", "end");

    g.selectAll(".line").remove();
    g.append("svg:path")
        .attr("class", "line")
        .attr("d", line(data));

    window.requestAnimFrame = (function(){
        return window.requestAnimationFrame ||
        window.webkitRequestAnimationFrame ||
        window.mozRequestAnimationFrame ||
            function( callback ){
                window.setTimeout(callback, 1000);
            };
    })();

    requestAnimFrame(setTimeout(updateData,3000));
    render();
};
```

Now, when the Update button has been clicked, from left a line begins to draw the values acquired by the function that generates random variations. Once the line reaches the right end of the chart, it will update every acquisition, showing only the last ten values (see Figure 9-1).

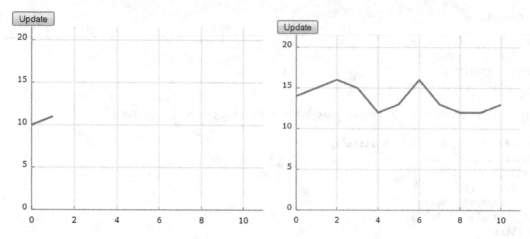

Figure 9-1. *A real-time chart with a start button*

Using PHP to Extract Data from a MySQL Table

Finally, the time has come to use data contained in a database, a scenario that is more likely to correspond with your daily needs. You choose MySQL as a database, and you use hypertext preprocessor (PHP) language to query the database and obtain the data in JavaScript Object Notation (JSON) format for it to be readable by D3. You will see that once a chart is built with D3, the transition to this stage is easy.

The following example is not intended to explain the use of PHP language or any other language, but to illustrate a typical and real case. The example shows how simple it is to interface all that you have learned with other programming languages. Often, languages such as Java and PHP provide an excellent interface for collecting and preparing data from their sources (a database, in this instance).

Starting with a TSV File

To understand more clearly the transition between what you already know and interfacing with PHP and databases, let us start with a case that should be familiar to you (see Listing 9-11). First, you write a tab-separated value (TSV) file with these series of data and save them as data_13.tsv.

Listing 9-11. data_13.tsv

```
day            income  expense
2012-02-12     52      40
2012-02-27     56      35
2012-03-02     31      45
2012-03-14     33      44
2012-03-30     44      54
2012-04-07     50      34
2012-04-18     65      36
2012-05-02     56      40
2012-05-19     41      56
2012-05-28     45      32
2012-06-03     54      44
2012-06-18     43      46
2012-06-29     39      52
```

■ **Note**   Notice that the values in a TSV file are tab separated, so when you write or copy Listing 9-11, remember to check that there is only a tab character between each value.

Actually, as hinted at, you have already seen these data, although in slightly different form; these are the same data in the data_03.tsv file (see Listing 3-60 in Chapter 3). You changed the column date to day and modified the format for dates. Now, you must add the JavaScript code in Listing 9-12, which will allow you to represent these data as a multiseries line chart. (This code is very similar to that used in the section "Difference Line Chart" in Chapter 3; see that section for explanations and details about the content of Listing 9-12.)

Listing 9-12. Ch9_02.html

```
<!DOCTYPE html>
<html>
<head>
<meta charset="utf-8">
<script src="http://d3js.org/d3.v3.js"></script>
<style>
body {
    font: 10px verdana;
}
.axis path,
.axis line {
    fill: none;
    stroke: #333;
}
.grid .tick {
  stroke: lightgrey;
  opacity: 0.7;
}
.grid path {
    stroke-width: 0;
}
.line {
    fill: none;
    stroke: darkgreen;
    stroke-width: 2.5px;
}
.line2 {
    fill: none;
    stroke: darkred;
    stroke-width: 2.5px;
}
</style>
</head>
```

```
<body>
<script type="text/javascript">

var margin = {top: 70, right: 20, bottom: 30, left: 50},
    w = 400 - margin.left - margin.right,
    h = 400 - margin.top - margin.bottom;

var parseDate = d3.time.format("%Y-%m-%d").parse;

var x = d3.time.scale().range([0, w]);
var y = d3.scale.linear().range([h, 0]);

var xAxis = d3.svg.axis()
    .scale(x)
    .orient("bottom")
    .ticks(5);

var yAxis = d3.svg.axis()
    .scale(y)
    .orient("left")
    .ticks(5);

var xGrid = d3.svg.axis()
    .scale(x)
    .orient("bottom")
    .ticks(5)
    .tickSize(-h, 0, 0)
    .tickFormat("");

var yGrid = d3.svg.axis()
    .scale(y)
    .orient("left")
    .ticks(5)
    .tickSize(-w, 0, 0)
    .tickFormat("");

var svg = d3.select("body").append("svg")
    .attr("width", w + margin.left + margin.right)
    .attr("height", h + margin.top + margin.bottom)
    .append("g")
    .attr("transform", "translate(" + margin.left + ", " + margin.top + ")");

var line = d3.svg.area()
    .interpolate("basis")
    .x(function(d) { return x(d.day); })
    .y(function(d) { return y(d["income"]); });

var line2 = d3.svg.area()
    .interpolate("basis")
    .x(function(d) { return x(d.day); })
    .y(function(d) { return y(d["expense"]); });
```

```
d3.tsv("data_13.tsv", function(error, data) {
    data.forEach(function(d) {
        d.day = parseDate(d.day);
        d.income = +d.income;
        d.expense = +d.expense;
    });

    x.domain(d3.extent(data, function(d) { return d.day; }));
    y.domain([
        d3.min(data, function(d) { return Math.min(d.income, d.expense); }),
        d3.max(data, function(d) { return Math.max(d.income, d.expense); })
    ]);

    svg.append("g")
        .attr("class", "x axis")
        .attr("transform", "translate(0, " + h + ")")
        .call(xAxis);

  svg.append("g")
      .attr("class", "y axis")
      .call(yAxis);

    svg.append("g")
        .attr("class", "grid")
        .attr("transform", "translate(0, " + h + ")")
        .call(xGrid);

    svg.append("g")
        .attr("class", "grid")
        .call(yGrid);

    svg.datum(data);

    svg.append("path")
        .attr("class", "line")
        .attr("d", line);

    svg.append("path")
        .attr("class", "line2")
        .attr("d", line2);
});

var labels = svg.append("g")
    .attr("class", "labels");

labels.append("text")
    .attr("transform", "translate(0, " + h + ")")
    .attr("x", (w-margin.right))
    .attr("dx", "-1.0em")
    .attr("dy", "2.0em")
    .text("[Months]");
```

```
labels.append("text")
    .attr("transform", "rotate(-90)")
    .attr("y", -40)
    .attr("dy", ".71em")
    .style("text-anchor", "end")
    .text("Millions ($)");

var title = svg.append("g")
    .attr("class", "title")

title.append("text")
    .attr("x", (w / 2))
    .attr("y", -30 )
    .attr("text-anchor", "middle")
    .style("font-size", "22px")
    .text("A Multiseries Line Chart");
</script>
</body>
</html>
```

With this code, you get the chart in Figure 9-2.

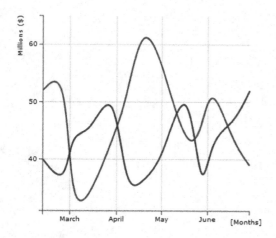

Figure 9-2. *A multiseries chart reading data from a TSV file*

Moving On to the Real Case

Now, let us move on to the real case, in which you will be dealing with tables in the database. For the data source, you choose a table called **sales** in a test database in MySQL.After you have created a table with this name, you can fill it with data executing an SQL sequence (see Listing 9-13).

Listing 9-13. sales.sql

```
insert into sales
values ('2012-02-12', 52, 40);
insert into sales
values ('2012-02-27', 56, 35);
insert into sales
values ('2012-03-02', 31, 45);
insert into sales
values ('2012-03-14', 33, 44);
insert into sales
values ('2012-03-30', 44, 54);
insert into sales
values ('2012-04-07', 50, 34);
insert into sales
values ('2012-04-18', 65, 36);
insert into sales
values ('2012-05-02', 56, 40);
insert into sales
values ('2012-05-19', 41, 56);
insert into sales
values ('2012-05-28', 45, 32);
insert into sales
values ('2012-06-03', 54, 44);
insert into sales
values ('2012-06-18', 43, 46);
insert into sales
values ('2012-06-29', 39, 52);
```

Preferably, you ought to write the PHP script in a separate file and save it as myPHP.php. The content of this file is shown in Listing 9-14.

Listing 9-14. myPHP.php

```php
<?php
    $username = "dbuser";
    $password = "dbuser";
    $host = "localhost";
    $database = "test";

    $server = mysql_connect($host, $username, $password);
    $connection = mysql_select_db($database, $server);
    $myquery = "SELECT * FROM sales";
    $query = mysql_query($myquery);

    if ( ! $myquery ) {
        echo mysql_error();
        die;
    }
```

```
    $data = array();
    for ($x = 0; $x < mysql_num_rows($query); $x++) {
        $data[] = mysql_fetch_assoc($query);
    }
    echo json_encode($data);
    mysql_close($server);
?>
```

Generally, a PHP script is recognizable by its enclosure in special start and end processing instructions: <?php and ?>. This short but powerful and versatile snippet of code is generally used whenever we need to connect to a database. Let us go through it and look at what it does.

In this example, dbuser has been chosen as user, with dbuser as password, but these values will depend on the database you want to connect to. The same applies to the database and hostname values. Thus, in order to connect to a dabase, you must first define a set of identifying variables, as shown in Listing 9-15.

Listing 9-15. myPHP.php

```
$username = "homedbuser";
$password = "homedbuser";
$host = "localhost";
$database = "homedb";
```

Once you have defined them, PHP provides a set of already implemented functions, in which you have only to pass these variables as parameters to make a connection with a database. In this example, you need to call the mysql_connect() and myqsl_select_db() functions to create a connection with a database without defining anything else (see Listing 9-16).

Listing 9-16. myPHP.php

```
$server = mysql_connect($host, $username, $password);
$connection = mysql_select_db($database, $server);
```

Even for entering SQL queries, PHP proves to be a truly practical tool. Listing 9-17 is a very simple example of how to make an SQL query for retrieving data from the database. If you are not familiar with SQL language, a query is a declarative statement addressed to a particular database in order to obtain the desired data contained inside. You can easily recognize a query, as it consists of a SELECT statement followed by a FROM statement and almost always a WHERE statement at the end..

■ **Note**   If you have no experience in SQL language and want to do a bit of practicing without having to install the database and everything else, I suggest visiting this web page from the w3schools web site: www.w3schools.com/sql. In it, you'll find complete documentation on the commands, with many examples and even the ability to query a database on evidence provided by the site by embedding an SQL test query (see the section "Try It Yourself").

In this simple example, the SELECT statement is followed by '*', which means that you want to receive the data in all the columns contained in the table specified in the FROM statement (sales, in this instance).

Listing 9-17. myPHP.php

```
$myquery = "SELECT * FROM sales";
$query = mysql_query($myquery);
```

Once you have made a query, you need to check if it was successful and handle the error if one occurs (see Listing 9-18).

Listing 9-18. myPHP.php

```
if ( ! $query ) {
    echo mysql_error();
    die;
}
```

If the query is successful, then you need to handle the returned data from the query. You place these values in an array you call $data, as illustrated in Listing 9-19. This part is very similar to the csv() and tsv() functions in D3, only instead of reading line by line from a file, it is reading them from a table retrieved from a database. The mysql_num_rows() function gives the number of rows in the table, similar to the length() function of JavaScript used in for() loops. The mysql_fetch_assoc() function assigns the data retrieved from the query to the data array, line by line.

Listing 9-19. myPHP.php

```
$data = array();
for ($x = 0; $x < mysql_num_rows($query); $x++) {
    $data[] = mysql_fetch_assoc($query);
}
echo json_encode($data);
```

The key to the script is the call to the PHP json_encode() method, which converts the data format into JSON and then, with echo, returns the data, which D3 will parse. Finally, you must close the connection to the server, as demonstrated in Listing 9-20.

Listing 9-20. myPHP.php

```
mysql_close($server);
```

Now, you come back to the JavaScript code, changing only one row (yes, only one!) (see Listing 9-21). You replace the tsv() function with the json() function, passing directly the PHP file as argument.

Listing 9-21. Ch9_02b.html

```
d3.json("myPHP.php", function(error, data) {
//d3.tsv("data_03.tsv", function(error, data) {
    data.forEach(function(d) {
        d.day = parseDate(d.day);
        d.income = +d.income;
        d.expense = +d.expense;
});
```

In the end, you get the same chart (see Figure 9-3).

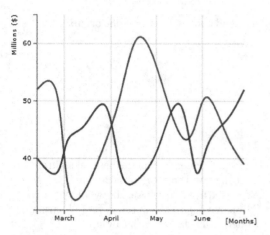

Figure 9-3. *A multiseries chart obtaining data directly from a database*

Summary

This chapter concluded by considering two different cases. In the first example, you saw how to create a web page in which it is possible to represent data you are generating or acquiring in real time. In the second example, you learned how to use the D3 library to read the data contained in a database.

In the next chapter, I will cover a new topic: **controls**. I will describe the importance of introducing controls in a chart, understanding how you can change the chart property using controls. This affords the user the opportunity to select a property's attributes in real time.

CHAPTER 10

■ ■ ■

Adding Controls to Charts

Sometimes, it can be useful to change settings directly from the browser at runtime and then replot the chart with these new settings. A typical way of doing this is to add active controls. These controls make the chart interactive, allowing the user to make choices in real time, such as deciding how the chart should be represented. By inserting controls, you give the user the ability to control the values of the chart's attributes.

In this chapter, you will look at introducing controls within your web page. You will also consider the factors that lead to the choice of one type of control over another. A series of examples featuring three of the most commonly used controls, will take you deeper into this topic.

Adding Controls

One way to group controls is according to their functionality. Some controls (e.g., buttons, menus) work as switches (command controls) with which the user can trigger a particular event or launch a command. Other controls (e.g., check boxes, radio buttons, combo boxes, sliders) are bound to a specific value or property. With this type of control, the user makes a choice or enters values through a text field (text area). Still other controls (e.g., scrollbars) have a navigation function and are especially suitable in situations in which it is necessary to move an object, such as a selected item in a list or a large image enclosed in a frame or in the web page.

Here, you will be investigating those controls that are linked to values and that let the user interact with a chart by making choices. These controls should, in some way, graphically represent the values that a particular property can assume (the same values that you would usually assign to some variables within your JavaScript code, limited to those that you want to make available to the user). Your choice of control will depend on the property to set and the values that it can assume:

- To enable the user to make a single selection from a set of values (e.g., one of three possible colors), the choice of mutually exclusive **radio buttons** as controls is optimal (see Figure 10-1a).

- To let the user select which series should be visible in a chart, you will need to use **check boxes** (see Figure 10-1b).

- To allow the user to choose within a range of values for a particular attribute (e.g., changing the color of an object through adjustment of the red-green-blue (RGB) values that define the color), a **slider** is generally the best choice (see Figure 10-1c) (in this case, you would use three sliders as controls, corresponding to the colors red, green, and blue).

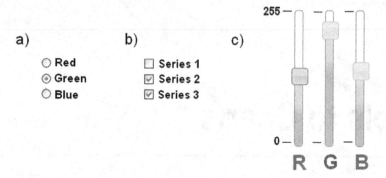

Figure 10-1. *Three of the most commonly used controls: (a) radio buttons, (b) check boxes, (c) sliders*

The list of possible controls does not end there. But, an understanding of the mechanisms that underlie these controls enables a chart developer to handle the vast majority of cases, including those that are the most complex.

In the following examples, you will discover how to apply these three controls to your chart.

Using Radio Buttons

To illustrate the use of controls, let us first look at radio buttons. Radio buttons are a set of small buttons grouped in list form (see Figure 10-1a). They are generally represented as small, empty circles, with text to the side. As previously stated, this type of control is linked to a certain value or property. The particularity of radio buttons is that their values are mutually exclusive; therefore, the user can choose only one of them.

By way of illustration, let us take a simple multiseries line chart, in which, instead of displaying all the series, you want to allow the user to decide which series will be shown. To make a selection, the user will click one of the radio buttons, filling the circle with a dot. The series corresponding to that control will then be drawn on the chart.

Adding Radio Button Controls

First, you need to write the HTML page importing all the necessary libraries (see Listing 10-1).

Listing 10-1. ch10_01.html

```
<HTML>
<HEAD>
<TITLE>Series selections with controls</TITLE>
<meta charset="utf-8">
<script src="http://code.jquery.com/jquery-1.9.1.min.js"></script>
<script src="http://d3js.org/d3.v3.min.js"></script>
<script src="./multiseries.js"></script>
<link rel="stylesheet" href="./multiseries.css"/>
<script>
$(document).ready(function(){

    //add your code here

});
</script>
</HEAD>
```

```
<BODY>
<div id="myChart"></div>
   <!-- add the table with the controls here -->
</BODY>
</HTML>
```

Or, if you prefer to use the content delivery network (CDN) service, you use the following code:

```
<script src="../src/js/jquery-1.9.1.js"></script>
<script src="../src/d3.v3.js"></script>
```

You start with a line chart in which you will be representing three sets of values. The chart that you're going to take as a point of reference is a multiseries line chart that you implemented in Chapter 3 (see Listing 3-51).

For convenience, here is the chart again (see Figure 10-2) and the code (see Listing 10-2) that generates it, on which you will work.

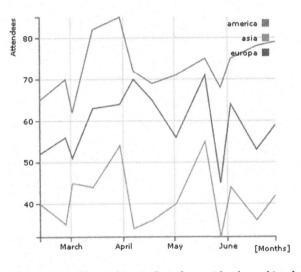

Figure 10-2. *The multiseries line chart with a legend implemented in Chapter 3*

Listing 10-2. Ch3_08a.html

```
<!DOCTYPE html>
<html>
<head>
<meta charset="utf-8">
<script src="http://d3js.org/d3.v3.min.js"></script>
<style>
body {
  font: 10px verdana;
}
```

```css
.axis path,
.axis line {
  fill: none;
  stroke: #333;
}

.grid .tick {
    stroke: lightgrey;
    opacity: 0.7;
}
.grid path {
    stroke-width: 0;
}

.line {
  fill: none;
  stroke: steelblue;
  stroke-width: 1.5px;
}
</style>
</head>
<body>
<script type="text/javascript">
var margin = {top: 70, right: 20, bottom: 30, left: 50},
    w = 400 - margin.left - margin.right,
    h = 400 - margin.top - margin.bottom;
var parseDate = d3.time.format("%d-%b-%y").parse;
var x = d3.time.scale().range([0, w]);
var y = d3.scale.linear().range([h, 0]);

var color = d3.scale.category10();

var xAxis = d3.svg.axis()
    .scale(x)
    .orient("bottom")
    .ticks(5);

var yAxis = d3.svg.axis()
    .scale(y)
    .orient("left")
    .ticks(5);

var xGrid = d3.svg.axis()
    .scale(x)
    .orient("bottom")
    .ticks(5)
    .tickSize(-h, 0, 0)
    .tickFormat("")
```

```javascript
var yGrid = d3.svg.axis()
    .scale(y)
    .orient("left")
    .ticks(5)
    .tickSize(-w, 0, 0)
    .tickFormat("")

var svg = d3.select("body").append("svg")
    .attr("width", w + margin.left + margin.right)
    .attr("height", h + margin.top + margin.bottom)
    .append("g")
    .attr("transform", "translate(" + margin.left + ", " + margin.top + ")");

var line = d3.svg.line()
    .x(function(d) { return x(d.date); })
    .y(function(d) { return y(d.attendee); });

d3.tsv("data_02.tsv", function(error, data) {

  data.forEach(function(d) {
    d.date = parseDate(d.date);
  });

  color.domain(d3.keys(data[0]).filter(function(key) {
    return key !== "date";
  }));

  var continents = color.domain().map(function(name) {
    return {
      name: name,
      values: data.map(function(d) {
          return {date: d.date, attendee: +d[name]};
      })
    };
  });

  x.domain(d3.extent(data, function(d) { return d.date; }));
  y.domain([
    d3.min(continents, function(c) {
        return d3.min(c.values, function(v) { return v.attendee; });
    }),
    d3.max(continents, function(c) {
        return d3.max(c.values, function(v) { return v.attendee; });
    })
  ]);

  svg.append("g")
      .attr("class", "x axis")
      .attr("transform", "translate(0, " + h + ")")
      .call(xAxis);
```

```
svg.append("g")
    .attr("class", "y axis")
    .call(yAxis)

svg.append("g")
    .attr("class", "grid")
    .attr("transform", "translate(0, " + h + ")")
    .call(xGrid)

svg.append("g")
    .attr("class", "grid")
    .call(yGrid);

var continent = svg.selectAll(".continent")
    .data(continents)
    .enter().append("g")
    .attr("class", "continent");

continent.append("path")
    .attr("class", "line")
    .attr("d", function(d) { return line(d.values); })
    .style("stroke", function(d) { return color(d.name); });

var legend = svg.selectAll(".legend")
    .data(color.domain().slice().reverse())
    .enter().append("g")
    .attr("class", "legend")
    .attr("transform", function(d, i) { return "translate(0, " + i * 20 + ")"; });

legend.append("rect")
    .attr("x", w - 18)
    .attr("y", 4)
    .attr("width", 10)
    .attr("height", 10)
    .style("fill", color);

legend.append("text")
    .attr("x", w - 24)
    .attr("y", 9)
    .attr("dy", ".35em")
    .style("text-anchor", "end")
    .text(function(d) { return d; });
});

var labels = svg.append("g")
    .attr("class", "labels")

labels.append("text")
    .attr("transform", "translate(0, " + h + ")")
    .attr("x", (w-margin.right))
    .attr("dx", "-1.0em")
    .attr("dy", "2.0em")
    .text("[Months]");
```

```
  labels.append("text")
      .attr("transform", "rotate(-90)")
      .attr("y", -40)
      .attr("dy", ".71em")
      .style("text-anchor", "end")
      .text("Attendees");

  var title = svg.append("g")
        .attr("class", "title")

  title.append("text")
      .attr("x", (w / 2))
      .attr("y", -30 )
      .attr("text-anchor", "middle")
      .style("font-size", "22px")
      .text("A multiseries line chart");
</script>
</body>
</html>
```

This chart does nothing more than display the data stored in an external TSV file (see Listing 10-3).

Listing 10-3. data2.tsv

date	europe	asia	america
12-Feb-12	52	40	65
27-Feb-12	56	35	70
02-Mar-12	51	45	62
14-Mar-12	63	44	82
30-Mar-12	64	54	85
07-Apr-12	70	34	72
18-Apr-12	65	36	69
02-May-12	56	40	71
19-May-12	71	55	75
28-May-12	45	32	68
03-Jun-12	64	44	75
18-Jun-12	53	36	78
29-Jun-12	59	42	79

But, instead of displaying all three series with lines of different colors, as seen previously, you provide the user the opportunity to display only one series at a time. Once the chart is loaded in the browser, the user will be able to select any one of the three series and switch between them, without having to load a new page.

Given that the examples are becoming increasingly complex, a good practice is to modularize the code as much as possible. Enclose all code relating exclusively to the display of the chart in an external js file. Let's call this file **multiseries.js**. This JS file will then be included in the HTML page.

```
<script src="./multiseries.js"></script>
```

You begin by enclosing all the code of the Listing 10-2 inside a function, called **draw_multiseries()** (see Listing 10-4). The parts of the code that have been added to the original example, are shown in bold.

Listing 10-4. Multiseries.js

```
function draw_multiseries(s,w,h,series){

var margin = {top: 70, right: 20, bottom: 30, left: 50},
    w = w - margin.left - margin.right,
    h = h - margin.top - margin.bottom;
var parseDate = d3.time.format("%d-%b-%y").parse;
var x = d3.time.scale().range([0, w]);
var y = d3.scale.linear().range([h, 0]);

var color = d3.scale.category10();

var xAxis = d3.svg.axis()
    .scale(x)
    .orient("bottom")
    .ticks(5);

var yAxis = d3.svg.axis()
    .scale(y)
    .orient("left")
    .ticks(5);

var xGrid = d3.svg.axis()
    .scale(x)
    .orient("bottom")
    .ticks(5)
    .tickSize(-h, 0, 0)
    .tickFormat("");

var yGrid = d3.svg.axis()
    .scale(y)
    .orient("left")
    .ticks(5)
    .tickSize(-w, 0, 0)
    .tickFormat("");

var svg = d3.select(s).append("svg")
    .attr("width", w + margin.left + margin.right)
    .attr("height", h + margin.top + margin.bottom)
    .append("g")
    .attr("transform", "translate(" + margin.left + ", " + margin.top + ")");

var line = d3.svg.line()
    .x(function(d) { return x(d.date); })
    .y(function(d) { return y(d.attendee); });
```

```
d3.tsv("data_02.tsv", function(error, data) {

    data.forEach(function(d) {
        d.date = parseDate(d.date);
    });

    color.domain(d3.keys(data[0]).filter(function(key) {
        return key !== "date";
    }));

    var continents = color.domain().map(function(name) {
        return {
            name: name,
            values: data.map(function(d) {
                return {date: d.date, attendee: +d[name]};
            })
        };
    });

    x.domain(d3.extent(data, function(d) { return d.date; }));
    y.domain([
        d3.min(continents, function(c) {
            return d3.min(c.values, function(v) { return v.attendee; });
        }),
        d3.max(continents, function(c) {
            return d3.max(c.values, function(v) { return v.attendee; });
        })
    ]);

    if( typeof series === 'number'){
        if (series < 3) {
            continents = [continents[series]];
        }
    }
    else if(typeof series === 'object'){
        var tmp = [];
        if(series[2])
            tmp.push(continents[2]);
        if(series[1])
            tmp.push(continents[1]);
        if(series[0])
            tmp.push(continents[0]);
        continents = tmp;
    }

    svg.append("g")
        .attr("class", "x axis")
        .attr("transform", "translate(0, " + h + ")")
        .call(xAxis);

    svg.append("g")
        .attr("class", "y axis")
        .call(yAxis);
```

```
    svg.append("g")
        .attr("class", "grid")
        .attr("transform", "translate(0, " + h + ")")
        .call(xGrid);

    svg.append("g")
      .attr("class", "grid")
      .call(yGrid);

    var continent = svg.selectAll(".continent")
        .data(continents)
        .enter().append("g")
        .attr("class", "continent");

    continent.append("path")
        .attr("class", "line")
        .attr("d", function(d) { return line(d.values); })
        .style("stroke", function(d) { return color(d.name); });

var legend = svg.selectAll(".legend")
        .data(color.domain().slice().reverse())
        .enter().append("g")
        .attr("class", "legend")
        .attr("transform", function(d, i) { return "translate(0, " + i * 20 + ")"; });

    Legend.append("rect")
        .attr("x", w - 18)
        .attr("y", 4)
        .attr("width", 10)
        .attr("height", 10)
        .style("fill", color);

    legend.append("text")
        .attr("x", w - 24)
        .attr("y", 9)
        .attr("dy", ".35em")
        .style("text-anchor", "end")
        .text(function(d) { return d; });
});

var labels = svg.append("g")
        .attr("class", "labels");

    labels.append("text")
        .attr("transform", "translate(0, " + h + ")")
        .attr("x", (w-margin.right))
        .attr("dx", "-1.0em")
        .attr("dy", "2.0em")
        .text("[Months]");
```

```
    labels.append("text")
        .attr("transform", "rotate(-90)")
        .attr("y", -40)
        .attr("dy", ".71em")
        .style("text-anchor", "end")
        .text("Attendees");

var title = svg.append("g")
        .attr("class", "title");

    title.append("text")
        .attr("x", (w / 2))
        .attr("y", -30 )
        .attr("text-anchor", "middle")
        .style("font-size", "22px")
        .text("A multiseries line chart");
} //end of the function
```

The function you just defined, accepts four parameters. The first parameter, **tag**, indicates from which tag in the HTML page the chart will begin to be drawn. The second and third parameters, **w** and **h** (width and height) are the dimensions of the canvas on which you're going to draw the chart. The last parameter, **series**, is a value that you will use to communicate to the function which series will be shown on the chart.

Having specified the code by supplying a function with parameters, you can draw the chart externally adjusting its properties each time without having to hack the code. For example, a simple property could be to decide whether or not to display a series in a multiseries chart.

The user will be selecting an option from a set of possible choices; the radio buttons is the best choice of control for this purpose. Therefore, let us assign one series to each radio button. As you can see in Listing 10-5, all the controls (buttons) are contained in an inner list within a table. Each button is specified by an <input> element in which the four series are also specified as values.

Listing 10-5. ch10_01.html

```
<table>
<tr>
  <td>
    <div>
       <ul>
           <li><input name="dataSeries" value="0" type="radio" checked />Europe</li>
           <li><input name="dataSeries" value="1" type="radio" />Asia</li>
           <li><input name="dataSeries" value="2" type="radio" />America</li>
           <li><input name="dataSeries" value="3" type="radio" />All</li>
       </ul>
    </div>
  </td>
</tr>
</table>
```

However, setting the controls definition in an HTML page is not enough; you must also create functions that relate the radio buttons to the D3 chart. Depending on which radio button is in the checked state, a different set from the data set will be loaded in the chart.

In selecting a different radio button, the user changes the checked attribute from 'false' to 'true'. The status change of a radio button involves the activation of the change() function, which detects this event. This function assigns a value to the series variable, indicating which series will be displayed in the chart (a value of 3 indicates that all series should be displayed) and finally forces the replot of the chart. The new data are thus represented in the chart, without having to reload the page (see Listing 10-6).

Listing 10-6. ch10_01.html

```
$(document).ready(function(){
    var series = 3;
    d3.select("#myChart").selectAll("svg").remove();
    draw_multiseries("#myChart",400,400,series);

    $("input[type=radio][name=dataSeries]").attr("checked", false);
    $("input[type=radio][name=dataSeries][value=3]").attr("checked", true);

    $("input[type=radio][name=dataSeries]").change(function(){
        series = parseInt($(this).val());
        d3.select("#myChart").selectAll("svg").remove();
        draw_multiseries("#myChart",400,400,series);
    });
});
```

To customize the elements within the table of controls, you can add a little bit of Cascading Style Sheets (CSS) style, as demonstrated in Listing 10-7.

Listing 10-7. ch10_01.html

```
<HTML>
<HEAD>
    <TITLE>Series selections with controls</TITLE>
<meta charset="utf-8">
<script src="http://code.jquery.com/jquery-1.9.1.min.js"></script>
<script src="http://d3js.org/d3.v3.min.js"></script>
<script src="./multiseries.js"></script>
<link rel="stylesheet" href="./multiseries.css"/>
<style>
li {
    font-family: "Verdana";
    font-size: 16px;
    font-weight: bold;
    text-shadow: 1px 2px 2px #555555;
    margin: 3px;
    list-style: none;
}
}
</style>
 <script>
$(document).ready(function(){
...
```

If you load this web page in the browser, you obtain the chart in Figure 10-3.

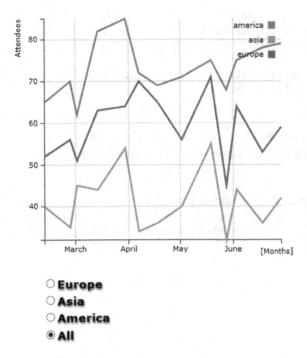

Figure 10-3. *With radio buttons it is possible to select only one series of data*

Now, the user can choose which series will be shown in the chart. Having selected the radio button as a control, the chart will display only one set of data at a time.

Using Sliders

In the previous example the user first set the series to display by checking one of the radio buttons. This time, selecting one of the series, you will keep unchanged all the other series, but you can modify the color of the selected series. In order to do this, you will insert a set of three sliders. In this scenario, the user selects a series in a predefined color, then he or she can modify this color by adjusting the three RGB values that compose it. Now, you have a selection, followed by a fine adjustment.

When you are required to change the value of an attribute by scrolling through contiguous values in a given range, sliders are the kind of control needed. In this case, three sliders are necessary, one for each color (red, green, blue), so that the user can adjust the RGB values to obtain the desired color.

Using the previous example (see Listings 10-3 and 10-4), first you choose the **jQuery Interface library (jQuery UI)** to obtain the sliders.

This library provides a whole range of tools, such as widgets, themes, effects, and interactions that enrich web pages, turning them into highly interactive web applications. For our purposes, widgets are of particular interest. These small graphic applications can prove a valuable tool that, when added to your web pages, makes your charts even more interactive. Widgets facilitate interaction with the program beneath the web page and very often are real mini-applications. In their simplest forms, widgets appear as tables, accordions, combo boxes, or even buttons.

Thus, before adding the sliders to the web page, you must import all the necessary files that are part of this library:

```
<script src="http://code.jquery.com/jquery-1.9.1.min.js"></script>
<link rel="stylesheet" href="http://code.jquery.com/ui/1.10.3/themes/smoothness/jquery-ui.css"/>
<script src="http://code.jquery.com/ui/1.10.3/jquery-ui.min.js"></script>
<script src="../src/js/jquery-1.9.1.js"></script>
<link rel="stylesheet" href="../src/css/smoothness/jquery-ui-1.10.3.custom.min.css"/>
<script src="../src/js/jquery-ui-1.10.3.custom.min.js"></script>
```

___

■ **Note**   If you are working in the workspace made available with the source code that accompanies this book (see Appendix A), you may access the libraries already contained in the workspace by using the following references:

___

Once you have imported all the files, you can start inserting the three sliders in the HTML table. As you can see in Listing 10-8, you eliminate the second column, containing the radio buttons, replacing it with a set of <div> elements (if you are starting directly from here, you can copy the entire listing instead of just the text in bold). The jQuery UI will convert them into sliders (see Chapter 2).

Listing 10-8. ch10_02.html

```
<table>
<tr>
  <td>
    <div>
        <ul>
            <li><input name="dataSeries" value="0" type="radio" checked />Europe</li>
            <li><input name="dataSeries" value="1" type="radio" />Asia</li>
            <li><input name="dataSeries" value="2" type="radio" />America</li>
        </ul>
    </div>
  </td>
  <td>
    <div id="red">
      <div id="slider-text">
        <div id="0">0</div>
        <div id="1">255</div>
      </div>
    </div>
    <div id="green">
      <div id="slider-text">
        <div id="0">0</div>
        <div id="1">255</div>
      </div>
    </div>
```

```
    <div id="blue">
      <div id="slider-text">
        <div id="0">0</div>
        <div id="1">255</div>
      </div>
    </div>
  </td>
</tr>
</table>
```

Furthermore, you have also added two numerical values to each slider with the slider-text id. These values are nothing more than labels that are used to display the minimum and maximum for the range of values (0–255) covered by the three sliders. This methodology can be very useful when you have to represent a scale for each slide in the web page.

Let us now add all the CSS style directives to make sure these new controls can be displayed correctly in the context of the existing page (see Listing 10-9).

Listing 10-9. ch10_02.html

```
<style>
...
#red, #green, #blue {
    float: left;
    margin: 15px;
    left: 50px;
}
#red .ui-slider-range {
    background: #ef2929;
}
#red .ui-slider-handle {
    border-color: #ef2929;
}
#green .ui-slider-range {
    background: #8ae234;
}
#green .ui-slider-handle {
    border-color: #8ae234;
}
#blue .ui-slider-range {
    background: #729fcf;
}
#blue .ui-slider-handle {
    border-color: #729fcf;
}
#slider-text div {
    font-family: "Verdana";
    font-size: 10px;
    position: relative;
    left: 17px;
}
</style>
```

With regard to the section of code in JavaScript, you keep only the part that manages the radio buttons for the selection of the desired series, integrating it with a new section of code that handles the RGB values, adjusted through the three sliders, as shown in Listing 10-10. The three RGB values are then converted to hexadecimal numbers through an appropriate function and combined to form the HTML color code, expressed by a pound sign (#), followed by six hexadecimal characters ('rrggbb'), where each pair represents a value from 0 to 255, translated into hexadecimal format.

Listing 10-10. ch10_02.html

```
$(document).ready(function(){

var colors = ["#ffc87c", "#ffeba8", "#f3b080"];
var series = 0;
d3.select("#myChart").selectAll("svg").remove();
draw_multiseries("#myChart",400,400,series,colors);

$("input[type=radio][name=dataSeries]").attr("checked", false);
$("input[type=radio][name=dataSeries][value=0]").attr("checked", true);

$("input[type=radio][name=dataSeries]").change(function(){
    series = parseInt($(this).val());
    d3.select("#myChart").selectAll("svg").remove();
    draw_multiseries("#myChart",400,400,series,colors);
});

function hexFromRGB(r, g, b) {
    var hex = [
        r.toString( 16 ),
        g.toString( 16 ),
        b.toString( 16 )
    ];
    $.each( hex, function( nr, val ) {
        if ( val.length === 1 ) {
            hex[ nr ] = "0" + val;
        }
    });
    return hex.join( "" ).toUpperCase();
};

$( "#red, #green, #blue" ).slider({
    orientation: "vertical",
    range: "min",
    max: 255,
    change: refreshPlot
});

$( "#red" ).slider( "value", 75 );
$( "#green" ).slider( "value", 178 );
$( "#blue" ).slider( "value", 197 );
```

```
function refreshPlot() {
    var r = $( "#red" ).slider( "value" );
    var g = $( "#green" ).slider( "value" );
    var b = $( "#blue" ).slider( "value" );
    var col = hexFromRGB(r, g, b);
    d3.select("#myChart").selectAll("svg").remove();
    colors[series] = "#"+col;
    draw_multiseries("#myChart",400,400,series,colors);
}
    $("[id=0]").css('top','90px');
    $("[id=1]").css('top','-20px');
});
```

For this specific example, you need an additional argument to be passed to the **draw_multiseries()** function, that is, the current color indicated by the three RGB sliders. In this regard, I prefer to pass as a fifth argument the entire **colors** array composed of three colors related to the three series. In this way you update the values of the three colors outside the function every time you go to change the position of one of the sliders and let the draw_multiseries() function have only the task of displaying the chart.

So you have to make some changes in the **draw_multiseries()** function in **multiseries.js** (see Listing 10-11), then save it as **multiseries2.js**. Do not forget to include this new file in place of the previous one in the HTML page.

```
<script src="./multiseries2.js"></script>
```

Listing 10-11. Multiseries2.js

```
function draw_multiseries(s,w,h,series,colors){

    ...
    //var color = d3.scale.category10();
    ...
    if( typeof series === 'number'){
       if (series < 3) {
          //continents = [continents[series]];
       }
    }
    ...
};
```

In Figure 10-4 the user can decide which series to display and change it by modifying the RBG values through three sliders.

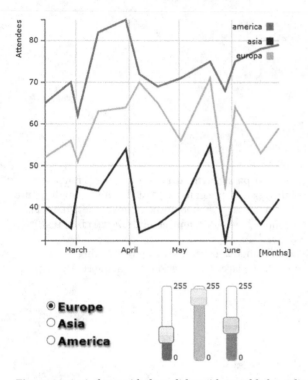

Figure 10-4. *A chart with three slider widgets added to adjust the RGB levels*

Using Check Boxes

In the previous examples, the user could choose only one among the number of series that could be displayed. However, typically the user will want to be able to decide which series should be displayed and which should not, choosing, for instance, to display two or more sets at the same time. This entails dealing with multiple choices within the same group. To enable the user to make this kind of choice, you have to opt for check boxes.

Generally, check boxes are grouped in a list, represented by empty boxes (see Figure 10-1). Unlike radio buttons, these controls are not mutually exclusive, but rather multiple choice. Thus, you can select all, some, or none of the values that they represent (whereas with radio buttons an item has to be selected).

Similar to radio buttons, there is a check box for each series, and if a check box is checked, the corresponding series is shown in the chart. Yet, unlike radio buttons, check boxes are independent of each other: their state (checked or unchecked) does not affect the status of the others.

Often, when you have a list of check boxes, it can be very useful to add two buttons with the "CheckAll/ UncheckAll" functionality, thereby allowing the choice of selecting/deselecting all the check boxes with one click.

Let's delete the table containing the previous controls (radio buttons, sliders) and substitute it with a new one containing check boxes, as shown in Listing 10-12 (if you are starting directly from here, you can copy the entire listing without considering the previous controls). Moreover, in addition to the four controls for as many series, you can add a button at the end to manage the feature "CheckAll/UncheckAll".

Listing 10-12. ch10_03.html

```
<table>
<tr>
   <td>
      <div>
        <ul>
          <li><input name="0" type="checkbox" checked />Europe</li>
          <li><input name="1" type="checkbox" checked />Asia</li>
          <li><input name="2" type="checkbox" checked />America</li>
          <li><input type="button" name="checkall" value="Uncheck All"></li>
        </ul>
      </div>
   </td>
</tr>
</table>
```

As with radio buttons, you have to add jQuery methods to bind the events that have occurred with these controls. First, you define the status of each check box. Normally, they should all be checked. Then, you define five jQuery methods, enabling or disabling the series to be represented, and then force the replot.

From the code, you must delete all the rows that handled the previous controls and in their place, write the methods in Listing 10-13.

Listing 10-13. ch10_03.html

```
$(document).ready(function(){

var series = [true,true,true];
d3.select("#myChart").selectAll("svg").remove();
draw_multiseries("#myChart",400,400,series);

$("input[type=checkbox][name=0]").change(function(){
    if(this.checked){
        series[0] = true;
    }else{
        series[0] = false;
    }
    d3.select("#myChart").selectAll("svg").remove();
    draw_multiseries("#myChart",400,400,series);
});

$("input[type=checkbox][name=1]").change(function(){
    if(this.checked){
        series[1] = true;
    }else{
        series[1] = false;
    }
    d3.select("#myChart").selectAll("svg").remove();
    draw_multiseries("#myChart",400,400,series);
});
```

```
$("input[type=checkbox][name=2]").change(function(){
    if(this.checked){
        series[2] = true;
    }else{
        series[2] = false;
    }
    d3.select("#myChart").selectAll("svg").remove();
    draw_multiseries("#myChart",400,400,series);
});

$("input[type=button][name=checkall]").click(function(){
    if(this.value == "Check All"){
        series = [true,true,true];
        $("input[type=checkbox][name=0]").prop("checked", true);
        $("input[type=checkbox][name=1]").prop("checked", true);
        $("input[type=checkbox][name=2]").prop("checked", true);
        d3.select("#myChart").selectAll("svg").remove();
        draw_multiseries("#myChart",400,400,series);
        this.value = "Uncheck All";
    }else{
        series = [false,false,false];
        $("input[type=checkbox][name=0]").prop("checked", false);
        $("input[type=checkbox][name=1]").prop("checked", false);
        $("input[type=checkbox][name=2]").prop("checked", false);
        d3.select("#myChart").selectAll("svg").remove();
        draw_multiseries("#myChart",400,400,series);
        this.value = "Check All";
    }
});

});
```

In this example we do not need to pass a property, perhaps the color of the previous example. Then you can go back to using the original function draw_multiseries (the one with four parameters).

```
<script src="./multiseries.js"></script>
```

As shown in Figure 10-5, the user can now select the series he or she wants to see displayed in the chart.

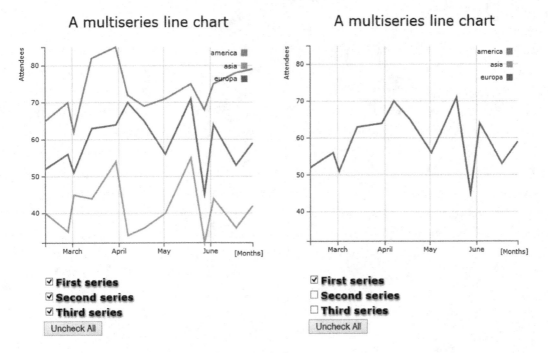

Figure 10-5. *A custom legend with check boxes and a button*

If you click the button labeled "Uncheck all", all the check boxes will be unchecked, and the corresponding series will be hidden in the plot. Subsequently, the button will show the label "Check All." When clicking it this time, all the check boxes will be checked, and the corresponding series will be shown in the chart.

Summary

In this chapter, you have seen how to use various controls, such as **radio buttons**, **sliders**, and **check boxes**, to increase the interactivity of a chart. With the introduction of controls, we, as programmers, are no longer the only ones to have direct control of the values of the properties of the chart; through such controls the user is also able to make the appropriate choices.

In addition, you learned how to integrate **jQuery UI widgets** with the D3 library, using these widgets **as controls**.

In the next chapter, you will complete this integration by using jQuery UI widgets **as containers** for your charts. This combination greatly expands the possibilities for development and representation of charts using the D3 library.

■ ■ ■

CHAPTER 11

Embedding D3 Charts in jQuery Widgets

In this chapter, you'll exploit the capability to represent the charts within some specific containers, often referred to as widgets, such as tabbed panels and accordions, provided by some libraries, including jQuery UI. This enables you to exploit the great potential of the jQuery UI widgets to further improve the way in which your charts are represented.

The advantages of combining jQuery UI and D3 libraries are various: you can display more charts occupying the same space in the web page, and at the same time keep the context of the page clean and tidy. Another advantage is that jQuery UI widgets can be resized, and even users can resize a D3 chart.

In this chapter, you'll explore three simple cases where the benefits just mentioned will be made evident.

jQuery UI: Widgets

Along with the D3 library, there is another library that can help you integrate your web page with interactive and graphic objects: the jQuery UI. This library provides an entire range of tools, such as widgets, themes, effects, and interactions, which enrich web pages, turning them into highly interactive web applications. For our purposes, widgets are of particular interest. These small graphic applications can prove a valuable tool that, when added to your web pages, make your charts even more interactive. Widgets facilitate interaction of the program beneath the web page and very often are real mini-applications. In their simplest forms, widgets appear as tables, accordions, combo boxes, or even buttons.

As with the D3 library, you will need to include the plug-in file in the web page if you want to integrate its widgets. In the examples that we will see in this chapter, we will use the jQuery UI version 1.10.3. You must also include the CSS file representing the theme. This can be done through the Google Hosted Libraries service:

```
<link rel="stylesheet" href="http://ajax.googleapis.com/ajax/libs/jqueryui/1.10.3/themes/smoothness/
jquery-ui.css"/>
<script src="http://ajax.googleapis.com/ajax/libs/jquery/1.9.1/jquery.min.js">
</script>
<script src="http://ajax.googleapis.com/ajax/libs/jqueryui/1.10.3/jquery-ui.min.js">
</script>
```

You can also download from the official CDN jQuery site:

```
<link rel="stylesheet" href="http://code.jquery.com/ui/1.10.3/themes/smoothness/jquery-ui.css"/>
<script src="http://code.jquery.com/jquery-1.9.1.min.js"></script>
<script src="http://code.jquery.com/ui/1.10.3/jquery-ui.min.js"></script>
```

If you prefer to download the libraries locally or to use the workspace in the source code accompanying this book (see Appendix A), you can refer to the libraries as follows:

```
<link rel="stylesheet" href="../src/css/smoothness/jquery-ui-1.10.3.custom.min.css"/>
<script src="../src/js/jquery-1.9.1.js"></script>
<script src="../src/js/jquery-ui-1.10.3.custom.min.js"></script>
```

▪ **Note** The theme for the jQuery UI widgets used in this book is **smoothness**. The list of available themes is vast and covers many combinations of colors and shapes. This well-stocked list is available on ThemeRoller (`http://jqueryui.com/themeroller`). ThemeRoller is a page on the official jQuery web site that allows you to preview widgets and to then download your favorite theme from those available.

On visiting the official jQuery UI web site (`http://jqueryui.com/`), you will notice that the widgets provided by this library are numerous. Here, I will discuss only the most common examples, especially those that are most likely to be integrated into a page containing charts.

As you will see throughout this book, some of these widgets will be used as containers, exploiting their particular capabilities, such as resizing and encapsulation, including these:

- Accordions

- Tabs

Other widgets will be used to replace the simple controls that HTML offers, as the former are much more advanced and rich in functionality, including the following:

- Buttons

- Combo boxes

- Menus

- Sliders

Still other widgets will also perform the function of indicators. With these, you will see how to integrate a particular widget class:

- Progress bars

Accordion

An accordion widget is a set of collapsible panels that enable the web page to show a large amount of information in a compact space panels (for more information, please refer to `http://jqueryui.com/accordion/`).

The jQuery UI accordion allows you to organize related content into distinct sections, called panels, with any one panel visible at a time. Each panel can hold a thematic area or, as you will see in later chapters, different types of charts. The content is revealed by clicking the tab for each panel, allowing the user to move from one panel to another without changing the page. The panels of the accordion expand and contract, according to the choice of the user, such that only one panel shows its content at any given time.

The HTML structure you need to write to obtain an accordion widget in the page is composed of an outer `<div>` tag containing all the panels. Each panel in turn is specified by a heading placed between two `<h3>` tags and a `<div></div>` pair, with the content inbetween. Listing 11-1 represents a simple accordion with four panels.

Listing 11-1. Ch11_01a.html

```
<div id="accordion">
    <h3>First header</h3>
    <div>First content panel</div>
    <h3>Second header</h3>
    <div>Second content panel</div>
    <h3>Third header</h3>
    <div>Third content panel</div>
    <h3>Fourth header</h3>
    <div>Fourth content panel</div>
</div>
```

In JavaScript code, you need to add the snippet in Listing 11-2 to obtain an accordion widget.

Listing 11-2. Ch11_01a.html

```
$(function() {
    $( "#accordion" ).accordion();
});
```

Figure 11-1 illustrates our accordion.

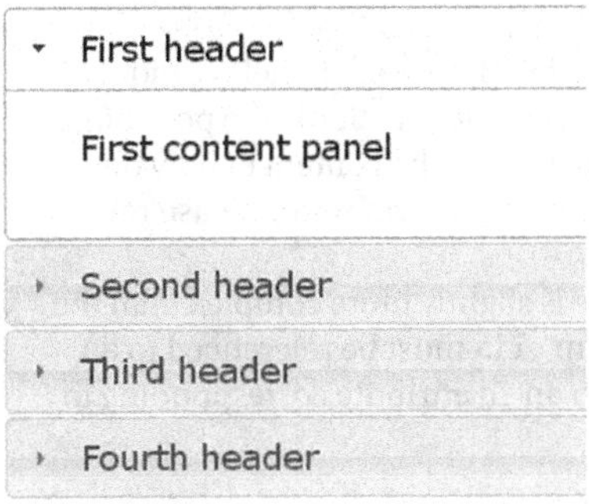

Figure 11-1. *An accordion consists of collapsible panels suitable for containing information in a limited amount of space*

But, that is not enough. It would be better if you could control the style of the accordion. This can be accomplished by adding the code given in Listing 11-3.

Listing 11-3. Ch11_01a.html

```
<style type="text/css">
    .ui-accordion {
        width: 690px;
        margin: 2em auto;
    }
    .ui-accordion-header {
        font-size: 15px;
        font-weight: bold;
    }
```

```
    .ui-accordion-content {
        font-size: 12px;
    }
</style>
```

The result is shown in Figure 11-2.

Figure 11-2. *By modifying the CSS style properties, you can change the accordion's appearance as you like*

Tab

A widget that is very similar to the accordion in its functionality is the panel with tabs. Here, each panel is unique, but there are several tabs at the top, identified by different headings. Nonetheless, this widget affords the possibility to show a large amount of information in a limited space, and the user can choose to view the content of only one tab at a time. More significant is the loss of the vertical expansion of panels (for more information, please refer to http://jqueryui.com/tabs/).

The HTML structure you need to write to obtain a tab widget in the web page is slightly more complex than the previous one. The headings are given in an unordered list <ul>, in which each item <li> must be referenced to an anchor tag <a>. The contents of every tab are enclosed in a <div></div> pair, with an id attribute corresponding to the references in the anchor tags (see Listing 11-4).

Listing 11-4. Ch11_01b.html

```
<div id="tabs">
  <ul>
    <li><a href="#tabs-1">First header</a></li>
    <li><a href="#tabs-2">Second header</a></li>
    <li><a href="#tabs-3">Third header</a></li>
    <li><a href="#tabs-4">Fourth header</a></li>
  </ul>
  <div id="tabs-1">
    <p>First tab panel</p>
  </div>
  <div id="tabs-2">
    <p>Second tab panel</p>
  </div>
   <div id="tabs-3">
    <p>Third tab panel</p>
  </div>
```

```
    <div id="tabs-4">
      <p>Fourth tab panel</p>
    </div>
  </div>
</div>
```

In JavaScript code, you need to specify the tab widget, as shown in Listing 11-5.

Listing 11-5. Ch11_01b.html

```
$(function() {
    $( "#tabs" ).tabs();
});
```

The CSS style classes must also be defined, as shown in Listing 11-6.

Listing 11-6. Ch11_01b.html

```
<style type="text/css">
    .ui-tabs {
      width: 690px;
      margin: 2em auto;
    }
    .ui-tabs-header {
      font-size: 15px;
      font-weight: bold;
    }
    .ui-tabs-panel {
      font-size: 12px;
    }
</style>
```

When the procedure is complete, you will get the widgets illustrated in Figure 11-3.

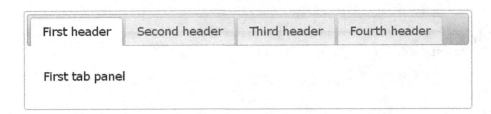

Figure 11-3. *The tab widget consists of multiple panels that occupy the same area*

D3 Charts on Tabs

The first widget you're going to use as a container is the *tab*. Inserting charts inside tabs allows you to display different charts on the same page within a limited area. In this example, you'll place three different D3 charts within three tabs, called Tab 1, Tab 2, and Tab 3. In the first tab you'll place a multiseries line chart, in the second tab you'll place a bar chart, and in the last tab a pie chart. You won't be analyzing these charts in detail, because they are exactly the same kind of charts used in previous chapters. Each type of chart will be enclosed in its corresponding JS file and expressed as a function (see Listings 11-7 through 11-9).

Listing 11-7. linechart.js

```
function draw_linechart(s,w,h){
margin_x = 32;
margin_y = 20;

var data = [{x:0,y:100},{x:10,y:110},{x:20,y:140},
                {x:30,y:130},{x:40,y:80},{x:50,y:75},
                {x:60,y:120},{x:70,y:130},{x:80,y:100}];

var ax = [];
var ay = [];
data.forEach(function(d,i){
    ax[i] = d.x;
    ay[i] = d.y;
})
var xMax = d3.max(ax);
var yMax = d3.max(ay);
var xLowLim = 0;
var xUpLim = d3.max(ax);
var yUpLim = 1.2 * d3.max(ay);
var yLowLim = 0.8 * d3.min(ay);

var line = d3.svg.line()
    .x(function(d) { return x(d.x); })
    .y(function(d) { return -y(d.y); })

y = d3.scale.linear().domain([yLowLim, yUpLim]).range([0 + margin_y, h - margin_y]);
x = d3.scale.linear().domain([xLowLim, xUpLim]).range([0 + margin_x, w - margin_x]);

var svg = d3.select(s)
    .append("svg:svg")
    .attr("width", w)
    .attr("height", h)

var g = svg.append("svg:g")
    .attr("transform", "translate(0, " + h + ")");

// draw the xLabels
g.selectAll(".xLabel")
    .data(x.ticks(5))
    .enter().append("svg:text")
    .attr("class", "xLabel")
    .text(String)
    .attr("x", function(d) { return x(d) })
    .attr("y", 0)
    .attr("text-anchor", "middle");

// draw the yLabels
g.selectAll(".yLabel")
    .data(y.ticks(5))
    .enter().append("svg:text")
```

```
        .attr("class", "yLabel")
        .text(String)
        .attr("x", 25)
        .attr("y", function(d) { return -y(d) })
        .attr("text-anchor", "end");

// draw the x ticks
g.selectAll(".xTicks")
    .data(x.ticks(5))
    .enter().append("svg:line")
    .attr("class", "xTicks")
    .attr("x1", function(d) { return x(d); })
    .attr("y1", -y(yLowLim))
    .attr("x2", function(d) { return x(d); })
    .attr("y2", -y(yLowLim)-5)

// draw the y ticks
g.selectAll(".yTicks")
    .data(y.ticks(5))
    .enter().append("svg:line")
    .attr("class", "yTicks")
    .attr("y1", function(d) { return -y(d); })
    .attr("x1", x(xLowLim))
    .attr("y2", function(d) { return -y(d); })
    .attr("x2", x(xLowLim)+5)

// draw the x grid
g.selectAll(".xGrids")
    .data(x.ticks(5))
    .enter().append("svg:line")
    .attr("class", "xGrids")
    .attr("x1", function(d) { return x(d); })
    .attr("y1", -y(yLowLim))
    .attr("x2", function(d) { return x(d); })
    .attr("y2", -y(yUpLim))

// draw the y grid
g.selectAll(".yGrids")
    .data(y.ticks(5))
    .enter().append("svg:line")
    .attr("class", "yGrids")
    .attr("y1", function(d) { return -y(d); })
    .attr("x1", x(xUpLim)+20)
    .attr("y2", function(d) { return -y(d); })
    .attr("x2", x(xLowLim))

// draw the x axis
g.append("svg:line")
    .attr("x1", x(xLowLim))
    .attr("y1", -y(yLowLim))
    .attr("x2", 1.2*x(xUpLim))
    .attr("y2", -y(yLowLim))
```

```
// draw the y axis
g.append("svg:line")
    .attr("x1", x(xLowLim))
    .attr("y1", -y(yLowLim))
    .attr("x2", x(xLowLim))
    .attr("y2", -1.2*y(yUpLim))

g.append("svg:path")
      .attr("class", "axisArrow")
      .attr("d", function() {
        var x1 = x(xUpLim)+23, x2 = x(xUpLim)+30;
        var y2 = -y(yLowLim), y1 = y2-3, y3 = y2+3
        return 'M'+x1+','+y1+','+x2+','+y2+','+x1+','+y3;
});

g.append("svg:path")
      .attr("class", "axisArrow")
      .attr("d", function() {
        var y1 = -y(yUpLim)-13, y2 = -y(yUpLim)-20;
        var x2 = x(xLowLim), x1 = x2-3, x3 = x2+3
        return 'M'+x1+','+y1+','+x2+','+y2+','+x3+','+y1;
});

// draw the line of data points
g.append("svg:path").attr("d", line(data));

};
```

Listing 11-8. barchart.js

```
function draw_barchart(s,w,h){

var margin = {top: 70, right: 20, bottom: 30, left: 40},
    w = w - margin.left - margin.right,
    h = h - margin.top - margin.bottom;

var color = d3.scale.category10();

var x = d3.scale.ordinal()
    .rangeRoundBands([0, w], .1);
var y = d3.scale.linear()
    .range([h, 0]);

var formatPercent = d3.format(".0%");

var xAxis = d3.svg.axis()
    .scale(x)
    .orient("bottom");
```

```
var yAxis = d3.svg.axis()
    .scale(y)
    .orient("left")
    //.tickFormat(formatPercent);
    .tickFormat(d3.format(".0%"));

var yGrid = d3.svg.axis()
    .scale(y)
    .orient("left")
    .ticks(5)
    .tickSize(-w, 0, 0)
    .tickFormat("")

var svg = d3.select(s).append("svg")
    .attr("width", w + margin.left + margin.right)
    .attr("height", h + margin.top + margin.bottom)
    .append("g")
    .attr("transform", "translate(" + margin.left + "," + margin.top + ")");

d3.csv("data_04.csv", function(error, data) {

  var sum = 0;
  data.forEach(function(d) {
    d.income = +d.income;
    sum += d.income;
  });

  x.domain(data.map(function(d) { return d.country; }));
  y.domain([0, d3.max(data, function(d) { return d.income/sum; })]);

  svg.append("g")
      .attr("class", "x axis")
      .attr("transform", "translate(0," + h + ")")
      .call(xAxis);

  svg.append("g")
      .attr("class", "y axis")
      .call(yAxis)

  svg.append("g")
      .attr("class", "grid")
      .call(yGrid);

var labels = svg.append("g")
      .attr("class", "labels")

  labels.append("text")
      .attr("transform", "rotate(-90)")
      .attr("y", 6)
      .attr("dy", ".71em")
      .style("text-anchor", "end")
      .text("Income [%]");
```

```
svg.selectAll(".bar")
    .data(data)
    .enter().append("rect")
    .attr("class", "bar")
    .attr("x", function(d) { return x(d.country); })
    .attr("width", x.rangeBand())
    .attr("y", function(d) { return y(d.income/sum); })
    .attr("height", function(d) { return h - y(d.income/sum); })
    .attr("fill", function(d) { return color(d.country); });

});

};
```

Listing 11-9. piechart.js

```
function draw_piechart(s,w,h){

var margin = {top: 10, right: 10, bottom: 10, left: 10},
    w = w - margin.left - margin.right,
    h = h - margin.top - margin.bottom;

var color = d3.scale.category10();

var radius = Math.min(w, h) / 2;

var arc = d3.svg.arc()
    .outerRadius(radius)
    .innerRadius(0);

var pie = d3.layout.pie()
    .sort(null)
    .value(function(d) { return d.income; });

var svg = d3.select(s).append("svg")
    .attr("width", w + margin.left + margin.right)
    .attr("height", h + margin.top + margin.bottom)
    .append("g")
    .attr("transform", "translate(" +(w/2+margin.left)+
                    "," +(h/2+margin.top)+ ")");

d3.csv("data_04.csv", function(error, data) {

  data.forEach(function(d) {
    d.income = +d.income;
  });

var g = svg.selectAll(".arc")
    .data(pie(data))
    .enter().append("g")
    .attr("class", "arc");
```

```
  g.append("path")
      .attr("d", arc)
      .style("fill", function(d) { return color(d.data.country); });

  g.append("text")
      .attr("transform", function(d) {
            return "translate(" + arc.centroid(d) + ")"; })
      .style("text-anchor", "middle")
      .text(function(d) { return d.data.country; });

});

};
```

With the introduction of so many graphic elements on the web page, the use of Cascading Style Sheets (CSS) styles becomes increasingly important. You need to define some settings in order to modify the tabs' appearance so that they will fit to your needs. Add the style settings in Listing 11-10.

Listing 11-10. Ch11-02.html

```
<style>
.ui-tabs {
    width: 690px;
    margin: 2em auto;
}
.ui-tabs-nav {
    font-size: 12px;
}
.ui-tabs-panel {
    font-size: 14px;
}
.jqplot-target {
    font-size: 18px;
}
ol.description {
    list-style-position: inside;
    font-size: 15px;
    margin: 1.5em auto;
    padding: 0 15px;
    width: 600px;
}
</style>
```

As you did previously for the JavaScript code, do the same for the CSS. Define separately Cascading Style Sheets (CSS) styles of the multiseries line chart by enclosing them in an external file called **linechart.css** (see Listing 11-11).

Listing 11-11. Linechart.css

```
path {
    stroke: black;
    stroke-width: 3;
    fill: none;
}
```

```
line {
    stroke: black;
}
.xGrids {
    stroke: lightgray;
}
.yGrids {
    stroke: lightgray;
}
text {
    font-family: Verdana;
    font-size: 9pt;
}
.axisArrow {
    stroke: black;
    stroke-width: 1;
    fill: black;
}
```

Now it is time to add the jQueryUI tabs() function at the end of the $(document).ready() function, as shown in Listing 11-12.

Listing 11-12. ch11_02.html

```
$(document).ready(function(){

  $("#tabs").tabs();

    draw_linechart("#tabs-1",400,300);
    draw_barchart("#tabs-2",400,300);
    draw_piechart("#tabs-3",400,300);

});
```

Selecting a tab will replot the content of the chart within it. Now, in the <body> part of the web page, you need to add the <div> elements that the jQuery UI library will convert into tabs. The way to do that is to specify a <div> element with tabs as id. Inside it, you define a list of three items, each representing a tab. After the list, you must define another three subdivisions of tabs: three additional <div> elements called tabs-1, tabs-2, and tabs-3. You are going to put these into your charts: chart1, chart2, and chart3 (see Listing 11-13).

Listing 11-13. ch11_02.html

```
<div id="tabs">
    <ul>
      <li><a href="#tabs-1">Tab 1</a></li>
      <li><a href="#tabs-2">Tab 2</a></li>
      <li><a href="#tabs-3">Tab 3</a></li>
    </ul>
    <div id="tabs-1">
      <p>This is the line chart</p>
    </div>
```

```
      <div id="tabs-2">
        <p>This is the bar chart</p>
      </div>
      <div id="tabs-3">
        <p>This is the pie chart</p>
      </div>
</div>
```

Figure 11-4 shows the final result.

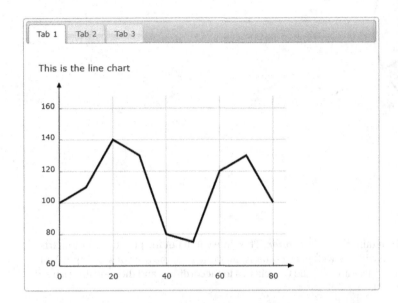

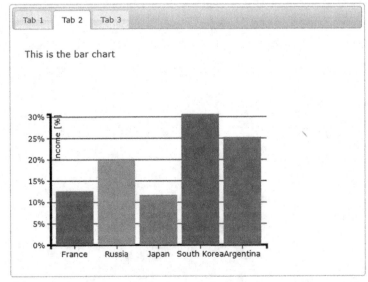

Figure 11-4. *A page with three tabs containing different charts*

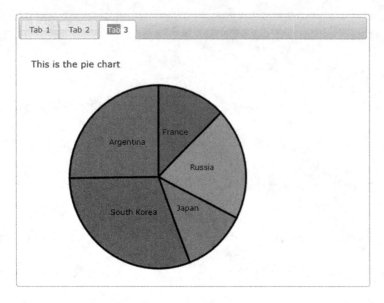

Figure 11-4. (*continued*)

D3 Charts on Accordions

Another commonly used type of jQuery UI container is the *accordion*. This time you'll put the previous three charts into accordions. The list of plug-ins to include with the web page remains the same as in the previous example. You need to make some changes in the CSS styles; there are specific CSS classes for accordions, and their attributes need to be specified. They are shown in Listing 11-14.

Listing 11-14. ch11_03.html

```
<style type="text/css">
.ui-accordion {
    width: 690px;
    margin: 2em auto;
}
.ui-accordion-header {
    font-size: 12px;
}
.ui-accordion-content {
    font-size: 14px;
}
.jqplot-target {
    font-size: 18px;
}
ol.description {
    list-style-position: inside;
    font-size: 15px;
    margin: 1.5em auto;
```

```
    padding: 0 15px;
    width: 600px;
}
.section {
    width: 400px;
    height: 200px;
    margin-top: 20px;
    margin-left: 20px;
}
</style>
```

As you did in the previous example, you must create the jQueryUi widget. You can do this by calling the accordion() function as shown in Listing 11-15:

Listing 11-15. ch11_03.html

```
$(document).ready(function(){

    $("#accordion").accordion();
    draw_linechart("#chart1",400,300);
    draw_barchart("#chart2",400,300);
    draw_piechart("#chart3",400,300);

});
```

As you can see, the way in which you define the accordions is very similar to the way you define the tabs. In the same way, you now define the <div> elements that will be converted into accordion tabs in the HTML code (see Listing 11-16).

Listing 11-16. ch11_03.html

```
<div id="accordion" style="margin-top:50px">
  <h3><a href="#">Section 1</a></h3>
  <div>
    <p>This is the bar chart</p>
    <div id="chart1"></div>
  </div>

  <h3><a href="#">Section 2</a></h3>
  <div>
    <p>This is the multiseries line chart</p>
    <div class="section" id="chart2"></div>
  </div>

  <h3><a href="#">Section 3</a></h3>
  <div>
    <p>This is the pie chart</p>
    <div class="section" id="chart3"></div>
  </div>
</div>
```

As you can see in Figure 11-5, the result is similar to the previous one, but this time the different charts are replaced by sliding the accordion tab vertically.

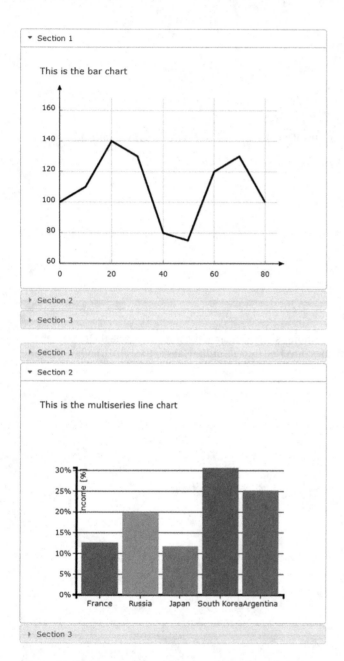

Figure 11-5. An accordion widget containing three charts

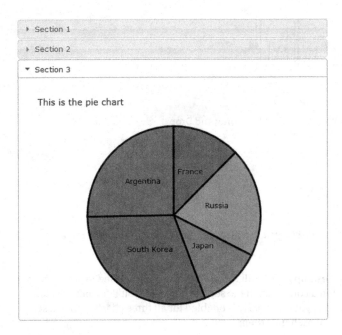

Figure 11-5. (*continued*)

By default, you have to click the accordion headers to activate the associated panel. But you can change this behavior, setting the event that will activate the section contained in each single panel. For example, you can set the mouseover as the activating event. To do this, you need to pass the event as an argument to the accordion() function.

```
$("#accordion").accordion({ event: "mouseover" });
```

If you change the code, you will see each section expanding whenever you mouseover the corresponding accordion header.

Resizable and Draggable Charts

Two other features that you can widely exploit in your charts enable users to resize and drag the container area. A resizable frame within a web page allows you to arbitrarily change its size and the size of the objects it contains. This feature could be combined with the ability to drag elements within the page, which would enable them to occupy different positions relative to the original.

In addition to giving fluidity to the layout of the page, this feature can sometimes be useful when you want the user to interactively manage spaces occupied by different frames on the page (see Figure 11-6).

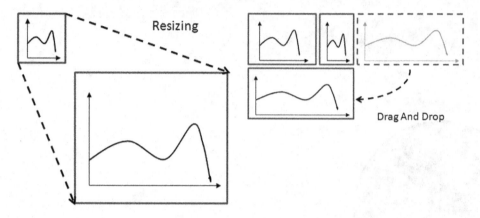

Figure 11-6. *Enclosing the charts in jQueryUI containers enables you to resize and move them around the page*

In this section, you'll see two examples. In the first example, you will focus on the resizing applied to a line chart. You'll see how easy it is to resize a chart contained within a container. In the second example, you'll further develop the example by adding two more line charts. Once the draggable property is enabled for all three charts, you will see how you can change their positions to your liking, or even exchange them.

A Resizable Line Chart

In this example you'll use a simple line chart. Thus, you'll need to include only the CSS and the **draw_linechart()** function contained in the file linechart.js (see Listings 11-7 and 11-11).

```
<link rel="stylesheet" href="./linechart.css" />
<script src="./linechart.js"></script>
```

Instead, add the CSS style relating to the jQuery UI container directly to your HTML page (see Listing 11-17).

Listing 11-17. ch11_04.html

```
<style type="text/css">
.chart-container {
    border: 1px solid darkblue;
    padding: 30px 0px 30px 30px;
    width: 900px;
    height: 400px;
}
#chart1 {
    width: 96%;
    height: 96%;
}
</style>
```

To the <body> part of the web page, you now add the <div> element, which will be the container enclosing the line chart(see Listing 11-18).

Listing 11-18. ch11_04.html

```
<div id="resizable" class="chart-container">
    <div id="chart1"></div>
</div>
```

Now, after you have defined the chart-container as container, you can handle it with two jQuery methods—the resizable() function adds the resizable functionality and the bind() function binds the event of resizing to the replotting of the chart (see Listing 11-19).

Listing 11-19. ch11_04.html

```
$(document).ready(function(){

  $('div.chart-container').resizable({delay:20});
  $('div.chart-container').bind('resize', function(event, ui) {
      d3.select("#chart1").selectAll("svg").remove();
      draw_linechart("#chart1", ui.size.width, ui.size.height);
  });
  draw_linechart("#chart1",400,300);
});
```

The result is a resizable chart, shown in Figure 11-7, with a small grey triangle in the bottom-right corner. By clicking on it, the user can resize the container and consequently the D3 chart.

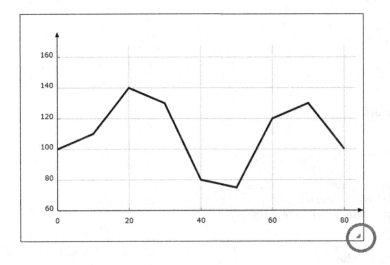

Figure 11-7. *A resizable line chart*

Three Draggable Line Charts

Starting from the previous example, you will add two more line charts by placing them in two independent containers. The goal here—in addition to making all three containers resizable—is to make the containers draggable. The final result is a web page with three line charts, the position of which can be changed by dragging them, even exchanging their positions.

Start by making some small additions to the previous example. In Listing 11-20, you add the other two containers (chart-container2 and chart-container3) with the new line charts inside, naming them chart2 and chart3, respectively.

Listing 11-20. ch11_04b.html

```
<BODY>
<div class="chart-container">
    <div id="chart1"></div>
</div>
<div class="chart-container2">
    <div id="chart2"></div>
</div>
<div class="chart-container3">
    <div id="chart3"></div>
</div>
</BODY>
```

Now that you have created three different containers, each of them may hold one of the three chart seen in the previous examples. Now you'll activate the draggable feature for the three containers. Doing this is really quite simple; you need to add the function to the three jQuery selections applied to each container, as shown in Listing 11-21. Moreover, you'll add the resizing feature for the two new containers the same way as was done for the first container.

Listing 11-21. ch11_04b.html

```
$(document).ready(function(){

    $('div.chart-container').draggable({
        cursor: 'move'
    });
    $('div.chart-container2').draggable({
        cursor: 'move'
    });
    $('div.chart-container3').draggable({
        cursor: 'move'
    });

    $('div.chart-container').resizable({delay:20});
    $('div.chart-container').bind('resize', function(event, ui) {
        d3.select("#chart1").selectAll("svg").remove();
        draw_linechart("#chart1", ui.size.width, ui.size.height);
    });

    $('div.chart-container2').resizable({delay:20});
    $('div.chart-container2').bind('resize', function(event, ui) {
        d3.select("#chart2").selectAll("svg").remove();
        draw_piechart("#chart2", ui.size.width, ui.size.height);
    });
    $('div.chart-container3').resizable({delay:20});
    $('div.chart-container3').bind('resize', function(event, ui) {
        d3.select("#chart3").selectAll("svg").remove();
        draw_barchart("#chart3", ui.size.width, ui.size.height);
    });
```

```
    draw_linechart("#chart1",300,200);
    draw_piechart("#chart2",200,200);
    draw_barchart("#chart3",500,200);

});
```

Nothing remains but to add CSS styles, thus defining the initial position and size of each container, as shown in Listing 11-22.

Listing 11-22. ch11_04b.html

```
<style type="text/css">
.chart-container {
    border: 1px solid darkblue;
    padding: 30px 0px 30px 30px;
    width: 300px;
    height: 200px;
    position: relative;
    float: left;
}
.chart-container2 {
    border: 1px solid darkblue;
    padding: 30px 0px 30px 30px;
    width: 200px;
    height: 200px;
    position: relative;
    float: left;
    margin-left: 20px;
}
.chart-container3 {
    border: 1px solid darkblue;
    padding: 30px 0px 30px 30px;
    width: 500px;
    height: 200px;
    position: relative;
    float: left;
    margin-left: 20px;
}
#chart1 {
    width: 96%;
    height: 96%;
}
#chart2 {
    width: 96%;
    height: 96%;
}
#chart3 {
    width: 96%;
    height: 96%;
}
</style>
```

In Figure 11-8, you can see the page layout when the page is initially loaded. Figure 11-9 shows a situation in which the user has changed the position and the size of the third chart to align it below the other two.

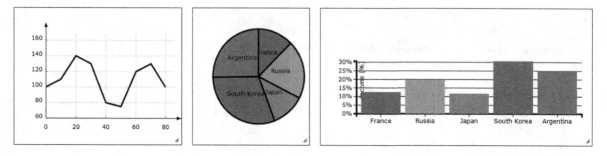

Figure 11-8. *The web page shows the three line charts enclosed in three different containers*

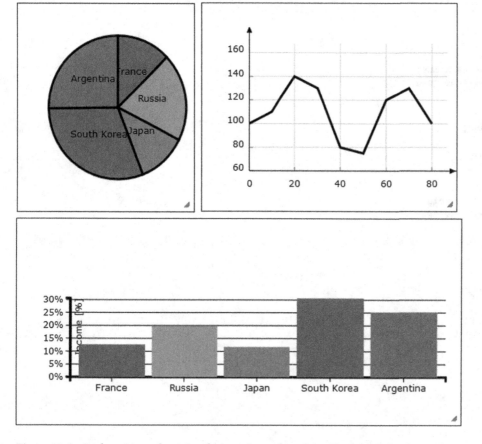

Figure 11-9. *By dragging and resizing the containers, the original layout can be changed*

Summary

In this chapter you have seen how to exploit the potential of widgets that the jQuery UI library makes available to you, widgets that help you improve the way your charts are represented. You have seen how to enclose more charts inside **containers, such as accordions and tabs**, so that you can view them one by one, even when they occupy the same area. You have also seen how to **resize** these **containers**, extending such capability to the charts developed with the jqPlot library.

In the next chapter and final chapter, you will see how you can handle structured data using the JSON format. You will see how it is "natural" working with highly structured data to get data visualizations that may be really challenging using other JavaScript libraries and other programming languages.

■ ■ ■

CHAPTER 12

JSON and Layouts—Handling Structured Data

Once you have dealt with all the graphical aspects of a chart, it is time to analyze input data in more detail. In the previous chapters, you started assigning the values of input data to arrays. Then you made use of tabulated data contained within CSV or TSV files. This step has allowed you to be able to handle most of the data for the visualization, but in reality there are more complex data structures, in a hierarchical form, such as trees.

In actuality, it is often necessary to interface with other technologies in order to obtain such data, and to do so you need to find a way that is well suited to any source of data. The need to use a common text format that can be easily handled by different scripting languages (especially JavaScript) and that remains comprehensible to humans, led to the use of the JavaScript Object Notation (JSON) format. You have briefly read about this kind of format in Chapter 1, but now you'll see how to use it concretely to handle input data from external sources.

This chapter studies in detail the JSON format. First of all, you will learn how there can be structured data in the JSON format, by analyzing some syntax diagrams. Then you will move on to practical examples.

The JSON Format

JSON (JavaScript Object Notation) is a data exchange format (see http://json.org for more details). Thanks to its tree structure, in which each element is referred as a name-value pair, it is easy for humans to read and write it and for machines to parse and generate it. This is the main reason for its increasingly prevalent use.

The JSON structure is built on the combination of two different structures: arrays and objects (see Figure 12-1). Within them you can define all of the classic primitive values commonly used, even in other languages: numbers, Booleans, strings, and null value. This allows values contained in it to be exchanged between various programming languages. (At www.json.org, you can find a list of all languages that handle the JSON format, along with a list of all the related technologies, such as libraries, modules, plug-ins, and so on.)

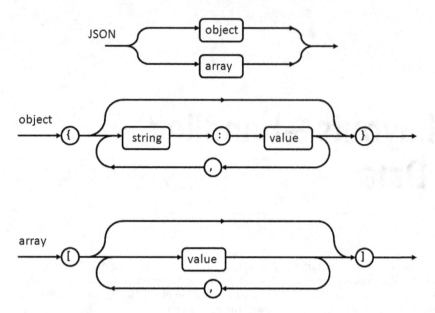

Figure 12-1. *Syntax diagrams for JSON*

Just to understand the syntax diagrams in Figure 12-1 better, you can analyze how a JSON format is structured. You must take into account two things. The first is that both the objects and the arrays contain a series of values identified by the value labels in the diagrams. value refers to any type of value, such as a string, a number, or a Boolean, and it can even be an object or an array.

In addition to this, you can easily guess that the JSON structure is a tree structure with different levels. The tree will have as nodes either arrays or objects; the leaves are the values contained in them.

Consider some examples. If you have a JSON structure with only one level, you will have only two possibilities:

- An array of values

- An object with values

If you extend the structure to two levels, the possibilities are four (assuming for simplicity that the tree is symmetrical):

- An array of arrays

- An array of objects

- An object with arrays

- An object with objects

And so on; the cases gradually become more complex. In this way you can generate all the possible data structures, such as trees (see Figure 12-2).

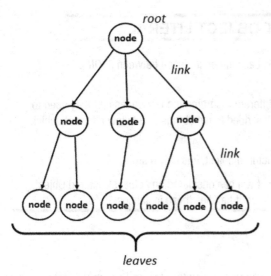

Figure 12-2. *A tree data structure*

Now, according to the directions on the JSON format described above, write the tree structure shown in Figure 12-2, then save the file as **tree.json**. As you can see in Listing 12-1, by alternating objects and arrays it is possible to describe any data structure, also much more complex.

Listing 12-1. Tree.json

```
{
  "name": "root",
  "children": [
    {
      "name": "parent A",
      "children": [
        {"name": "child A1"},
        {"name": "child A2"}
      ]
    },{
      "name": "parent B",
      "children": [
        {"name": "child B1"}
      ]
    },{
      "name": "parent C",
      "children": [
        {"name": "child C1"},
        {"name": "child C2"},
        {"name": "child C3"}     ]
    }
  ]
}
```

JSON IS NOT A JAVASCRIPT OBJECT LITERAL

This is a point that is good to discuss in more detail, because it is easy to get confused between JSON and JavaScript Object Literal.

When you have two different systems, probably making use of different programming languages and they need to communicate, they will use strings to exchange data. The data described in the strings, will follow a format, which in your case is JSON.

Even if the JSON string has the same format of a JavaScript structured object, it is only a string.

Instead, once the JSON file is interpreted by `d3.json()` function, it will be considered an actual structured Object, with data stored in variables, arrays, and objects, in the way JavaScript handles these instances.

The D3 Layouts

The library provides D3 modules, called **layouts**, which help the developer to structure to handle complex data. In addition, the D3 layouts, thanks to their internal implementations, present themselves as very useful tools in the management of the calculation of the coordinates of the elements that go to make up the chart then. In fact once loaded, the data structure in a layout, such as a tree, the layout will calculate the x and y coordinates for each node that will occupy in the drawing area.

   Precisely because of the large number of possible data structures, the D3 library provides a set of built-in layouts. In particular, for the handling of hierarchical data structures, the D3 library provides the following layouts:

- partition
- tree
- cluster
- pack
- treemap

Starting with a Simple Tree

As a first example, you implement an HTML page that will display a tree. The data for the hierarchical structure are precisely those contained in the file **tree.json** (see Listing 12-1). So far you've seen how easy it is to read the data in a CSV or TSV file thanks to the **d3.csv()** and **d3.tsv()** functions. In a similar way, the library D3 provides a function called **d3.json()**.

```
d3.json("path/to/file.json", function(error, root){
   ...
});
```

   Among the various D3 layouts available specifically for hierarchical data structures, **d3.layout.tree** is the most suitable to the example chosen. As a point of reference, I chose a complex dendrogram representation, M. Bostock's example #4063570 (http://bl.ocks.org/mbostock/4063570).

Listing 12-2. Ch12-1.html

```html
<HTML>
<HEAD>
<meta charset="utf-8">
<script src="http://d3js.org/d3.v3.js"></script>
<STYLE>
.node circle {
    fill: #fff;
    stroke: steelblue;
    stroke-width: 1.5px;
}
.node {
    font: 20px sans-serif;
}
.link {
    fill: none;
    stroke: #ccc;
    stroke-width: 1.5px;
}
</STYLE>
</HEAD>
<body>
<script>
var width = 600;
var height = 500;
var tree = d3.layout.tree()
    .size([height, width-200]);
var diagonal = d3.svg.diagonal()
    .projection (function(d) {return [d.y, d.x];});
var svg = d3.select("body").append("svg")
    .attr("width",width)
    .attr("height",height)
    .append("g")
    .attr("transform", "translate(100, 0)");
d3.json("tree.json", function(error, root){
    var nodes = tree.nodes(root);
    var links = tree.links(nodes);
    var link = svg.selectAll(".link")
      .data(links)
      .enter().append("path")
      .attr("class", "link")
      .attr("d", diagonal);
    var node = svg.selectAll(".node")
      .data(nodes)
      .enter().append("g")
      .attr("class", "node")
      .attr("transform", function(d) { return "translate(" + d.y + ", " + d.x + ")"; });
    node.append("circle")
      .attr("r", 4.5);
```

```
      node.append("text")
        .attr("dx", function(d) { return d.children ? -8 : 8; })
        .attr("dy", 3)
        .style("text-anchor", function(d) { return d.children ? "end" : "start"; })
        .text( function(d){return d.name;});
});
</script>
</BODY>
</HTML>
```

In this way you get a tree (see Figure 12-3), which is very similar to the tree represented in Figure 12-2.

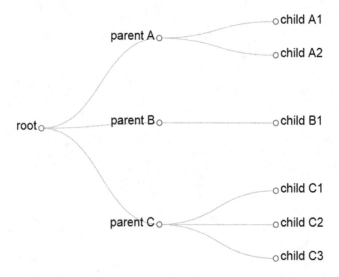

Figure 12-3. *A tree dynamically generated from a JSON file*

Analysis of the Tree Layout

If you look in detail at the tree in Figure 12-3, this is nothing more than the dynamic representation of the hierarchical structure described in JSON format in the file **tree.js**. The code you implemented in this example is capable of representing any tree structure, regardless of the number of levels, nodes, and leaves present.

One such efficient data management JSON and their correct visualization is due in large part to the role played by the D3 layout. In this example you used the d3.layout.tree. Now you will see in detail how it works and how it manipulates data internally read from JSON file.

By analyzing the code shown in Listing 12-2, you can see the declaration of the layout. The next step is to declare the size of the drawing area with the **size()** function (see Listing 12-3). This step is very important because one of the main purposes of the layout is to automatically calculate all the x and y coordinates of all the nodes of the tree. Then the x and y values calculated depend exclusively on two parameters passed to the **size()** function.

Listing 12-3. Ch12-1.html

```
var tree = d3.layout.tree()
    .size([height, width-200]);
```

The data read from the JSON file is stored in the **root** variable. Then, it is loaded into the layout through the **nodes()** function (see Listing 12-4). This operation generates an array containing all the nodes that make up the tree, which you're going to store in the variable **nodes**. The next operation will be to generate an array **links** containing all the links connecting the nodes of the tree. You can create this using the **links()** function.

Listing 12-4. Ch12-1.html

```
d3.json("tree.json", function(error, root){
    var nodes = tree.nodes(root);
    var links = tree.links(nodes);
...
});
```

Taking a look at the contents of the two arrays just created, you can discover a series of nested data structures much more complex than what was described in the JSON file. The tree consists of 10 nodes and 9 links, as many objects are contained in two arrays nodes and links (see Figure 12-4). In addition you will also notice that each node is accompanied by two new fields, x and y, which are precisely the coordinates computed from the layout.

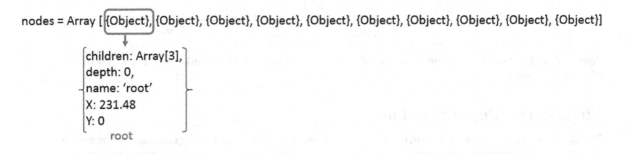

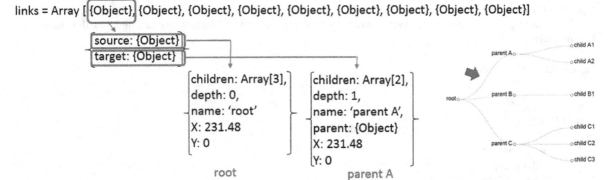

Figure 12-4. *The d3.layout.tree has an internal structure which is quite complex*

Figure 12-5 clearly shows how the x and y coordinates within the nodes of the layout match the drawing area that will be represented on the tree.

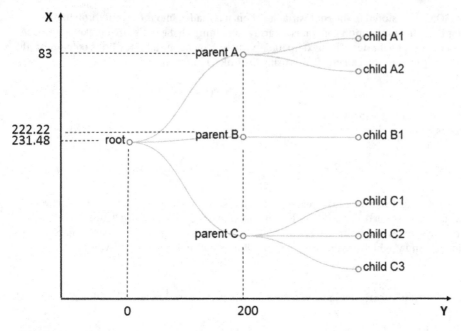

Figure 12-5. *The d3.layout.tree automatically calculates the coordinates for each node depending on the size of the drawing area*

Circular Tree Representation

The tree structure that you have seen in the previous example was a simple structure, gradually that the number of nodes and levels is growing the structure becomes increasingly complex. At this level, a general practice is to represent the tree in a circular shape.

First, increase the complexity of the tree, writing a new structure in JSON format (see Listing 12-5), then save it as **tree2.json**.

Listing 12-5. tree2.json

```
{
 "name": "root",
 "children": [
  {
     "name": "parent A",
     "children": [
       {"name": "child A1"},
       {"name": "child A2"},
       {"name": "child A3"},
       {"name": "child A4"},
       {"name": "child A5"},
       {"name": "child A6"}
     ]
},{
     "name": "parent B",
     "children": [
       {"name": "child B1"},
```

```
        {"name": "child B2"},
        {"name": "child B3"},
        {"name": "child B4"},
        {"name": "child B5"},
        {"name": "child B6"},
        {"name": "child B7"},
        {"name": "child B8"}
      ]
  },{
     "name": "parent C",
     "children": [
        {"name": "child C1"},
        {"name": "child C2"},
        {"name": "child C3"},
        {"name": "child C4"}
      ]
  }]
}
```

Now type the code from the HTML page for the representation of circular trees (see Listing 12-6).

Listing 12-6. ch12-2.html

```
<HTML>
<HEAD>
<meta charset="utf-8">
<script src="http://d3js.org/d3.v3.js"></script>
<style type="text/css">
.node circle {
  fill: #fff;
  stroke: steelblue;
  stroke-width: 1.5px;
}
.node {
  font: 20px sans-serif;
}
.link {
  fill: none;
  stroke: #ccc;
  stroke-width: 1.5px;
}
</style>
</HEAD>
<body>
<script>
var radius = 350;
var margin = 120;
var angle = 360;
var tree = d3.layout.tree()
  .size([angle, radius-margin]);
```

```
var diagonal = d3.svg.diagonal.radial()
 .projection (function(d) {return [d.y, d.x / 180* Math.PI];});

var svg = d3.select("body").append("svg")
 .attr("width", 2*radius)
 .attr("height", 2*radius)
 .append("g")
 .attr("transform", "translate("+radius + ", " + radius + ")");

d3.json("tree2.json", function(error, root){
 var nodes = tree.nodes(root);
 var links = tree.links(nodes);
 var link = svg.selectAll(".link")
 .data(links)
 .enter().append("path")
 .attr("class", "link")
 .attr("d", diagonal);

 var node = svg.selectAll(".node")
 .data(nodes)
 .enter().append("g")
 .attr("class", "node")
 .attr("transform", function(d) { return "rotate(" + (d.x - 90) + ")translate(" + d.y + ")"; });

 node.append("circle")
 .attr("r", 4.5);

 node.append("text")
 .attr("dy", ".31em")
 .attr("text-anchor", function(d) { return d.x > 180 ? "start" : "end"; })
 .attr("transform", function(d) { return d.x > 180 ? "translate(8)" : "rotate(180)translate(-8)"; })
 .text(function(d) { return d.name; });
});
</script>
</body>
</HTML>
```

Figure 12-6 shows the circular representation of a tree read from a JSON file.

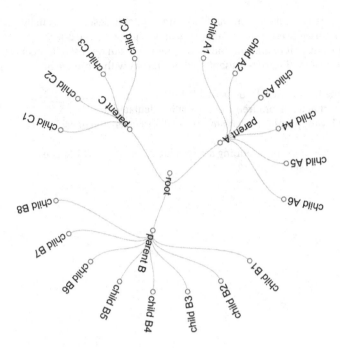

Figure 12-6. *The circular representation of a tree*

The Partition Layout

In the previous example you saw the circular representation of a tree. In this section you will see an alternative representation, much like the donuts chart (see Chapter 5, Figure 5-10). (see Figure 12-7). In general it will produce adjacency diagrams such as a space-filling variant of a node-link tree diagram. Rather than drawing a link between parent and child in the hierarchy, nodes are drawn as solid areas (either arcs or rectangles), and their placement relative to other nodes reveals their position in the hierarchy.

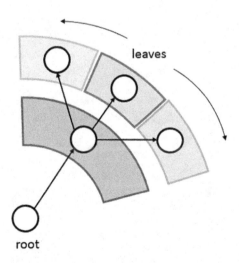

Figure 12-7. *An alternative circular representation of a tree*

So in this representation, the nodes are represented by circular sectors and links are implicitly described radially. The information on the hierarchy of a typical tree structure is preserved. But there is something more. The nodes represented in the form of circular sectors allows us to add a more information to our graph: we can represent as each leaf weights compared to the other. Indeed, we have the possibility of representing this quantity with the angle of extension of the circular sector.

Also in this case the library D3 provides us with the hierarchical layout suitable for this purpose: the **d3.layout.partition**. In the previous examples you saw that d3.layout.tree automatically calculated the x and y coordinates for each node. Well, the same way the d3.layout.partition calculates the angles of extension of each circular sector, that is, of each node.

First, change the data structure you used in the previous example adding a **size** value to each leaf. This value expresses the 'weight' of each leaf with respect to the other (see Listing 12-7).

Listing 12-7. tree4.json

```json
{
 "name": "root",
 "children": [
 {
     "name": "parent A",
     "children": [
       {"name": "child A1", "size": 25},
       {"name": "child A2", "size": 31},
       {"name": "child A3", "size": 11},
       {"name": "child A4", "size": 21},
       {"name": "child A5", "size": 44},
       {"name": "child A6", "size": 22}
     ]
 },{
     "name": "parent B",
     "children": [
       {"name": "child B1", "size": 5},
       {"name": "child B2", "size": 11},
       {"name": "child B3", "size": 35},
       {"name": "child B4", "size": 36},
       {"name": "child B5", "size": 28},
       {"name": "child B6", "size": 22},
       {"name": "child B7", "size": 26},
       {"name": "child B8", "size": 41}
     ]
 },{
     "name": "parent C",
     "children": [
       {"name": "child C1", "size": 23},
       {"name": "child C2", "size": 51},
       {"name": "child C3", "size": 33},
       {"name": "child C4", "size": 4}
     ]
 }]
}
```

While Listing 12-8 shows the code of the HTML page to display a circular sectors of the tree. As a point of reference, I chose a "sunburst" representation, M. Bostock's example #4063423 (http://bl.ocks.org/mbostock/4063423).

Listing 12-8. ch12_03.html

```
<HTML>
<HEAD>
<meta charset="utf-8">
<script src="http://d3js.org/d3.v3.js"></script>
</HEAD>
<body>
<script>
var radius = 250;
var angle = 360;
var color = d3.scale.category10();

var svg = d3.select("body").append("svg")
    .attr("width", 2*radius)
    .attr("height", 2* radius)
    .append("g")
    .attr("transform", "translate("+radius + ", " + radius + ")");

var partition = d3.layout.partition()
    .size([2 * Math.PI, radius]);

var arc = d3.svg.arc()
    .startAngle(function(d) { return d.x; })
    .endAngle(function(d) { return d.x + d.dx; })
    .innerRadius(function(d) { return d.y; })
    .outerRadius(function(d) { return d.y + d.dy; });

d3.json("tree3.json", function(error, root) {

  var size = function(d) { return d.size; };
  var nodes = partition.value(size).nodes(root);

  var path = svg.datum(root).selectAll("path")
      .data(nodes)
      .enter().append("path")
      .attr("display", function(d) { return d.depth ? null : "none"; })
      .attr("d", arc)
      .style("stroke", "#fff")
      .style("fill", function(d) { return color((d.children ? d : d.parent).name); })
      .style("fill-rule", "evenodd");

});
</script>
</body>
</HTML>
```

Figure 12-8 shows the result of the code.

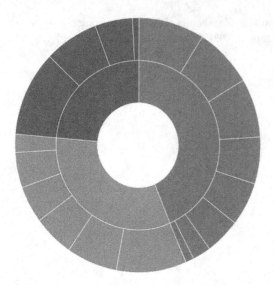

Figure 12-8. *An alternative circular representation of a tree*

Now let's analyze in detail how the project works d3.layout.partition. The declaration of the partition layout is very similar to that of the tree layout (see Listing 12-9). With the two parameters passed to the **size()** function you can establish the extent circular as the first argument (in this case a round angle) and the radius as the second argument.

Listing 12-9. ch12_03.html

```
var partition = d3.layout.partition()
    .size([2 * Math.PI, radius]);
```

Inside the **json()** function, you can assign the structured data contained in the JSON file through the **root** variable to the partition layout. The **size** values of the leaves are passed through recursion to the value() function (see Listing 12-10).

Listing 12-10. ch12_03.html

```
d3.json("tree3.json", function(error, root) {

  var size = function(d) { return d.size; };
  var nodes = partition.value(size).nodes(root);
```

If you go to analyze in detail the internal structure of the partition layout you can see how it is structured in the Figure 12-9.

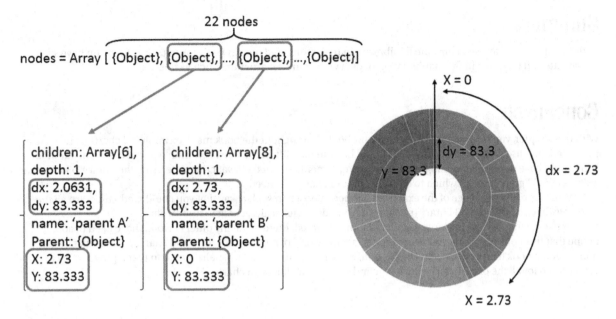

Figure 12-9. *The partition layout structure in detail*

Finally, the function **d3.svg.arc ()** will convert the values x, y, dx, and dy in the circular sectors that will make up the chart in its entirety (see Listing 12-11).

Listing 12-11. ch12_03.html

```
var arc = d3.svg.arc()
    .startAngle(function(d) { return d.x; })
    .endAngle(function(d) { return d.x + d.dx; })
    .innerRadius(function(d) { return d.y; })
    .outerRadius(function(d) { return d.y + d.dy; });{
```

Endless Possibilities with JSON and Layouts

In the two previous examples you have seen first hand just the tip of the iceberg of the infinite possibilities that the library D3, integrated technology JSON for data input, can provide.

For anyone interested in further extending the topic I highly recommend going to https://github.com/mbostock/d3/wiki/Gallery. Within this page are a large number of examples developed with the library D3.

Summary

In this chapter you have seen how the D3 library can read structured data in JSON format. Moreover, you have seen the layouts and their role in the manipulation of data with complex structures such as trees.

Conclusion

With this chapter, you have come to the end of this book. Throughout the book many examples of charts were presented and discussed. At this point you should be familiar with all the most common types of charts. In addition, you should have developed a good practice in the implementation of the JavaScript code using the library D3 to create a series of SVG graphics with which to build all kinds of charts you need.

In addition, the sequence of the examples has been chosen in such a way that you could gradually learn all the concepts that underlie the D3 library (selectors, layout, domains, scales, chain methods, etc.)

I must say that despite the large number of topics covered, there are many others I would have liked to add. I hope that this book has made you better appreciate the world of data visualization and charts in particular. I also hope that the book has provided you with a good, basic knowledge of data visualization and that it proves to be a valuable aid for all the occasions in which you find yourself dealing with charts.

■ ■ ■

Guidelines for the Examples in the Book

This appendix provides guidelines on how to use XAMPP and Aptana Studios together to create a development environment on your PC that will allow you to develop, run, and fix the examples given in the book.

Installing a Web Server

Nowadays, on the , you can easily find free software packages containing everything you need to set up a test environment for all your examples and for everything related to the web world in general.

These packages minimize the number of programs that need to be installed.More important, they may be acquired with a single installation. The packages generally consist of an Apache HTTP server; a MySQL database; and interpreters for the programming languages PHP, Perl, and Python. The most complete package is XAMPP (available for download at the Apache Friends web site [`www.apachefriends.org/en/index.html`]). XAMPP is totally free, and its key feature is that it is a cross-platform package (Windows, Linux, Solaris, MacOS). Furthermore, XAMPP also includes a Tomcat application server (for the programming language Java) and a FileZilla FTP server (for file transfer). Other solutions are platform specific, as suggested by the initial letter of their name:

- **WAMP** (Windows)
- **MAMP** (MacOS)
- **LAMP** (Linux)
- **SAMP** (Solaris)
- **FAMP** (FreeBSD)

In fact, XAMPP is an acronym; its letters stand for the following terms:

- **X**, for the operating system
- **A**, for Apache, the web server
- **M**, for MySQL, the database management system
- **P**, for PHP, Perl, or Python, the programming languages

Thus, choose the web server solution that best fits your platform, and install it on your PC.

Installing Aptana Studio IDE

Once the Web server has been installed, it is necessary to install an integrated development environment (IDE), which you need to develop your JavaScript code. In this appendix, you will install Aptana Studio as your development environment.

Visit the Aptana site (www.aptana.com), and click the Products tab for the Aptana Studio 3 software (at the time of writing, the most recent version is 3.4.2). Download the stand-alone edition (with the Eclipse IDE already integrated): Aptana_Studio_3_Setup_3.4.2.exe.

After the download is complete, launch the executable file to install the Aptana Studio IDE. At the end of the installation, in launching the application, you should see the workbench opening, as shown in Figure A-1.

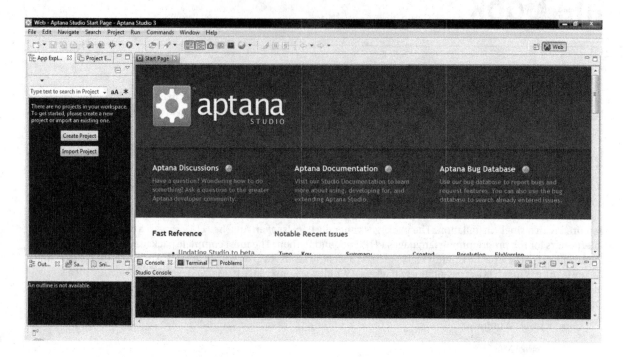

Figure A-1. *The Aptana Studio IDE workbench*

During the installation of Aptana Studio, the software detects the various browsers and the web server installed and configures itself accordingly.

Setting the Aptana Studio Workspace

Before starting to develop the examples in the book, you must create a workspace. First, you should set the workspace on Aptana Studio, where the Web server document root is.

These are typical paths with XAMPP:

- Windows: C:\xampp\htdocs

- Linux: /opt/lamp/htdocs

- MacOS: /Applications/XAMPP/xamppfiles/htdocs

Whereas with WAMP, this is the path:

- `C:\WAMP\www`

Thus, select File ➤ Switch Workspace ➤ Other . . . from the menu. Then, insert the path of the web server document root in the field, as demonstrated in Figure A-2.

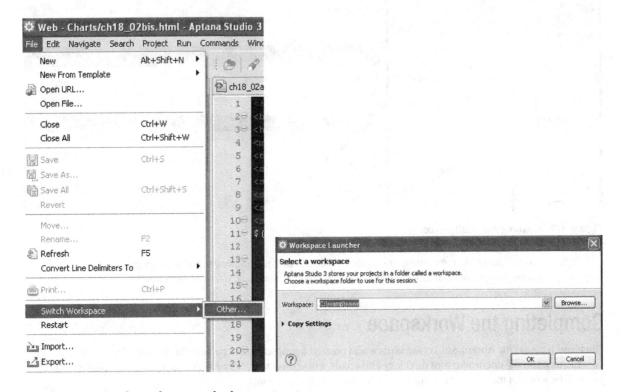

Figure A-2. *Setting the workspace on the document root*

Creating a Project

The next step in creating your workspace consists of creating a project in Aptana Studio:

1. Select New ➤ Web Project from the menu.

2. A window such as that shown in Figure A-3 appears. Select Default Project, and click Next.

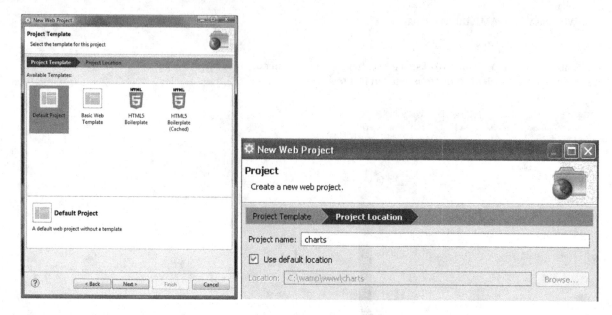

Figure A-3. *Creating a default project*

3. Insert "'charts" as the name of the project. This will be the directory in the workspace in which you will write all the example files described in the book, using Aptana Studio.

Completing the Workspace

Once you have set the Aptana Studio workspace and created a project, you complete the workspace.

Let us open the document root directory and create a new directory, named src. Now, the workspace on which you will be working throughout the book is composed of two directories:

- src
- charts

The src directory should contain all the files related to libraries.

The charts directory should contain all HTML, images and Cascading Style Sheets (CSS) files related to the examples in the book (which is in fact a project). Each example file should be created in this directory (if you prefer to do things differently, that's fine, but it is important to take note of the different path reference in HTML pages in order to include the library files and images).

■ **Note** The source code that accompanies this book (available from the Source Code/Download area of the Apress web site [www.apress.com]) is practically already packaged in a workspace. With it, you will find two versions of the charts project: content delivery network (CDN) and local. The charts_CDN directory contains all the examples referring to libraries remotely distributed from services. The charts_local directory offers all the examples referring to libraries found within the src directory.

Filling the src Directory with the Libraries

If you have chosen to develop HTML pages by referring to libraries locally, it is necessary to download all their files. These files will be collected in the src directory. This is a good approach, as you can develop several projects that will make use of the same libraries without having to copy them for each project.

The versions listed in this appendix are those used to implement the examples in the book. If you install other versions, there may be issues of incompatibility, or you may observe behavior different from that described.

D3 library version 3

1. Visit the D3 site (http://d3js.org), and download the library: d3.v3.zip.

2. Extract all content directly, and place in the src directory. Now, you should have two new files in the src directory:

   - d3.v3.js

   - d3.v3.min.js

You have thus obtained the src directory, which should contain the subdirectories and files shown in Figure A-4.

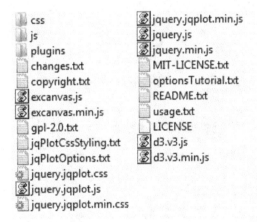

Figure A-4. *The files and subdirectories contained in the src directory*

■ **Note** By convention you are developing the examples in the charts directory. If you want to do otherwise, you need to consider the new path when you will include the other files in a web page.

If you are developing the HTML page inside the charts directory, you need to use the following code:

```
<script type="text/javascript" src="../src/d3.v3.js"></script>
```

In contrast, if you prefer to develop it directly, in the document root, you use this:

```
<script type="text/javascript" src="src/d3.v3.js"></script>
```

In short, it is important to take the path of the file you are including into account, with respect to the page you are implementing.

Running the Examples

Once you have created or copied an HTML file in the workspace, to run it in Aptana Studio IDE, select Run ➤ Run from the menu, or click the Run button on the toolbar (see Figure A-5).

Figure A-5. *The Run button from the toolbar*

Immediately, your default browser will open, with the selected HTML page loaded.

Look at Run Configurations (see Figure A-6), selecting Run Configurations . . . from the context menu of the Run icon. Let us set, for example, `http://localhost/` as your base URL; to do so, you select the Append project name option, as shown. Then, you click the Apply button to confirm your settings.

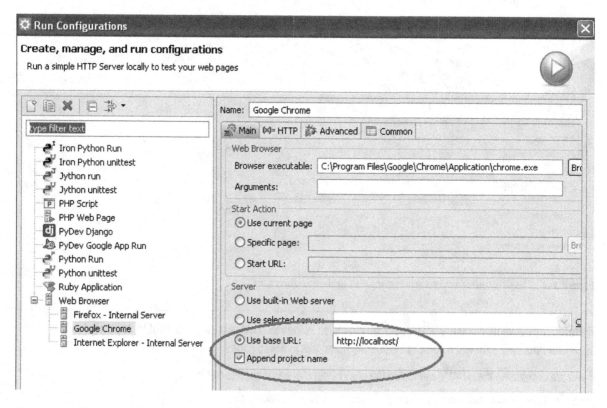

Figure A-6. *The run configuration for each browser must be set correctly*

Now, you have everything required to work easily on all the examples in the book.

Once you reach a certain familiarity with the Aptana IDE, you will find that it is an excellent environment for developing many other projects, both in JavaScript and in other programming languages (e.g., PHP).

And, now, have fun!

Summary

This appendix provides guidelines on how to use XAMPP and Aptana Studios together to create a development environment on your PC. The choice of using these applications is not mandatory, and many other solutions are possible; there are many applications available on the Internet for performing similar operations. But, if you wish to implement and quickly test the examples described in the book, this environment will prove a good choice.

Index

Get the eBook for only $10!

Now you can take the weightless companion with you anywhere, anytime. Your purchase of this book entitles you to 3 electronic versions for only $10.

This Apress title will prove so indispensible that you'll want to carry it with you everywhere, which is why we are offering the eBook in **3 formats** for only $10 if you have already purchased the print book.

Convenient and fully searchable, the PDF version enables you to easily find and copy code—or perform examples by quickly toggling between instructions and applications. The MOBI format is ideal for your Kindle, while the ePUB can be utilized on a variety of mobile devices.

Go to www.apress.com/promo/tendollars to purchase your companion eBook.